*Transitions from Authoritarian Rule: Prospects for Democracy*
edited by Guillermo O'Donnell, Philippe C. Schmitter, and
Laurence Whitehead, is available in separate paperback editions:

*Transitions from Authoritarian Rule: Southern Europe*
edited by Guillermo O'Donnell, Philippe C. Schmitter, and
Laurence Whitehead

*Transitions from Authoritarian Rule: Latin America*
edited by Guillermo O'Donnell, Philippe C. Schmitter, and
Laurence Whitehead

*Transitions from Authoritarian Rule: Comparative Perspectives*
edited by Guillermo O'Donnell, Philippe C. Schmitter, and
Laurence Whitehead

*Transitions from Authoritarian Rule:*
*Tentative Conclusions about Uncertain Democracies*
by Guillermo O'Donnell and Philippe C. Schmitter

## Contributors

**P. Nikiforos Diamandouros**   *Social Science Research Council, New York*

**Salvador Giner**   *Brunel University, London*

**Abraham F. Lowenthal**   *University of Southern California, Los Angeles*

**José María Maravall**   *Universidad Complutense de Madrid*

**Kenneth Maxwell**   *The Tinker Foundation, New York*

**Gianfranco Pasquino**   *University of Bologna*

**Julián Santamaría**   *Universidad Complutense de Madrid*

**Sabri Sayari**   *Bogazici Universitesi, Istanbul*

**Philippe C. Schmitter**   *European University Institute, Florence*

**Ilkay Sunar**   *Bogazici Universitesi, Istanbul*

# Transitions from Authoritarian Rule

## Southern Europe

*edited by*
*Guillermo O'Donnell,*
*Philippe C. Schmitter, and*
*Laurence Whitehead*

*The Johns Hopkins University Press*
**Baltimore and London**

The Johns Hopkins University Press,
2715 North Charles Street
Baltimore, Maryland 21218-4319
The Johns Hopkins Press Ltd., London

Library of Congress Cataloging-in-Publications Data

Transitions from authoritarian rule. Southern Europe.

   Papers originally commissioned for a conference sponsored by the
Latin American Program of the Woodrow Wilson International Center
for Scholars between 1979 and 1981.
   Bibliography: p.
   Includes index.
   Contents: An introduction to southern European transitions from
authoritarian rule: Italy, Greece, Portugal, Spain, and Turkey /
Philippe C. Schmitter—Political economy, legitimation, and the state
in southern Europe / Salvador Giner—The demise of the first Fascist
regime and Italy's transition to democracy, 1943–1948 / Gianfranco
Pasquino—[etc.]
   1. Representative government and representation—Europe,
Southern—Case studies.   2. Authoritarianism—Europe,
Southern—Case studies.   3. Democracy—Case
studies.   I. O'Donnell, Guillermo A.   II. Schmitter, Philippe
C.   III. Whitehead, Laurence.   IV. Woodrow Wilson International
Center for Scholars.   Latin American Program.
JN12.T73   1986       321.09'094          86-2713
ISBN  0-8018-3190-3 (pbk. : alk. paper)


A catalog record for this book is available from the British Library.

# Contents

# Foreword

## Abraham F. Lowenthal

The three coeditors of *Transitions from Authoritarian Rule* have kindly invited me to introduce this effort because it resulted from the Woodrow Wilson Center's project on "Transitions from Authoritarian Rule: Prospects for Democracy in Latin America and Southern Europe."

The "Transitions" project was the most significant undertaking of the Wilson Center's Latin American Program during the seven years I had the privilege of directing its activities. The resulting four-volume book contributes substantially on a topic of vital scholarly and political importance. I want to highlight both these points, to underline some of its strengths, and finally to say a bit about what is still left to be done.

The Woodrow Wilson International Center for Scholars was created by an act of the United States Congress in 1968 as a "living memorial" to the twentieth president of the United States, a man remembered for his idealism and for his commitment to democracy, for his scholarship, for his political leadership, and for his international vision, but also for his interventionist attitudes and actions toward Latin America and the Caribbean. The Center supports advanced research and systematic discussion on national and international issues by scholars and practitioners from all over the world. It aims to bring together the realms of academic and public affairs, as Wilson himself did.

The Latin American Program was established early in 1977, within the Center's overall framework, to focus attention on the Western Hemisphere. The Program has tried, from the start, to serve as a bridge between Latin Americans and North Americans of diverse backgrounds, to facilitate comparative research that draws on the Center's special capacity to bring people together, to emphasize the highest standards of scholarship, to stress privileged topics that merit intense cooperative efforts, and to help assure that opinion leaders in the United States and Latin America focus more attentively and more sensitively on Latin America and the Caribbean and on their relation with the United States.

In all its undertakings, the Program has been striving to assure that diverse viewpoints—from men and women with varying national, professional, disciplinary, methodological, and political perspectives—are presented, and that complex issues are illuminated through the confrontation of different analyses. But the Program's orientation has never been value-free; it has stood for vigorous exchange among persons who disagree about many things but who fundamentally respect the academic enterprise and who share a commitment to the core values all the nations of the Americas profess. The Program has sought diversity of many kinds, but not artificial balance. It awarded fellowships in the same semester to writers exiled because of their convictions from Argentina and from Cuba, for example, but it has never invited their censors on an equal basis. It has sponsored research on human rights from many different standpoints, but never from the perspective of the torturers. And it sponsored the project on "Transitions from Authoritarian Rule" with a frank bias for democracy, for the restoration in Latin America of the fundamental rights of political participation.

The "Transitions" project was begun in 1979 on the initiative of two charter members of the Latin American Program's nine-person Academic Council: Guillermo O'Donnell (then of CEDES in Buenos Aires) and Philippe Schmitter (then of the University of Chicago), with the active encouragement and support of the Council's chairman, Albert O. Hirschman, and of Council member Fernando Henrique Cardoso of Brazil. During the project's first phase, I served as its coordinator. As the project grew in scope and complexity, it became clear that another Center-based person was needed to focus more fully on it; we were fortunate to recruit Laurence Whitehead of Oxford University, a former Wilson Center fellow, who then worked closely with O'Donnell and Schmitter and became coeditor of the project volume.

The "Transitions" project illustrates the Wilson Center's aspirations in several respects:

Its leaders are recognized as among the world's foremost academic authorities in Latin America, the United States, and Europe.

It attracted the participation of other top-flight scholars from all three continents and encouraged them to work closely together in a structured and linked series of workshops and conferences.

It emphasized comparative analysis, and sharpened the focus on Latin American cases by putting them into a broader perspective.

In its various workshops, the project drew on the perspective not only of scholars but of several persons—from Latin America and from among former U.S. government officials—experienced in politics and public affairs.

Its findings have been made available to opinion leaders from different sectors through specially organized discussion sessions in Washington.

It maintained a creative tension between its normative bias, its theoretical ambitions, and its empirical and case-oriented approach. The project's animus, as I had occasion to say at its first meeting, was never wishful thinking but rather "thoughtful wishing," that is, it was guided by a normative orientation that was rigorous and deliberate in its method.

Finally, the project illustrated a point the Wilson Center's director, Dr. James H. Billington, has often emphasized: to seek tentative answers to fundamental questions rather than definitive responses to trivial ones. All the project's participants know that the complex issues involved in transitions to democracy have not been dealt with conclusively in this volume, but they can take great satisfaction in what they have contributed.

## Transitions from Authoritarian Rule

Ultimate evaluations of this book's import, obviously, will have to come from analysts less involved in the project's inception and management than I. I would like, however, to suggest some of the reasons why I think *Transitions from Authoritarian Rule* is important.

It is the first book in any language that systematically and comparatively focuses on the process of transition from authoritarian regimes, making this the central question of scholarship as it is today in Latin American politics.

Its analytic and normative focus on the prospects of building democratic or polyarchic politics in the wake of an authoritarian transition provides a vantage point that organizes the materials in ways useful not only to scholars and observers but to political actors as well.

Its comparisons of cases in Latin America and in Southern Europe and of cases of transition from bureaucratic authoritarianism, military populism, and sultanistic despotism allow for considering several different variables.

*Transitions from Authoritarian Rule* is rich in nuanced, contextually sensitive analysis, and each of the case studies is written by a leading authority. Although the methods, perspectives, and styles of the various authors understandably differ, their agreement on shared assumptions makes this a coherent volume. The book is filled with subtleties, complexity, and a keen sense of paradox.

Throughout, disaggregation is emphasized. All authoritarian regimes are not equated with each other. No authoritarian regime is regarded as monolithic, nor are the forces pushing for democratization so regarded. Distinctions are drawn between "democracy" and "polyarchy"; between "democratization" and "liberalization"; between "transition" and "consolidation"; between "hard-liners" and "soft-liners" or accommodationists within the authoritarian coalition; and among "maximalists," "moderates," and "opportunists" in the coalition supporting *abertura* (liberalization).

From the various cases, several points emerge that deserve special mention here. These cases show that, although international factors, direct and indirect, may condition and affect the course of transition, the major participants and the dominant influences in every case have been national. They demonstrate the importance of institutions, of mediating procedures and forums that help make the rules of political discourse legitimate and credible in a period of change. They illustrate the vital significance of political leadership and judgment, of the role of single individuals in complex historical processes. They point out, again and again, the importance of timing, the complexity of inter-active processes carried out over extensive periods, the various ways in which transitions produce surprises, and some of the ironies and paradoxes that result.

Above all, the cases analyze the ways in which transitions from authoritar-ian rule are conditioned and shaped by historical circumstances, unique in each country but patterned in predictable ways, by the way in which a pre-vious democratic regime broke down, by the nature and duration of the authoritarian period, by the means the authoritarian regime uses to obtain legitimacy and to handle threats to its grip on power, by the initiative and the timing of experimental moves toward *abertura*, by the degree of security and self-confidence of the regime's elites and by the confidence and competence of those pushing for opening the political process, by the presence or absence of financial resources, by the counseling of outsiders, and by the prevailing inter-national *fashions* that provide legitimacy to certain forms of transition.

## The Tasks Ahead

I do not wish to detain the reader longer before he or she enters the reading of *Transitions from Authoritarian Rule*. It remains only to concede, as all the authors would, that this book is incomplete, and that much remains to be done. The cases of transition are still few in number, and each one merits a much more detailed and sustained analysis. The processes of consolidation, so important if these transitions are to be meaningful, are barely considered in this volume, and require separate treatment. The sensitivity that the authors in their chapters show to the dilemmas and choices faced by opposition groups pressing for *abertura* needs to be matched by equally empathetic and well-informed assessments of the choices made by those within authoritarian regimes who permit *abertura* to occur and push for its extension. Some of the categories of analysis—of hard-liners (*duros*) and soft-liners (*blandos*), for example—need to be further specified and refined.

All this and more needs to be done. No doubt the editors and authors of *Transitions from Authoritarian Rule* will be among the leaders in carrying out this research. Some of them will be leaders, as well, in the very processes of building democracies. They, and many others, will go much further than this volume can, but they will build upon a solid foundation.

# Preface

Between 1979 and 1981 the Latin American Program of the Woodrow Wilson International Center for Scholars, in Washington, D.C., sponsored a series of meetings and conferences entitled "Transitions from Authoritarian Rule: Prospects for Democracy in Latin America and Southern Europe." As this project grew in scope and complexity, Abraham Lowenthal, program secretary from 1977 to 1983, provided indispensable encouragement that enabled us to turn it into the present four-volume study. We wish to acknowledge our special debt of gratitude to him, and also to thank the Woodrow Wilson Center, the Aspen Institute for Humanistic Study, the Inter-American Foundation, the Helen Kellogg Institute of the University of Notre Dame, the European University Institute in Florence, and Nuffield College, Oxford, for their financial and logistical support. Louis Goodman, acting secretary of the Latin American Program in 1983–84, also gave us much-needed assistance. Needless to add, only those named in the table of contents are responsible for the views expressed here.

All of the papers published in these four volumes were originally commissioned for a Woodrow Wilson Center conference or were circulated, discussed, and revised in the course of the "Transitions" project. They have, therefore, some commonality of approach and outlook, but it was never our intention to impose a uniformity of interpretation and terminology. On the contrary, we deliberately set out to widen the range of serious discussion about regime transitions in general, and to promote informed debate comparing specific cases. In Volume 4, O'Donnell and Schmitter present the lessons they have drawn from this experience of collaboration among scholars working on Latin America and Southern Europe. Volume 3 contains a series of discussion papers analyzing common themes from different perspectives. Volume 1 (on Southern Europe) and Volume 2 (on Latin America) contain country studies, some of which were written during or immediately after the launching of a democratic transition, and some even before it had begun. Two cases (Uruguay and Turkey) were added to our sample at a later stage in the project as developments in these countries called for their inclusion, whereas the chapter on Italy refers to a transition completed more than thirty years earlier. Because of these differences in timing, and the delay in publication, readers should be warned that not all chapters carry the analysis right up to date (end of 1984).

Although the three editors are listed alphabetically in volumes 1, 2, and 3, they, of course, established some division of labor among themselves. Primary responsibility for Volume 1 rests with Philippe C. Schmitter; Laurence Whitehead took the lead in editing Volume 2; and Guillermo O'Donnell had first responsibility for Volume 3. This has been very much a collective endeavor, however, and all three of us share credit or blame for the overall result.

*Transitions from Authoritarian Rule*

**Southern Europe**

# 1 •

# An Introduction to Southern European Transitions from Authoritarian Rule: Italy, Greece, Portugal, Spain, and Turkey

**Philippe C. Schmitter**

The countries on the northern rim of the Mediterranean have long been the "stepchildren" of the study of Western European politics and society. With the notable exception of Italy (and then only since its democratization after World War II), they have been routinely placed outside the mainstream of inquiry and generalization about political developments in that part of the world. Scholars shied away from studying them. Textbooks simply ignored their existence. Classification systems assigned them the status of "exceptions," or simply placed them in the ignominious category of "other." In the crosstabs, factor analyses, and scatterplots that sought the socioeconomic correlates of political democracy, the Southern European countries kept popping up in the off-cell, adhering to the wrong cluster, or outlying with a whopping negative residual.

The conviction grew that they somehow did not belong in Western Europe. Spain and Portugal were placed on the other side of the Pyrenees, "in Africa." Greece, when it fell to the despotism of the colonels, became Balkan. Turkey, despite all its efforts at Western secularization and modernization, was exiled to the Middle East.

Explicitly, the chapters in this volume deal with the demise of authoritarian rule in Southern Europe and the struggle to establish political democracy in its stead. Implicitly, they argue that these countries—Italy some time ago; Portugal, Spain, and Greece more recently; and Turkey more ambiguously—have entered into, and can be expected to remain within, the range of institutional variation and patterns of political conflict characteristic of Western Europe as a whole.

Perhaps more than anything else, this conclusion marks the strongest contrast with the Latin American cases which have also been a part of this project. The authors of these studies—with the notable exception of the Sunar-Sayari chapter on Turkey—are relatively confident that a regime transition has indeed occurred in Southern Europe and that, despite persistent uncertainties

3

and unresolved problems, the political democracies that have emerged to replace authoritarian rule stand a reasonable chance of surviving. Their Latin American colleagues exhibit no such optimism. Some of them doubt whether a transition has even begun; others are uncertain about what mode of political domination is going to replace the defunct autocracies; still others are hesitant in assuming that fledgling successor democracies will be able to consolidate themselves in the near future.

There is a measure of irony in this difference in evaluation, for compared to Latin America, the Southern European countries have not only experienced bureaucratic-authoritarian rule more continuously and for a longer period of time but its presence has had a more pervasive effect upon their social and economic structures, political and civic institutions, and, perhaps, individual values and group aspirations. Only Greece in this subset has followed a "Latin American" pattern of oligarchic democracy, personal dictatorship, populist pressures, military-bureaucratic autocracy, and liberal democracy in varying sequence and combination. In Portugal and Spain, and to a lesser extent, Italy, consolidated authoritarian rule lasted so long that a whole generation or more grew up without any direct experience of democratic processes or rights. Substantial social and economic transformations, not to mention major political events, occurred under its aegis. In Latin America, such a regime has been a more recent and episodic phenomenon. Its leaders have not had the time, the will, or the capacity to intervene as extensively and protractedly in the social, economic, and political institutions of the societies they were attempting to govern. Indeed, they were compelled to expend a great deal of their scarce resources just on protecting their tenure in office. Turkey and Mexico stand out as roughly analogous exceptions in that, as the regime successors to successful nationalist revolutions, their rulers were able to preside over a relatively continuous project of institutional and cultural transformation of their respective societies.

Why, then, have the liberalizations/democratizations of Southern Europe got off to what seems to be a better and more reassuring start? A partial explanation is that the international context in that part of the world and at this point in time is more supportive of such an outcome. Italy earlier and Greece, Portugal, and Spain later—the Turkish case is more ambiguous—have become enmeshed in a complex network of regional institutions, commercial exchanges, political pressures, party linkages, treaty obligations, citizen contacts, and normative expectations that reward conformity to democracy and punish transgressions from it. Extraregional powers have also played a significant role. The United States, whose policies toward democratization in Latin America have been ambiguous and variant from one case to another, has consistently supported it in Southern Europe—at least once it became evident that protecting or reinstating former authoritarian allies was no longer a viable option. Not only has the geostrategic location of these countries given them important assets with which to bargain, but the presence of a plausible threat to their national security from the Soviet Union, as well as the negative example furnished by the practices of "real existing socialism," has provided additional motives for their reaching domestic political compromises and not pushing momentary partisan conflicts or even longstanding social cleavages too far.

But such international factors cannot be made to bear the entire explanatory burden. Indeed, one of the firmest conclusions that emerged from our Working Group was that transitions from authoritarian rule and immediate prospects for political democracy were largely to be explained in terms of national forces and calculations. External actors tended to play an indirect and usually marginal role, with the obvious exception of those instances in which a foreign occupying power was present.

One enormous advantage enjoyed by at least three of the Southern European cases was the relatively modest, not to say minor, role played by the armed forces in the defunct regime. As Gianfranco Pasquino demonstrates, the Italian military may have facilitated the advent to power of Mussolini, but it was hardly a predominant or even an integral element in the ensuing Fascist regime. Indeed, high-ranking officers were part of the conspiracy that forced Mussolini out of power and surrendered the country to the Allies in 1943. In any case, subsequent military defeat and occupation by a foreign army effectively removed the armed forces as a power contender during the transition to democracy. In Spain, by the time Franco died, the military were securely, if not shabbily, confined to barracks. This demobilization has not precluded their playing a threatening role—witness the events of February 1981—but it is perhaps relevant that the leading elements in that conspiracy to arrest democratization came from the Guardia Civil, not the regular armed forces. Portugal, of course, followed a quite different course in which the transition was triggered by a rebellion from within the ranks of the army itself. Here the problem, discussed at some length in Kenneth Maxwell's chapter, was not the usual one of getting a conservative military to stay out of power, but of getting a radicalized military to hand over power. Even in the Greek case, perhaps the closest in Southern Europe to the Latin American "model," the relatively narrow and isolated status of the clique of colonels who ran the outgoing regime greatly reduced the subsequent danger they could pose to civilian rule.

Perhaps of even greater significance than the general pattern of civil-military relations has been the absence of direct responsibility in these countries—again with the notable exception of Greece under the colonels—of the armed forces as such for acts of official and unofficial violence against the civilian population. Indeed, by comparative standards, the levels of repression in the period preceding regime change were low. Even in countries where they had been high in the past, for example, in the savagery that accompanied and followed the Spanish Civil War, the memory of repressive acts had faded and few of the victims were still around to demand restitution and justice. Consequently these countries are free of one of the central issues that is plaguing the current transition in Argentina and that will certainly affect the one yet to occur in Chile. Only in the Greek case was this issue a significant problem and the Karamanlis government proceeded cautiously and selectively in dealing with it.

But a more favorable geostrategic location and international context, even coupled with a lesser responsibility of the military for policy-making and repression, do not suffice in my view to explain the interregional differences explicitly and implicitly raised in these chapters. Much was said—however inconclusively—about the possibility that the "civil societies" of Southern Europe and Latin America might be differently configured and differentially viable. The root hypothesis is that for an effective and enduring challenge to authoritarian rule to be mounted, and for political democracy to become and remain an alternative mode of political domination, a country must possess a civil society in which certain community and group identities exist independent of the state and in which certain types of self-constituted units are capable of acting autonomously in defense of their own interests and ideals. Moreover, these identities and interests must not only be dispersed throughout the country, they must also be capable of being concentrated when the occasion demands, that is, they must be organized for coherent collective action. In democracies, such participation is accomplished in large part consensually through political parties which compete to win electoral majorities, ally with others in dominant coalitions, or enter into consociational arrangements. Underneath these "superstructural" expressions of territorial and partisan representation lies a particular social configuration—"a historical bloc" to use Antonio Gramsci's expression—that orients the direction of change, provides the dominant ideology, and organizes the distribution of benefits.

Could it be that the countries of Southern Europe, or at least some of them, possess more viable civil societies and hegemonic blocs than those of Latin America? This observation is obviously not something that can be proven. In any case, transition from authoritarian rule is clearly not merely a matter of economic development or societal complexity, as the earlier literature on the "social requisites of democracy" put it. Italy and Spain may be demonstrably more economically developed and diverse than any country in Latin America, but Portugal, Greece, and certainly Turkey are not. What is relevant to an understanding of these differences are the obscure historical conditions that have given rise to independent territorial communities, especially towns and cities, and to distinctive functional identities, especially of social classes, economic sectors, and professions. Ethnic and linguistic groups, religions and sects, voluntary associations and social service organizations, gender and generational groupings have also prominently contributed to the institutionalized social pluralism that supports a strong civil society. What is particularly important about these groups, as opposed to the families, clans, cliques, cabals, and clienteles that predominate in other social formations, is that they have a public status, a *bürgerliche* quality about them. They not only acquire, often through lengthy struggle, a recognized right to exist, but they also can openly deliberate about their common affairs and publicly act in defense of justifiable interests. This public status constitutes their "civicness" and gives them the capacity to escape subordination to state authority or governmental manipulation and, hence, to contribute to eventual democratization.

Within the study of Western Europe, it is a commonplace to observe that the countries on its southern flank lack these qualities of "civicness." Salvador Giner in his carefully balanced chapter in this volume assesses these alleged peculiarities. In less skillful hands, these societies have been frequently depicted as awash in "amoral familism," "clientelism," and "personalism," supposedly to explain their deviance from normal, that is, Northern and Central European, patterns of citizen behavior and public authority. Not only is this North-South contrast within Europe frequently exaggerated, but it ignores the substantial social, economic, and even normative transformations that have taken place in recent decades behind the facade of authoritarian immobilism. Spain is certainly the clearest case, and the Maravall-Santamaría chapter stresses the extent to which that country has "caught up" with the region, not just in terms of productive capacity, distribution of income, and availability of services, but also in terms of individual values, group identities, and collective aspirations. Admittedly, Portugal and Greece have not moved so far or so fast to close the gap. Turkey, with its strong and persistent "statist tradition," seems a different case altogether.

Nevertheless, we have a potential explanation for some of the contrasts observed in these chapters if we assume that certain historical factors produced—in very different mixes from one country to another—more resilient and viable civil societies in Southern Europe than in Latin America.[1] The potential list of historical factors seems endless: greater population density, more compact settlement patterns, lesser internal mobility, frequent warfare, religious nonconformity, emigration flows, dispersed land ownership, less ethnic stratification, greater diversity in languages and dialects, more widely distributed and specialized occupational skills, higher levels of preindustrial literacy, less central city predominance and greater provincial city autonomy, more deeply rooted traditions of guild organization, and so forth. The authors on Southern Europe more than those writing on Latin America stress the extent to which mobilization and pressure from below were factors leading to a liberalization of authoritarian rule, although most would probably agree with the generalization that calculations and conflicts within the dominant group and among its privileged supporters/beneficiaries provide the major motivation for beginning a regime transformation. Even more striking, however, is their emphasis on the revival of civil society that almost immediately ensues upon liberalization and makes it virtually impossible for the process to stop short of a more thoroughgoing democratization. "Franco-ism without Franco," "Spinolismo" in Portugal, or monarchic oligarchy without the colonels in Greece were simply not viable options.

Another possible "unobtrusive" indicator of the greater strength of civil societies in Southern Europe compared with Latin America can be seen in the parties and factions that have emerged to fill the new spaces for political action. They tend to be associated closely (organically?) with class and status divisions and, in the case of Spain, with ethnic, linguistic, and regional differentiations. Populist movements and personalistic followings play a less significant role, although Greece and Turkey are notable exceptions, confirming our "suspicion" that the civil societies of these two countries are more analogous to those in Latin America. Centrist or Center-Right parties performed surprisingly well in the founding elections in all the Southern European countries. This fact is particularly striking given the dubious heritage of complicity they had to defend and the initially high level of citizen expectation for change they had to face. Even when, in subsequent contests, voter preferences swung to the Left (and, in the cases of Greece and Spain, brought Socialist governments to power), conservative forces have chosen to continue within the electoral game—presumably because they remained confident of their popular support and eventual capacity to return to power—something only a variegated civil society enjoying widespread consent could guarantee. Left parties did not win the initial elections held after the demise of authoritarian rule in Southern Europe, but they quickly became a formidable presence with a strong stake in the electoral game, a stake that subsequently increased. Especially crucial in Italy and Spain, and to a lesser extent in Greece after the colonels, was the moderate strategy adopted by national Communist parties. Despite their often militant rejection of "bourgeois democracy" in the past, their leaders somehow became convinced that such a maximalist strategy was no longer viable during the transition. Again, the existence of a civil society with complex patterns of cleavage and identity encouraged such a calculation. In other words, the Southern European countries have been less threatened by hard-line (*duro*) factions, either from the ranks of previous supporters of authoritarian rule, or from those of its most intransigent opponents, and they have been better able to rely upon shifting, even rotating, coalitions of softliners (*blandos*) than have the countries of Latin America.

Finally, one can speculate about some ideological and ideational factors. Are the procedures and symbols of political democracy simply more legitimate (or better stated, less discredited) in Western Europe than in Latin America? Given the convergence of regime type that has occurred in Western Europe is there a fundamental consensus that democracy represents the only political mode appropriate to contemporary circumstances? In Latin America a much greater variety of political experiences is simultaneously present. More groups seem convinced that political or "bourgeois" democracy is either too hazardous to their interests or too prosaic for their ideals. If one excludes the problematic case of Turkey, only marginal groups in the other four Southern European countries advocate such positions. At the height of the Portuguese Revolution, more radical models such as "Mediterranean Socialism" or "Popular Democracy" seemed possible, but these illusions have passed and the country has settled into a liberal bourgeois/social democratic consensus. Terrorist movements which sought to propel these polities into another configuration by violence have failed utterly to do so and, perhaps, have succeeded only in convincing the citizenry that no other alternative is currently possible.

The bankruptcy of the Soviet model has become evident to all but the most diehard elements of national Communist parties.

The Southern European countries may have also benefited from their distance from the American system of government. Western Europe may seem to be monolithically democratic in the contemporary period, but beneath that overall similarity lie many differences in institutional configuration. For example, pure parliamentarism, semipresidentialism, and consociationalism, coupled with a wide range of party systems, electoral arrangements, and territorial distributions of authority, all coexist within the area. They offer a variety of experiences and formulas from which prospective democratizers can learn and all provide some assurance of legitimate acceptance. There is evidence that the regime builders in Southern Europe have creatively sampled this extensive "menu." Witness, for example, the use to which Greece and Portugal have put the "semipresidentialist" model pioneered by Gaullist France, and Spain's borrowing of the West German device of "a constructive vote of no-confidence." This is not to say that they have not exploited their own institutional traditions. The Spaniards even accepted a formula, left to them by the outgoing authoritarian regime, which many thought *démodé:* constitutional monarchy. By the account of José Maravall and Julián Santamaría, it has proven to be a wise and significant choice.

Latin American regime builders may be compelled to choose from a more restricted menu. The hegemony of the United States as a model of political democracy, not to mention the legacy of their own nineteenth-century constitutions, makes it less likely that they will deviate from the presidentialist, bicameral, formal checks-and-balances, first-past-the-post "ideal" with its implied two-party system. Because of the complex interest structures and mass electorates of the contemporary world the U.S. model may be a much more difficult system to implement and operate than the more flexible arrangements that parliamentarism, coalitional politics, and proportional representation can offer. In any case, the countries of Southern Europe have opted for the latter and, so far, have managed to avoid the extremes of polarization or immobilism which are alleged to be its pitfalls.

To some, perhaps to the authors of the chapters that follow, this introduction may seem excessively optimistic. This optimism is largely the result of my having stressed the contrast with the Latin American cases, in which the transitions from authoritarian rule have been much more incomplete, inconclusive, and uncertain. Greece, Portugal, and Spain still have some way to go before their nascent democracies can safely be considered to be consolidated and capable of meeting conceivable challenges. Their having already passed one of the most critical thresholds in democratization—the peaceful rotation of previous opposition parties into power—is an especially encouraging sign. Nevertheless, in all three some diehard remnants of authoritarian rule continue to conspire, and a sizable faction on the Left persists in rejecting political democracy in principle, even if it has accommodated to its presence in practice. In Spain the greatest challenge comes from regionalism or ethnonationalism which threatens the territorial integrity of the state and, with it, the institutional survival of the regime. Italy, of course, has been a consolidated democracy for some time. It has yet to cross the threshold of party rotation, but it has survived protracted mobilization of regime opponents, threats to its territorial integrity, high levels of social and labor conflict, and more recently, terrorism of both the Left and Right. Currently, its principal problem is whether it can adapt the flexible parliamentary institutions, which initially facilitated its transition from authoritarian rule and enabled it to meet successfully a wide range of challenges, to the imperatives of governing what has subsequently become a much more complex society and an internationalized economy. Turkey is still at an uncertain point in its transition from authoritarian rule. It is too early to judge whether its present limited democracy will survive, much less whether it will evolve toward single-party predominance, Italian style; shifting coalition politics, Portuguese style; or two-party rotation, Greek or Spanish style.

With these transitions, four of the five Southern European countries have been belatedly entering into the range of institutional and behavioral variation characteristic of contemporary Western European politics. We can anticipate that, in the future, social scientists will increasingly treat them more like siblings and less like stepchildren. In the meantime, however, before the transition is over and political life in these countries has settled into the trenches of party identification, electoral competition, interest associability, and corporatist bargaining, it may be more useful to look elsewhere for similarities and contrasts. As long as the outcome is dominated by highly uncertain skirmishes between shifting and vaguely delineated "hard-line" and "soft-line" factions, by the impact of a momentary popular upsurge, and by the effect of transient pacts and emergent procedures, the comparison with analogous experiences in Latin America, especially its more developed Southern Cone countries, seems promising. The Woodrow Wilson Center's working group was based on this premise.

# 2 •

# Political Economy, Legitimation, and the State in Southern Europe

## Salvador Giner

### Introduction

Is Southern Europe a distinct, identifiable universe? Can the sociological imagination capture it? Are the obvious discontinuities and acute varieties of the area it encompasses too salient for the expression "Southern Europe" to have any useful meaning beyond that attributed to it by strategists, geographers, and politicians? Minimally rigorous answers to these questions are bound to be complex, for they will have to reflect faithfully the intricacy of the Mediterranean world, the ambiguities and contradictions that are its very stuff. It is with them that this chapter will attempt to grapple.

As a region, Southern Europe has often been seen as standing halfway between an advanced, capitalist, and industrial world, and those lands farther removed from the historical center of modernization. The belated and, no doubt, incomplete passage of its societies from a peripheral (or, more accurately, semiperipheral) position in the world of labor and power into a far more central one has been awkward.[1] Compounding this difficulty in certain cities and regions of this part of Europe has been a domestic bourgeoisie endowed with a fully modern or Western outlook. These societies never "imported" capitalism or the industrial mode of production. Except for Turkey, they have always been substantially European, save perhaps to the occasional unperceptive Northern traveler in search of exoticism. Two of them, Spain and Portugal, became vast and enduring overseas empires, a role crucial to the development of the modern Eurocentric world system. A third, Italy, managed to get its share of late European imperial expansionism in Africa. By contrast, of course, Greece was never an imperial nation, but was itself a part, until 1821, of an oriental one. And Turkey emerged at the core of a crumbling Eurasian Empire, which disintegrated precisely because of its incapacity to cope with the forces of change with which we are here primarily concerned.

These societies have been subject to the ambiguities, strains, and endemic polarizations generated by the simultaneous presence of a number of contradictory trends, uneven stages of economic development, and, in some cases, heterogeneous ethnic, class, and cultural components. Vigorously asserting themselves within their boundaries were the most diverse and apparently irreconcilable trends: cultural universalism and local and kinship bonds of patronage; religious legitimation of public institutions and militant secularism; classless and doctrinaire political commitments and uncompromisingly classbound ideologies; dependent industrialization through foreign capitalist investment and a substantial degree of national capitalism, later followed by state capitalist intervention. Consequently it has not been easy to rank Southern European societies along conventional and imaginary continua, or axes, often used (perhaps quite carelessly) for the rough classification of countries, such as backwardness/modernity, preindustrial capitalism/advanced capitalism, traditional fatalism/enterprising individualism, intuitive religiosity/scientific rationalism. The confrontation of these conflicting forces, the strife and strains and the successive undemocratic solutions that have frequently been reached at the political level give the Northern rim of the Mediterranean, in spite of its striking internal varieties, an unmistakable commonality and distinctiveness within the larger framework of European society.

This distinctiveness, together with certain historical continuities and a common geopolitical and economic location on Europe's southern flank, allows the analyst to advance a number of cautious and limited generalizations. In this chapter I propose to make and substantiate such generalizations by analyzing some important aspects of the class and power structures resulting from the cleavages and many-sided confrontations that characterize Southern Europe, as the basis for a macrosociological explanation of social change in the region. I will discuss historical periods appropriate to the four societies and hope to show that their troubled national experiences possess a much higher degree of consistency than is often thought to be the case. Certain general patterns, cutting across countries and states, do emerge, and consequently belie the image of haphazard instability, volatility, and unpredictability so often held by observers of Europe's southern world.

The recognition of these historical and structural patterns does not mean that all Mediterranean societies on the northern rim can be made to fit a single Procrustean bed, only that they exhibit a number of interesting common traits with respect to their historical evolution, predominant modes of political domination, the form and tempo of their economic development (or stagnation, as the case may be), and systems of class relations. By comparing them and looking at their common traits as much as at their divergences, we will be in a better position to know not only why these countries are economically late developers, but also why they began to improve their status at a given moment in their recent history, or, more accurately, why they have not done even better. Unfortunately, the very scope of the analysis, together with the length of this chapter, will not allow me to go into the details of every particular historical event in each one of the countries: Portugal, Spain, Italy, Greece, and, to a much lesser extent for obvious reasons, Turkey.

Merely for heuristic purposes, the historical evolution of the region since the early nineteenth century can be subdivided into four distinct periods, separated by three modes of transition. In this respect, the following discussion shows the emergence of a remarkable degree of overlap and synchronism among the four that are clearly Southern European countries. (Turkey appears to be quite marginal to the process in the early stages, and thus receives little attention in this chapter. With the passing of time, however, its progressive if unsteady incorporation into the Western sphere has become more pronounced, so that today its share in the evolution of the Southern European world can no longer be considered as altogether questionable.) More important for my argument than the relative synchronism of key events and structural changes, however, is the sequential and episodic similarity among the countries. The four suggested phases are oligarchic control, bourgeois consolidation, Fascist dictatorship, and constitutional order.

### Oligarchic Rule and Extreme Popular Exclusion

The immediate breakdown of the *anciens régimes* allowed exceptional popular participation in wars of liberation and independence, linked to ephemeral moments of radical liberal access to power. Yet these events were soon harnessed by the oligarchic monopoly of the state and the systematic exclusion of the subordinate classes from any form of participation in the political sphere by means of a restricted franchise and frequent military intervention. (The longest-lasting case seems to have been Greece where court and *tzakia* control by notables lasted from 1820 to 1869.) This type of domination was made possible by the small scale of the local industrial bourgeoisie, the nature of international capitalist penetration, based largely on foreign dealings with state officials and foreign loans, and the size and dispersion of the rural population. Nevertheless, in this period certain parliamentary processes and a limited opposition were established.

### Bourgeois Consolidation and Continued Popular Exclusion

At one point the facade of parliamentary institutions created in the first phase began to be used by rising commercial, rural, and industrial bourgeoisie allied to "respectable" middle classes everywhere. These emergent propertied groups often rallied to incipient modern (so-called mass) parties. Popular exclusion and lack of lower-class representation (persecution of trade unions, rigged elections, and so on) resulted in alternating bourgeois regimes, that is, governments that rotated between conservatives and liberals. Between them, they tightly controlled the small sphere of "legitimate" political activity. Thus efforts by Venizelists in Greece, Giolittists in Italy, Mauraists in Spain, and other similar movements toward "national regeneration" from within the established order were doomed by their incapacity or unwillingness to incorporate the peasantry, the proletariat, and other popular forces. Exceptions to this form of class and political exclusion at the end of the period, however, produced the deradicalization and acceptance of some Socialist parties as legitimate participants, but did little to alter the overall conservative nature of the regimes. The transition to the next phase occurred when the political order of such monarchist, parliamentary, and thoroughly bourgeois hegemonic regimes failed to achieve two aims: (1) the successful incorporation (or, alternatively, neutralization and control) of the growing radical extra-parliamentary opposition; and (2) the successful implantation of a privately financed imperialist state. The latter aspect of the phenomenon was illustrated by the Italian defeat in Abyssinia (1895), the Portuguese humiliation in Angola and Mozambique (1896 rebellion), the Spanish colonial disaster (Spanish-American War, 1898), and the Greek holocaust in Asia Minor (1922), not to mention the steady erosion and final collapse of the Ottoman Empire.

### Fascist and Fascistoid Military Dictatorships

The transition to this period came with the "disorders" bred by the onslaughts of the excluded and persecuted radical bourgeoisie and their allies against the old ruling groups, now in disarray largely because of their own political failures. In a number of cases these newly mobilized groups managed to bring about quasi-revolutionary republican regimes but, as a response to their serious challenge, law-and-order militaristic or militarily consolidated reactionary coalitions soon came to power. They set about complementing the endemic shortcomings of private capital accumulation with state intervention. Thus, despite the cultural archaism of some of the dictatorships (Italian Fascism was certainly more of a novelty), modernization from above continued everywhere. The civil freedoms allowed to exist precariously under the second phase as part of its basic arrangements were now abolished.

### Constitutional Order within Advanced Capitalist Corporatism

The exhaustion of the dictatorial praxis was caused by the continued rise of the middle classes, further urbanization and depeasantization, secularization, working-class opposition, state capitalism, and the international penetration of the economy. A series of crises, some of them linked to military defeats and adventurism, others to a renewed upsurge of popular and democratic forces, brought about the end of the dictatorships and the present parliamentary democratic regimes in Southern Europe. Although the radical rhetoric of the Left has been kept alive, its virtually unprecedented political inclusion has come in exchange for its almost complete abandonment of revolutionary pretensions. The left-wing opposition accepts class distinctions and economic exclusion based on the relative permanence of the inherited social inequality as a compensation for its incorporation into the legitimate sphere of political life. Thus general moderation in respect to the traditional political demands of the radicals and a commitment to a minimum of welfare state policies by the conservatives form the basis of a new consensus. Yet, given the region's inherited political culture, the levels of ideological dissent, extremism of every kind, including both nihilism and maximalism, continue to be higher, by contrast, than they are in certain other European societies, though much lower than those prevalent in the region earlier. Given the nature of international tensions today, however, it is not prudent to predict that these phenomena will continue to diminish. Meanwhile, this general moderation is taking place with the full participation of these societies in the development of contemporary "corporatist" tendencies in the economy. In the four countries a tripartite process of agreement among government, the employers, and the trade unions has become an important feature of their economic life, whereas several of the other features often attributed to contemporary corporatism have also taken root. It is now possible to speak, albeit tentatively, of a limited degree of "convergence" with the arrangements prevalent elsewhere in the West.

### The Rise of Capitalism in Late Developing Societies

The political and intellectual history of Southern Europe in modern times cannot be explained without the anguished self-consciousness of the members of certain elite groups—from enlightened ministers of *ancien régime* governments to bourgeois reformers and educators—about the problem of relative backwardness. Their practical initiatives have ranged from notable improvements in education, health, and transportation to the most foolish imperialist adventurism, from the patient and skillful introduction of tolerance and liberalism to the hurried and crude recourse to reactionary dictatorship for the violent, involuntary accumulation of private and state capital. The Southern European preoccupation with what was seen as its endemic backwardness and the search for ways to overcome it did not suddenly appear, as did the related concept of underdevelopment when it burst out in the midst of ex-colonial countries in the twentieth century.[2] Ironically, theories of underdevelopment and economic dependence were later extended to the Southern European region, despite the fact that the evolution of their economies and political life has been very different from that of the so-called Third World.

Having witnessed the emergence and consolidation of certain social structures and cultural innovations that were in due course to transform the face of the European world, the peoples of the northern rim of the Mediterranean suffered a sharp and profound reversal in their fortunes toward the end of the Renaissance. Though the prosperity of the entire European Atlantic seaboard affected Castile and Portugal through their ports at Seville and Lisbon, the fortunes of the great patrician republics—the imperial cities of Barcelona and Venice—suffered irreparable damage under Ottoman expansion, as did the entire Byzantine Greek world, which fell entirely within the power of the Porte. Catalonia, Barcelona's hinterland, had become by the Renaissance one of the most advanced areas in Europe.[3] Subsequently excluded from trading with the overseas colonies of the Spanish monarchy, Catalans had hardly any choice but retrenchment and occasional revolts against the crown. Commercial stagnation combined with agricultural decline in the southern half of Europe, precisely when momentous innovations were taking place in commerce and agriculture elsewhere on the same continent.[4]

The industrial revolution began in those countries (first in England, to be followed by Belgium) which had earlier experienced certain far-reaching and unprecedented inovations in agriculture. Whereas the majority of European farmers were subsistence peasants living on small holdings (or on large latifundia in certain areas of Southern Europe), by the sixteenth century the situation in the Low Countries and Great Britain had already begun to change. By 1800 a profound agricultural revolution had produced a capitalist, commercialized, and highly efficient farming system, which enhanced the further development of nonagricultural capitalism. In England, the existence of coal and iron ore provided a special encouragement to industrialization. By contrast, the Mediterranean countries were immensely poor in natural resources. Italian industrialization throughout the nineteenth century, especially in the development of its nontextile industries, went hand in hand with the costly importation of coal. Because of the low quality of its coal, up to the eve of World War I, Spain had to be supplied by the United Kingdom with well over 40 percent of its coal and coke needs.[5] Given the technological knowledge, specific resources, and consumer needs of those times, Southern Europe was poor both in relative and absolute terms.

The formidable rise of industrial and financial capitalism in Northwestern Europe, followed by intense international competition among its national powers in search of new markets and areas of influence, had serious consequences for the development of bourgeois industrial society in the southern semiperiphery. The seeds of that development had been planted much earlier, and were unmistakably to be found in Catalonia, Lombardy, Piedmont, and Porto, as well as in the far-flung merchant classes of the Greek nation. Yet massive advanced capitalist intervention in the guise of both political interference and the *diktat* of much more powerful foreign buyers and sellers imposed two forms of constraint.

In certain cases, such as Portugal and Greece, early promises of development were frustrated. Greek efforts to create a textile and shipbuilding industry had already floundered before the 1821 War of Independence against the Turks.[6] On the other hand, although Pombal's eighteenth-century reforms in Portugal had obvious limitations, they might ultimately have led the country into nonagricultural growth and modernization, had Portugal not been forced to become a client nation with a client empire under British tutelage in order to survive as a relatively independent state. In the larger societies, Italy and Spain, there occurred less a complete destruction of autochthonous possibilities for capitalist development than a special process of subordinate development. I use the term "special" because, in the first place, competition and dissension among the great powers (and the private companies and finance institutions operating from them) often slackened foreign surveillance and allowed for important bursts of nondependent economic development in both countries, leading to the consolidation of national capitalist industries. In the second place, their national bourgeoisie, sheltered behind weak and inefficient but nevertheless somewhat effective states, managed to build up their strength by creating markets in their own territories, allowing them to enter the international arena when conditions were favorable. The consolidation of this pattern occurred in Italy during the expansion of 1878–89, when the "leap forward" from textiles—silk, cotton, wool—to railway machinery and engineering opened the way for full transformation in the first decade of the twentieth century, with the establishment of chemicals, light and heavy machinery, and hydroelectric plants. The meager participation of foreign capital over the period (the years 1889–96 witnessed a serious international depression) only emphasized the pattern. A similar phenomenon occurred in Spain, though it lagged behind in both time and consequence. The same diversification from textiles to chemistry, iron and steel, and hydroelectric power occurred there. Although it began in the years before World War I, the process gathered momentum under the advantageous conditions for export enjoyed by the nonbelligerent economies during the conflict.[7]

The belated rise of industrial capitalism in Southern Europe before and during World War I was only the most visible trace of a deeper current, with a much longer past: the qualitative transformation of all the economies in question into commercial, market economies, with wage payments for labor, proletarianization, and capital accumulation—often, of course, "primitive" capital accumulation. The initial defeat of the industrial revolution in some parts (Portugal, Greece) and its circumscribed success in others (Italy, Spain) meant that capitalism had to confine itself for a long time to the commercial and property spheres. To oversimplify this complex issue: the societies of the South had long ceased to be precapitalist, but their new-found capitalism became stunted—its transition to industrialism systematically blocked by the forces that have already been described and others that will be analyzed. These countries were not so much "late joiners" to the capitalist industrial transformation; rather, their respective bourgeoisie had failed in their efforts to put them among the "first comers."

## The Peripheral State and the Path towards Reactionary Despotism

When Southern Europe entered the post-Napoleonic era, its political map was extremely varied. Yet important common traits and developments may be discerned. Despite a number of initial reforms (save in Greece) begun under the auspices of the *ancien régime*, nineteenth-century efforts to continue the process met with stiff resistance and counterattacks which drew their strength from the still massive precapitalist component of those societies. Liberal and reformist forces managed to reach power and introduce modernizing innovations only precariously and during brief periods, usually when the traditionalist ruling classes were caught off guard. On the whole, the liberal bourgeoisie managed to continue furthering capitalism only at the price of its continual alliance with the most backward-looking elements in the society. They thereby forsook some of the civic and political facets of the liberal creed to which they claimed adherence. In exchange, the initially anticapitalist stance of the upper classes of the surviving *ancien régime* was for the most part abandoned, though their own view of profit maximization remained rather peculiar in a number of cases. The seigneural ethos of the great rural landlords of Sicily and Andalusia is a typical example of this survival, and a paradoxical one at that, since feudal ties were themselves weakly defined in Southern Europe. Defeudalization took the line of least resistance, as shown by the forcible sale of church lands and properties in the middle and latter part of the nineteenth century.

With some variations, the process was everywhere similar. Thus, throughout the 1808–1914 period the Iberian bourgeoisie were too small and weak for their aspirations of economic and political supremacy. In Portugal, compromise with an immobilist and patriarchal establishment was their lasting option. Moreover, the Portuguese ruling classes were also forced to accept "free exchange" by their British ally, thus dooming all chances for the development of a substantial national industry.[8] The far larger and more complicated Spanish society offered somewhat greater possibilities. Yet the Catalan bourgeoisie and later the Basque were rooted ethnically and economically in a distinct and limited way. Their ability to control the huge, cumbersome, remote, and, as they saw it, archaic state apparatus in Madrid became problematic. As a consequence, significant sectors of the Catalan bourgeoisie soon began to appreciate the attractiveness of regionalism and, later, to engage in a persistent demand for home rule.[9] Eventually, the bourgeoisie of both regions would settle for a protectionism that allowed them to enjoy unmolested the exploitation of the Spanish market (including the remaining overseas possessions) for their own industries. Tariff protection, however, reinforced the familistic structure of Catalan capitalism and, by eliminating competition, made industrial renewal and innovation less necessary, thus widening the serious gap that existed between industry in Spain and that in the more advanced areas abroad.[10]

The reverse situation obtained in Italy at the time of the unification. Whereas the Catalans possessed a relatively advanced society which was subordinated to a larger preindustrial political unit, the Piedmontese, Lombards, and Ligurians formed the base on which a modern state structure was being erected. The Northern Italian elites were also, initially, the elites of the new state. Yet the rapid inclusion of heavily populated backward areas and consequent demographic weight of Southern Italians meant a rapid loss of the elites' control over the emergent public administration. The new state provided vast and relatively more attractive opportunities for employment for the urban nonindustrial middle classes from the dismantled Papal States and the Kingdom of the Two Sicilies. Moreover, clientelistic favoritism and electoral manipulation helped to inflate the ranks of officialdom. This last phenomenon, of course, was not restricted to Italy. Greece, for instance, suffered from even greater bureaucratic inflation as soon as the nation acquired an independent state.[11] What is significant in each case is that, no matter where the initiative to reform or build the state came from, the result was similar. The circumscribed or hardly existent industrial sector combined with the needs of an aspirant modern state and oligarchic democracy, overloading the public administration with parasitical personnel. This has remained a feature of Southern Europe down to the present.

During its early stages, the modern state itself did not engage in production, save perhaps as a subsidiary to entrepreneurs for whom certain functionally necessary investments were not yet or no longer profitable. Certainly, the states of Southern Europe were in no position to engage in subsidizing production. Under the new conditions, earlier traditions of state investment—Venice had had the earliest and longest-lasting state industry of any European polity— were of no avail. Nor were well-established habits of state control and redistribution of wealth of any use; they did not respond to a modern conception of investment but rather reflected a form of centralized preindustrial state patrimonialism, as in the paradigmatic case of the Ottomans, for whom the Porte had become the central economic institution in the empire.[12] It is not surprising, then, that when state investment for industrialization and modernization finally made its appearance it did so with a vengeance, often under the aegis of fascistic autarkic economic notions. However, until such time, the chief service rendered by state expenditure and policies to the respective industrial bourgeoisie was an inconsistent protectionism, some public works, and police and army protection. Economic protectionism was not restricted to tariffs against foreign manufacturers: privileged contracts for local suppliers also played an important role. Even this approach happened late and haphazardly, and only after convoluted and protracted political battles within the ruling classes. For example, the introduction of the protective tariff in Italy did not occur until 1887. The endemic financial weakness of the national treasuries forced governments to accept foreign investment as a solution. Even if one recognizes some beneficial effects on the standard of living of the people directly affected by it, it could never by itself help create an independent and fully advanced economy, on a par with those from whence investment came. (The United States was at the time also dependent on foreign capital, but national capital formation was intense, and did not have to struggle against precapitalist or "primitive" capitalist forces, once the Civil War was over.) Nevertheless, there were different degrees of success in the bourgeois "nationalization" of capital investment: Italy was most effective in developing a strong capitalist class; Spain came nearest; Portugal lacked one; Greece possessed an absentee merchant bourgeois class. This observation raises a number of important questions in the economic history of international development, dependence, and arrested development that still remain unresolved.[13]

The long road to fascistic and semifascistic autarky was paved with the frustrations of a chronic dependence on foreign powers. The hegemonic classes of the Southern European countries until the rise of the interwar dictatorships were plagued by their own ideology of international free trade among unequal nations which they tried to make compatible with certain doses of protectionism. They were undermined by the free trade interests of their own agricultural exporters and of their government officials, so often open to foreign pressures and bribery. Foreign investments poured into the countries without regard to the specific needs of their populations and profits were repatriated without substantial reinvestments in the host country. Often and for a long period of time, foreign companies at ridiculously low tax rates exploited great mineral wealth. The governments were too ill equipped both ideologically and technically to face the implications of such dependence. Often, during the crucial early stages of the new era, their attention was absorbed by a deadly struggle with backward hinterlands (brigandage in Greece, Carlist warbands in Spain) and their resources were wasted by an incompetent officialdom. One can hardly wonder why they did not act otherwise; they often raised loans abroad, not to modernize or to industrialize, but simply to put down such awkward rebellions. In contrast with, say Prussia, poised to lead the final transformation of Germany into a great industrial power and without serious internal dissensions (at least, not after 1848), the political leaders of the Southern European countries were usually not in a position to see beyond their immediate, pressing, and often bewildering concerns. Furthermore, international threats and competition varied in Southern, Central, and Northern Europe, being least favorable—given the nature of their economy—for the southerners.

Until the outbreak of World War I substantially changed the political frame of reference for many countries, the universe in which these southern ruling classes moved was certainly nontotalitarian. Their model for national aggrandizement, industrialization, and progress was embodied in the great parliamentary democracies, especially Great Britain. Alternative "routes to modernity" were, of course, being devised; the political formulas of Bismarckian Germany and Meiji Japan are now the best known, but their solution to the problem through "modernization from above" was not yet understood as a "model" by Southern Europeans, however much they might have copied specific military and banking institutions. The implications of the "initially liberal" nature of state control and class inequality for the political order of the South were interesting. In the very early stages, when preindustrial, *ancien régime*-based upper strata were still powerful, they attempted to rule according to an overtly atavistic system of semifeudal privilege. The set of oligarchic families crowding around the Greek throne (the *tzakia*, as they were known) and literally owning and running the Greek state is perhaps the ultimate example of this phenomenon. The *tzakia* even managed to survive the sweeping 1864 electoral reforms by a form of vote control.[14] Its Spanish counterpart was the institution of political bossism known as *caciquismo*. Although it would be an overly simplistic view of any Mediterranean country to describe it as dominated by a handful of families, at least in one case, Portugal, the role of oligarchic lineages and family coteries in the power structure of the state played a vital role until recently. Thus according to some authors the small Portuguese nepotistic oligarchy developed a symbiotic relationship with Salazarism, and its power actually increased as time went on, reinforcing its strength in the regime's most typical institutions.[15] The opposite seems to be the case, however, for the Southern European world. Even in Portugal, the maintenance of such primitive arrangements as pivots of the political order soon grew too complicated.[16]

The most accomplished, lasting, and characteristic political formula arrived at by these societies before the rise of Fascism involved the accommodation of the then paradigmatic "Northwestern" European pattern of liberal-democratic bourgeois government to their own backward environments. (Such a formula, of course, cannot be extended to Turkey, which only began to approximate other Southern European paths toward political modernity after its national War of Independence of 1919–22.) The political formula in question found its most accomplished expression in Giolitian Italy (1878–1914) and Restoration Spain (1876–1923) but it could, almost as well, describe the Greece of Venizelos after 1910, and long periods of Portuguese "republicanism" from 1822 to 1926.

It is essential, however, not to regard these regimes, as they so often have been, as mere aberrations of some ideal European model, an ideal that existed only in the realm of liberal political theory. Rather, they were the specific forms that liberal/conservative class domination took under the sociostructural, economic, and cultural circumstances of the South. The specific elements of the Southern European hegemonic political formula for that age could perhaps be sketchily described under four headings.

**Restrictive Parliamentarianism** This practice was based on a limited, albeit expanding, degree of class pluralism. The incorporated political class was drawn, almost exclusively, from the upper and upper middle classes. Recruitment from other social classes into the "legitimate" political class could occur only after individuals had been safely separated from their social origins through their integration into one of the three main recognized vertical corporations: the church, the army, or the civil service. The stability (and instability) of such a highly conservative political order was underpinned by the actual and promised extent of the franchise. Barriers to its expansion were erected, as elsewhere, on the basis of literacy, property ownership, and so forth. Their demolition, however, was too slow and erratic for the efficient assimilation or neutralization of certain strategically located, hostile sectors of the society. As a consequence, a radicalization of lower middle-class intellectuals ensued. Elsewhere, disappointment and bitter skepticism grew—often connected with the growing urban proletariat and the increasingly commercialized peasantry. The real crisis came when the ruling classes, trapped in their own intransigent ultraconservative ideologies, ran out of concessions. It is true, however, that some leaders (notably Gioliti) were hardly ever ideologically trapped and that they were notably open to making concessions.

**The Liberal Creed** The ultimate sanction of the political order of that period was not autocracy in any of its known guises. Thus, even military dictators often issued their rallying calls (pronunciamentos) by presenting themselves only as emergency saviors of a "monarchic-liberal" order. Nor was it the application of sheer physical coercion. It was the liberal creed, usually in its conservative version, but also occasionally and uneasily combined with more radical (often anticlerical) and doctrinaire ideologies. In fact, the combined version, known often as "radicalism," frequently functioned as the accepted opposition. The split into two distinctive forms of liberalism—or rather, of capitalist bourgeois ideology—did not, however, involve a drastic cleavage in political life. In fact, the distinction became less and less intense as time went on. We find its roots split at the very beginning of the period—for instance, in the juxtaposition of Mazzini's Young Italy Movement (which was secular, republican, and democratic) and Cavour's constitutionalism (ready to find a role for the monarchy and an accommodation with the church). The Greek *dichasmos*, or schism, between monarchists and Venizelists (after 1916) is another example. The virulence of the struggles between the two branches of the accepted political spectrum should not blind us to the fact of their complementarity and shared dominance within the political arena. The problem, which led much later to the ultimate breakdown of the system, was the inability of both wings (more glaring in the case of the radicals) to encompass, coopt, or otherwise integrate the vast sections of the civil society that fell outside the class-bound liberal creed. Unlike the Social Democrats in Northern and Central Europe, anarchists, Socialists, and other system-challenging movements—Left and Right—in the South were never offered the chance of entering into a real and lasting compromise, save perhaps in Italy in 1910 and 1911. In that country, however, the chance was ruined by the Libyan War; once again the effects of colonialism upon the internal affairs of these countries appear as highly disruptive. In a word, the radical opposition, by and large, was constantly kept beyond the pale and led to some form of final confrontation.

*Societal "Dualism"*  Under circumstances of societal "dualism," reform and modernization occurred through an exceedingly slow process of accommodation between the interests of the ruling classes and the pressures from below. The dominant interests included the maintenance of low wages, the avoidance of agrarian reform whenever possible, and the advantageous private participation in state-sponsored projects through loans and other means. Pressures from below included, of course, the workers' movement, middle-class revolutionary intellectuals, and academic and peasant unrest. The built-in lag in responsiveness explains the enormous volume of accumulated contradictions that characterized Southern European societies on the eve of Fascism. On the one hand, some essential structural changes, such as agrarian reform, had not taken place at all.[17] (In some areas, however, external factors had forced reform upon the government; for example, in Greece war led to an influx of citizens. In 1917 Venizelos was able to break up the large Thessalian latifundia, or *chiftliks*; subsequently, the 1922 Asia Minor debacle put further pressure on land occupation and distribution among the people.) On the other hand, little or no effort was made to meet the demands of a sizable industrial sector, with its urban proletariat and a small but growing middle class. In the specific sense of these cleavages, but not in the sense that there were "two" societies and "two" economic orders in each country, the Southern European region possessed a degree of structural dualism.[18]

*The Utopian Element* In this social and political context, governing elites of the southern countries promoted fantasies of national aggrandizement. They spoke a language and manipulated the symbols of belligerent expansionism or imperialism—often as a means of diverting attention from their failure to implement domestic reform. Certainly, realistic (and materialistic) bourgeois imperialist aims were present, for example, in the Spanish mining interests in the Riffian wars in Morocco, the Portuguese share, however meager, of the economic exploitation of the country's own vast overseas territories, the desire of Italian industrialists to acquire greater markets for an economy becoming substantial in world terms by the turn of the century. Such bourgeois factors loom large in the explanation of imperialist expansionism. Yet only hurt pride, not political calculation, could have inspired the Spaniards to send their antiquated and feeble fleet against the American aggressors in the Caribbean and the Philippines in 1898. Other cases, such as the Greek Anatolian adventure (posthumously defined as "folly" by Greek critics), may have been objectively less foolish because it was perhaps reasonable at the time to assume the extreme weakness of the Turks, especially after they had been so thoroughly routed in World War I. The uneasy success of Italian expansion in Africa may also weaken claims that southern imperialism was utopian. Yet only a perception of national realities in terms of ethnocentric European ideological distortion can help us understand the behavior of governments that refused to improve their internal markets, raise the educational level of their peoples, or even promote further capital accumulation in their own economies and that instead embarked on disastrous wars in hopeless emulation of the Great Powers—even though that emulation sometimes served the immediate purpose of diverting popular discontent from much graver social issues.

The inner contradictions of each one of these basic components—limited parliamentarianism, restricted and divided liberalism, stunted reformism, and utopian imperialism—irrevocably led these societies toward a specific form of class despotism, namely, Fascist or *fascistisant* dictatorship, when the social transformations created under the aegis of the "paternalistic" political order came to be too much at odds with that order. A new solution had to be found that would, on the one hand, allow the continued legitimation of the inherited system of inequality, foster the widespread aim of national aggrandizement, and further capitalist industrialization while, on the other, successfully destroy the revolutionary movements of the Left which had begun seriously to challenge the existing order. Such a solution was found and imposed through various forms of violence at somewhat different points in time. Its triumph meant the end of the old liberal bourgeois order as well as a redefinition of the political and economic functions of the state. It meant, also, the demise of the revolutionary path to modernization in Southern Europe.

## "Fascism" and Class Domination

The question of the precise nature of Fascism has long been a puzzling one. No less confusing is the question of "how Fascist" Italy, Spain, and the other Mediterranean countries really were.[19] Fascism, *in abstracto*, possesses characteristics of varying degrees of intensity in the area analyzed here. "Pure" Fascism entails a political cult under one single chief; a mode of class domination closely related to single-party control of the society; extreme nationalism; the systematic neutralization of the opposition, up to, and including, its physical extermination; autarkic economic policies linked to state enterprise; the myth of ethnic, national, or cultural superiority; extreme anti-Communism and the reduction of all opposition to Communism; imperialism; political paranoia. In real life, however, this construct appears as part and parcel of a larger political universe in which other, less explicit, structures of power and inequality play a considerable role.

Not only the degree of "Fascistization" but also the kind of Fascist experience varied considerably from society to society. In the Mediterranean area, the nearest thing to the Fascist ideal type was, of course, Mussolini's regime, which dominated Italy from 1922 to 1943. Some observers may claim that only Italy was Fascist as it was the only country with a popular, charismatic leader. This observation ignores the perhaps unpalatable fact that Franco and Salazar were as popular and, indeed, as cherished, in several substantial sections of their countries as Mussolini was in Italy. One could even argue that they were more "legitimate," for they were rather more closely identified with certain mentalities and deeply engrained class attitudes than Mussolini, who was committed to a party and a movement. Others may claim that authentically Fascist economic policies of national autarky were carried out in only two of the four countries. Despite these and other differences at certain stages of their history, the other Mediterranean dictatorial regimes— Salazarism in Portugal (1926–74) and Francoism in Spain (1936–76)—came quite close to the Italian formula. The Greek Metaxas regime (1936–40) shared important characteristics with the others; certainly the outspokenly Fascist beliefs of that dictator himself firmly placed the country within the sphere of European Mediterranean "Fascism." Moreover, certain other regimes, either preceding or succeeding the hard-core Fascist periods just mentioned—for example, the Primo de Rivera dictatorship in Spain (1923–31) and the colonels' dictatorship in Greece (1967–74)—may have been less completely Fascist, but they can be analyzed as either starting or completing the historical process. For Southern Europe must be viewed as a whole, rather than as a number of discrete and unrelated instances of praetorian right-wing rule. The Fascist or *fascistisant* solution in that part of the world must be understood as an essentially "long-wave" counterrevolutionary phenomenon.[20]

All these societies passed through at least one variety of that kind of solution and did so under relatively similar historical conditions. Basically, Fascist and semi-Fascist dictatorships appeared at periods when the traditional political formulas of bourgeois parliamentary domination began to break down. The crises came to a head at different times after World War I, though earlier "warnings" of what was coming could be detected (e.g., the Barcelona insurrection of 1909 and the Lisbon insurrection and proclamation of the Republic in 1910). They occurred when the pressures of increasingly radical and revolutionary movements combined with serious setbacks in the economy. Both became all the more serious because important structural transformations had previously taken place in the societies concerned. These were beginning to be felt by political orders quite unsuited to cope with new demands and forms of political action. Then several varieties of modern despotism which go under the generic name of "Fascism" came to the rescue. This new order possessed several common characteristics.[21]

### A Specific Mode of Class Domination

In Southern Europe, the form of reactionary despotism that may be defined as "Fascist" or that adopted certain forms of "Fascist state corporatism" was essentially a mode of class domination brought about by a right-wing political coalition.[22] Regimes that followed its pattern invariably claimed to represent everyone's interests—hence their frequent recourse to populistic nationalism for the control of the collective means of emotional production—but from the start they were deliberately entrusted with the preservation of the interests of a reactionary coalition.[23] Usually they paved the way for further capital accumulation and the development of capitalism in accordance with the wishes of the ruling classes, though this aspect of the situation soon ran into difficulties when confronted by other, equally important, imperatives. At any rate, these regimes neutralized the working classes and other threatening groups (such as dissident intellectuals and students) so that internal peace was assured. In the countries of Southern Europe, with the notable exception of Italy, the reactionary coalition—landowners, industrialists, financiers—controlled the state through the army, whose highest echelons were amply rewarded, although the concrete mode of articulation between ruling groups varied from country to country. Thus, the key office of chief of state was taken over by the military in Spain and Greece, though Portugal's dictatorial head of government was a civilian. In Italy, intense militarization of the Fascist party largely made up for the less prominent weight its army had in the general arrangements of the Fascist dictatorship. In Greece, the right-wing forces went through a long and tortuous path of coalition formation; the 1936 Metaxas's dictatorship suppressed and temporarily superseded the *dichasmos* between the radical, middle-class Venizelists and the monarchists, but the two sides were not really reconciled until confronted with their common enemy in the Civil War, at the earliest. Full reconciliation took place in the 1970s, under a new dictatorship, as well as under the pressures of considerable social change and the relentless passage of time. By then, however, the colonels' dictatorship was approaching matters quite differently. Their government went out of its way to woo the established bourgeoisie and the "unreliable" sections of the armed forces—the navy and air force—but was notoriously unsuccessful in welding the ruling classes into one firm reactionary coalition. This major structural weakness allowed the notables of the right-wing parties, whose democratic credentials were more than doubtful, to convert to democracy and come to power in 1974. For the first time they shed the accepted double standards of Greek pseudodemocratic rule in the past: government under a liberal constitution with the help of a set of illiberal and thoroughly repressive unconstitutional laws, forming a "paraconstitutional order" in themselves.

These reactionary coalitions assured the centralized control of the political and administrative apparatus in its intermediate and lower rungs through a *Dienstklasse* or "service class," drawn from a relatively wide spectrum of the population.[24] The easy recruitment and loyalty of this "class" were assured by the backward or semideveloped nature of the economy; job security, a steady income, and health and medical advantages were even more highly valued in Southern Europe than farther north. An arrangement with the service class also helped consolidate the alliance of the rulers with the middle classes.

These regimes therefore combined traditional forms of class domination with a tight control of the public administration, an effective distribution of state rewards, and a fairly adequate neutralization of the subordinate classes, not necessarily involving political mobilization. Consequently they can be seen neither as mere reflections of a mode of production (or, to use the expression, of an articulation of modes of production into a complex whole) nor as mere tools of the ruling classes. Each despotic regime may be, of course, partly a "tool" of that nature, but the vested interests of the institutions and corporations on which it has to rely themselves become constraints at the level of domination, that is, limitations on power and orientations for policy stemming from the makeup of the regime itself. For these reasons modern despotic regimes and their states are among the most important structuring agents of the societies over which they rule. Once established they generate and maintain certain patterns of opportunity, occupation, and inequality that cannot be explained solely by the mere presence of inherited class structures or by the dynamics of market trends, capital accumulation, and other aspects of the economy. Nevertheless, their capacity to reshape the social structure is less than that of genuine totalitarian states. In fact, in the latter, the party is the central institution of power, privilege, and class, whereas in the former it is secondary to the ruling class coalition. Consequently modern despotisms can more easily dismantle their party, police, and "trade union" facades and give way to other, historically or economically more adequate political arrangements, including, of course, parliamentarian democracy.

### Restricted Ideological Sphere and Limited Political Pluralism
Insofar as a coalition of different classes differentially but firmly represents each one of them at the center of political power, the officially sanctioned ideological spectrum also includes ideological components drawn from each

class. Likewise, the official ideological amalgam explicitly excludes the ideologies and values of all the subordinate classes and outlawed parties and movements, although some rhetorical and symbolic concessions may have to be made to "democracy," the "common good," and other altruistic notions. This exclusion entails a sustained and virulent propagandist attack on one main culprit (and its "allies") whose progress is said to have been arrested by the establishment of the dictatorship. The culprit is usually "Communism," invariably not only the permanent scapegoat of reactionary despotism but also the convenient label attached to any liberal, Socialist, separatist, or simply democratic opponents of the regime. In Southern Europe, Communism tended to be singled out as a real internal menace and the source of all evils even when it was nonexistent as in the Greek *Idionym* of 1929, or Special Law for the Security of the Social Regime, or when it was only one force—often a small one—among others on the Left, as in Portugal before 1933.

The southern dictatorships possessed a syncretic ideological substratum, ranging from Fascism to ultramontane monarchical legitimism from which the dictator and the ruling clique could choose at every political juncture. In fact, one of the main tasks of the chief of state was to establish the successive adequate balances within the amalgam and to emphasize each one of its aspects according to time and place. One of the most arduous tasks was to produce a convincing doctrine by reconciling the essentially reactionary nature of the regime with officially acknowledged rhetorical expressions of support for the subordinate classes.

A limited, but qualitatively highly important, degree of political pluralism corresponds to this ideology. It was restricted to the ruling classes, to factions and movements of the reactionary coalition, extending to the employees of the regime's political police, propaganda personnel, single-party members, high civil servants, sympathizers among the local notables, and so forth, though they had to show a high degree of discipline and subservience to the chief of state at all times.

### Coercion and State Control through the Service Classes

The victorious reactionary coalition inherited the state administration but in order to govern set up a large number of new institutions for repression, economic development, welfare, and education. A traditional straightforward military-bourgeois dictatorship could no longer be successfully implemented because of the new complex economic conditions and mass aspiration characteristic of the postwar period.

Associations and movements not sanctioned by the government were outlawed, excluded, or suffered tight surveillance on the part of the forces of repression and manipulation. Nonorganized individuals and persons not stigmatized by their past political activity—a majority of the population—were left alone in the enjoyment of their property, the carrying out of their private lives, their search for employment, their expression of religious belief, and their adherence to cultural norms. Cautious noninterference with vast areas of social life thus became the hallmark of modern dictatorial regimes in Southern Europe, coupled with a keen protection and encouragement of recognized "apolitical" institutions such as the established national church and other associations devoted to the control of the means of emotional production, especially those geared toward popular distraction and national patriotism.

State power was thus implemented through service classes. They legitimated the regimes, and their members were given, in return, the intermediate rungs in the diverse chains of authority. Part of the personnel in these classes did not directly belong to the state apparatus. Such was the case of the religious legitimizers of the traditional order upheld by the reactionary government: Catholic priests and Greek orthodox popes.[25] At any rate, given the ultimately nontotalitarian nature of these states, the service classes did not interfere with everyday life in civil society. Surveillance and, especially, the use of institutionalized violence—political terror, torture, arbitrary imprisonment—tended to be selective, that is, to be applied only to suspects and "troublemakers," real or potential.[26] The political formula of the Fascist or *fascistisant* regimes in the Mediterranean inherited and incorporated the "live and let live" tenet of traditional despotism as an essential unwritten rule of their existence.

### Political Cooptation and Passive Obedience

Under political cooptation and passive obedience recruitment into the sphere of state employment tended to be more pragmatic than ideological, especially after the phase of regime consolidation was over. Members of the service classes—mayors of towns, high and middling civil servants, university professors—were asked to express allegiance to the official doctrine, yet what was decisive was their personal loyalty to the chief or arbiter of the reactionary coalition and their explicit promise not to question the legitimacy of the dominant political arrangement.

This sort of allegiance found its counterpart in the selective form of repression noted earlier, which blocked the access to political participation for the perennial *classes dangereuses*—workers, students—and aggravated discrimination against ethnic, religious, and national minorities, but also avoided the unnecessary harassment of well-behaved and law-abiding citizens. Tight control of the mass media and the strict censorship of public opinion made these tasks easier. Yet the entire repressive apparatus of the state was geared toward obtaining the passive obedience of the subordinate majority rather than, as already indicated, its active mobilization. Large-scale militancy, even in favor of the regime, was avoided. Public celebrations of multitudinous support were often arranged on special occasions, but tended to be as orderly and ritualized as possible. Obviously, insofar as the Italian regime was far more Fascist than the other three, this last characteristic, low popular mobilization, did not apply. However, as many observers have pointed out, the mobilization and penetration of the civil society by the Partito Fascista did not go so far as that of the Nazi party and declined considerably after the late 1930s. Moreover, the

Italian Fascist party, in a country without the tradition of praetorian right-wing rule such as existed in the Greek and Iberian peninsulas, filled many of the functions carried out by the Portuguese, Spanish, and Greek armies in their respective societies. Its martial role was therefore even more prominent than, say, that of the Spanish Falange. Likewise, the Italian party can also be seen as part of a reactionary coalition of the kind described above. This broke down after Stalingrad and the Allied invasion of Sicily. That such a coalition was still not ready for a switch to pluralist democracy is shown by Badoglio's immediate prohibition of all political parties after the deposition of Mussolini in 1942. Yet, under Allied pressure and with Communist support for constitutional rule (Togliatti's *svolta di Salerno* in 1943), Italy became the first Mediterranean country on the northern rim to enter the parliamentarian camp on a relatively secure basis.

## Cultural Legitimation in the Southern Polities

It seems appropriate, at this juncture, to look briefly at some important issues involving the cultural legitimation of power and authority in the Southern European countries. I have so far treated culture as unproblematic, concentrating on class domination and sheer political control in the context of a period of rapid economic transformation. This treatment could give the impression that my entire argument is committed to a vision of culture as a mere byproduct of other, supposedly more powerful, realities. The political economy and the structure of a society may remain the best starting points in any macrosociological analysis but, if taken alone, they fail to explain the success or failure of a political order.

I have already referred to the failure of the Enlightenment to erode significantly the inherited traditional world and its culture, both in the Iberian Peninsula and in Italy. Greece, of course, remained utterly beyond the pale during that great European current. Interestingly enough, the participation of these countries in the Enlightenment itself was quite considerable, but the tensions and confrontations unleashed by the Napoleonic Wars and their aftermath put an end to the orderly and, in so many ways, spectacular evolutionary path initiated by them during the eighteenth century. A final and most remarkable effort at modernization without chaos and generalized revolutionary and counterrevolutionary violence was the Spanish Cortes at Cadiz in 1812. The constitution elaborated and proclaimed there was destined to have wide international repercussions, not least in the Mediterranean world. It inspired the Portuguese Constitution of 1822 after the Oporto 1820 Revolution, the Neapolitan rising of 1820, and the Piedmontese rising and Constitution of 1822.

The immense resilience of the cultural edifice built by the Counterreformation was certainly not confined to religious and clerical support for the interests of backward-looking ruling classes, essential as that was for the subsequent politics of reaction. Such classes were interested in the maintenance of, say, slavery, for that was vital to the plantation economy and seignorial domination overseas, but they were less united as to whether obscurantist policies were to be pursued in higher education, and even less in agreement with respect to the new emerging forms of capital accumulation. Extreme conservatism had a popular (and later, populistic) basis in regions with a profoundly pious agricultural population. The popularity of such conservatism might have been less so in more "pagan" areas such as Sicily, or "de-Christianized" ones such as Andalusia, both latifundia regions with uprooted rural proletariats, but the areas in which legitimist slogans of "God, Altar, Throne" were to triumph were deeply committed to ancient pieties. Their mode of distinguishing between the sacred and the profane and of defining the relationship of both to earthly authority had not been much affected by secularization. They were rather violently and suddenly confronted, if not with "satanic mills"—though these were not entirely unknown—then at least with "satanic powers," that is, with liberal, atheistic, and masonic governments, intent on undermining the ultimate unity of earthly power and holiness. That background must be understood in order to grasp the historical bitterness and virulence of the religious/secular tension, and the nonclass components of confessional parties and political allegiances in all the countries concerned. Thus religious allegiance continues to be a factor in contemporary political alignments in varying degrees according to country and region.[27]

The degradation of the tensions between the sacred and the secular into a ruthless confrontation of clericalism and anticlericalism seemed inevitable in the absence of Protestantism, which had found a solution for the creative reconciliation of the two in Northern Europe. In Italy the Carbonari, for example, were immediately forced to take a conspiratorial stance against institutions that embodied a religiously sanctioned legitimacy for the immense majority of the population. Later still, Vatican resistance to the political unification of Italy not only exacerbated the confrontation, but created a rift between two primordial, *Gemeinschaftlich*, levels of the collective consciousness: national loyalty and religious identification. In other countries, such as Ireland and Poland, these forces went (and still go) together. In Southern Europe, their unity has been essential for the collective identity of the Basque people, and the same can be said of the Greeks, at least for as long as the Ottoman yoke had not been overthrown. In the latter case, though, the early antagonism of the Orthodox church hierarchy to the War of Liberation also made the rift inevitable, despite important differences between the nature of anticlericalism in the Eastern and Western Mediterranean.

A chance to heal the wounds of the liberal/traditionalist cleavage which rent asunder and largely paralyzed the Mediterranean countries was missed during the late decades of the nineteenth century and the years up to 1914, when the rule of conservative liberalism and limited constitutionalism prevailed throughout the region. A thoroughly cynical political culture had grown among the political class and had spread skepticism and apathy in the electorate. Perhaps no other outcome could have been expected from the inherited structure of class domination, the difficulties encountered by industrial and financial capitalism, and the virulence of the radical opposition, which had so many reasons to be aggressive and so few reasons to expect understanding from the rulers and their allies. This institutionalized cynicism penetrated the Portuguese *rotavismo*, or alternation in power between Regenerators (conservatives) and Progressives (liberals) during the 1861–89 period. It was embedded in the same rotation between similar parties during the Spanish Restoration, linked in Spain as in Portugal to *caciquismo* and other undemocratic forms of vote control. It found its supreme example in Italian *trasformismo*, the practice whereby cabinets were set up without regard for the party affiliations or political principles of its members. For the sake of office, politicians would abandon their electoral mandate altogether.[28] Meanwhile, in Greece, the semblance of a two-party system had arisen. It lasted for much of the twenty years after 1883. When the "alternating," modernizing governments led by Charilaos Trikoupis were in power during that period they managed to carry out significant reforms, with the support of business interests in the country. In all countries, however, if reforms from above were sometimes notable they never managed to do away with the nefarious practices of the closed parliamentary system and its narrow dedication to the class interests it served.[29]

In the long run this institutionalized cynicism would prove fatal for the prospects of democracy. The liberal intelligentsia itself began to desert the basic creed of enlightened, orderly, and progressive democracy. Thus Costa in Spain began to veer toward a technocratic theory of government and of economic reform, whereas Pareto in Italy elaborated a theory of political elites which severed all links with progressive liberalism. It is not accidental that both authors have been seen by some as ideological forerunners of Fascism. At any rate, the weakening of the liberal moral fiber, caught between denial of the legitimacy of the state on the one side (so strongly expressed by the substantial anarchist movement of Southern Europe, among other forces), and unflagging resistance to cultural change by the traditionalists on the other were decisive factors in the ultimate triumph of the Fascist doctrine in all its varieties. Commendably, some analysts have pointed out that despotism or Fascism was not fatally destined to take over government and that democratic regimes, even in those countries, did not necessarily have to break down.[30] While strongly sympathizing with the importance of skillful strategies and democratic statesmanship over structural determinants, one is bound to reach quite pessimistic conclusions about the real possibilities of liberal republicanism in the area for the period in question. Only after further economic development and changes in the class structure had transformed the situation almost beyond recognition was parliamentarian democracy to be given a solid chance.

The cultural polarization represented by the dichotomy of religious traditionalism versus liberal radicalism entailed more opposing sets of attitudes than are explicit in its two terms. It encompassed, for instance, opposing attitudes toward industrialization, the spread of literacy, and the conception of social justice and public welfare. Social justice stemmed, for some, from Christian charity, and for others it was to be based on philanthropy and the natural duties of the state. Polarization created in these countries, as well as in others such as France, a duality and a cleavage that consumed energies and paralyzed minds. The great Andalusian poet, Antonio Machado, warned every Spaniard who came into the world that, whichever camp he was born into, the "other half" of his fatherland was bound to "freeze his heart." An appalling Civil War (1936–39) fought over these two irreconcilable modes of legitimation soon proved him right. The same could be said of situations elsewhere, *mutatis mutandis*. The terror generated by the Portuguese secret police (PIDE), the Metaxas police, the Fascist thugs, was directly linked to the Manichaean paranoia bred by extreme cultural polarization, as was also true, needless to say, of the political terror of the Left, for instance, in those areas in Greece and in Spain dominated by Stalinist Communists during their respective civil wars.

The ideological "solutions" arrived at by the Fascist or ultranationalist forces to cope with this fatal cultural cleavage merit some attention. By and large they consisted of an amalgam of historical myths, racist doctrines, sublimations of imperial frustrations, and inherited pseudoscientific theories about society. Wrong and ridiculous as they may seem today, as they indeed already were when they were first put forward, they were used in a manner that led, quite inevitably, to their own exhaustion by dint of a sheer *reductio ad absurdum*. Random examples of this motley collection might include the "theory" advanced by a Portuguese mythmonger in 1914 that his countrymen were neither *homini europeii* nor specimens of *homo mediterranensis*, but rather the far superior members of an imaginary *homo atlanticus* race. Such ideas would later become marginal to Salazarist pragmatism, but a thoroughly distorted view of the "Christian civilizing mission of the Lusitanian nation" was not. A similar daydream formed an essential element in the rhetoric of *Hispanidad* ideology under Francoism. The Greek megali idea, which had evolved out of the anxieties, illusions, and frustrations of the early Panhellenic liberation movement, was likewise appropriated by the Right and conveniently distorted by it out of all recognition. Italian Fascist notions of Roman Empire and *civiltà* are too well known to need discussion here. In all these cases no regard whatsoever was paid to the glaring contradictions of the ideology. Cultural dissonance would have reached an unprecedented pitch had the thoroughly skeptical populations of the ancient Mediterranean ever fallen, as so many Germans did, for such official nonsense. Thus the Greek colonels, in the late 1960s, claimed that they were synthesizing the (essentially contradictory) values of ancient Hellas and later Byzantium.[31] Their relatively short dictatorship, which in so many practical ways completed the unpalatable tasks initiated by the earlier Metaxas regime, floundered amid general indifference and universal derision. Derision may speak well of the Greek people's sense of humor (though it was not absent from the other Mediterranean peoples either), but it was largely made possible by the colonels' "lateness." By the time the colonels had come to power, the cultural and ideological situation had already profoundly changed everywhere in the West, including Mediterranean Europe.

The manner in which each Fascist ideology—each extreme right-wing formulation and justification of the reactionary social order—collapsed differed from country to country. Defeat, either in war or by virtue of foolish adventurism, brought the ideology into eventual total disrepute in Italy (1943) and Greece (1974). In Spain it was eroded, slowly, by the regime's own policies, especially after 1959 when the Opus Dei began to displace certain old-fashioned clericalist and Falangist sectors from power and led the country into pragmatic neocapitalist policies by repealing the autarkic economic policies in force until then. By the time Franco died in 1975, the official ideology of the regime had practically evaporated. As for Salazar, he was the wisest of the Fascistoid leaders. He saw from the beginning the dangers of real "modernity" for the stability of his own rule and quite successfully kept the population as ignorant as possible of the vain enticements of the industrial, technologically advanced, and secularized world.

The ultimate failure of this syncretic Fascist culture by its own *reductio ad absurdum* was nowhere more spectacular than under the "Fascist-clericalist" Spanish regime; seminaries began to empty and church attendance declined despite the official protection of the state religion. Worse than that for the Francoist government, a powerful oppositional movement from the ranks of the church itself, led by Christian radicals, began in the early 1960s. By contrast, a limited "back to the church" movement was perceptible in Greece in the 1970s, heralding similar movements elsewhere in the Mediterranean. And Turkey, after many years of militant official secularism as established by the Ataturkian legacy, witnessed a revival of often violent Muslim fundamentalism, which played its part in the conditions of widespread terrorism and political disorder that led to the Evren coup d'etat in 1980. However, the intensification of fundamentalist piety in Turkey was not a mere contagion of Muslim fundamentalism elsewhere; the revolutionary reforms of Mustapha Kemal may have forged modern Turkey, but they also rent asunder the collective consciousness and cultural identifications of its people.[32] All things considered, perhaps all these movements may ultimately have more to do with wider cultural and religious fluctuations in the West and elsewhere than with a true renaissance of today's embattled older sources of religious legitimation.

As for the oppositional or radical side of the traditional cultural cleavage, its basis shifted from one sector of the political challengers to another. Thus, once liberalism lost its credibility as an opposition movement (if not as a plausible framework for peaceful coexistence and pluralism) Socialism and Communism took over the radical strand of militant secularism and anticlericalism. Therefore, the politicocultural mix described above was not lost, but rather recast into the terms of newly emerging ideologies. The problem now is to establish whether it has been merely redefined after decades of post–World War II prosperity, urbanization, labor migrations, growing international interdependence, and the inroads of the new hedonism and consumerism, or whether it is really on the wane. Although one may agree with many observers that in Southern Europe a relatively new "alternative" subculture linked to the several Socialist and Communist parties has arisen, one should be wary of attributing to it the aggressive and antagonistic qualities such divisions once possessed. Accommodation with the church, Christianity, and with the liberal, lay (noncollectivistic) subcultures has gone a very long way everywhere, even if nostalgic or extremist groups are still easily identifiable here and there. Enrico Berlinguer's launching in 1973 of the theme of a "historic compromise" may have been part of his party's momentary political and cultural strategy just as his and Santiago Carrillo's later profession of faith in "Eurocommunism" may be considered as a passing phase of the partisan struggle. Nevertheless, there is little doubt that the commitments implicit in such policies—the social-democratic maintenance of welfare capitalism, the open acceptance of political pluralism, and so on—imply, if not a "waning of opposition" as some have suggested, at least a serious weakening of the deepest split in the traditional political culture, and a reinforcement from the Left of a much greater degree of consensual legitimation throughout the polity.[33]

It is perhaps in this light that some forms of extremist militancy—from political terrorism to acute forms of "extraparliamentary" opposition—can be best understood, especially in Italy and in Spain, in the 1970s and early 1980s. In fact, the creation of terrorist groups and extremist militant movements and parties may be linked to the weakening of the inherited cleavage between the two cultures of legitimation. In turn, every act of violence forges a greater degree of unity among all parliamentary parties. Witness the massive support for democratic parliamentarism and law and order generated by the assassination of Prime Minister Aldo Moro in 1978, and stemming from the Communist party of Italy. At another level the tactics of the Euskadi Ta Askatasuna-Basgne Homeland and Freedom party (ETA), the military branch of the Basque separatist movement, may be seen as uniting, rather than weakening, the ties among the most diverse parties of Spain, forcing them to find a common political culture in establishing the rules of the political game, an impetus certainly absent before 1936.

Polarities and cleavages in the cultural universe of Southern Europe are not restricted to the confrontation of conservative consensus and radical challenge. There are those which arise from the mosaiclike character of national cultures, such as the linguistic-ethnic pluralism of the Iberian Peninsula. The usual distinction between North and South Italy, accepted by the most acute and demanding critics, appears as paradigmatic. It may also be applied, albeit with quite different implications, to Portugal, north and south of the Ribatejo, although to the Portuguese themselves, the Lusitanian cultural world often seems to divide elsewhere, perhaps on the banks of the Mondego at Coimbra. These distinctions do not always find parallels nor do they correspond to the questionable assertion of economic dualism in the societies concerned. Marxists are right when they reject the notion of the "dual economy" as it has often been applied to Italy or Spain. It is true that in some areas of those countries rudimentary agricultural and simple commodity production predominated whereas in others production was industrially advanced, but it is misleading to conceive of them as separate parts of the same economy. Once the national capitalist market was created, the entire economic system and its different class and inequality patterns became linked into one single and evidently complex "social formation" with mutually dependent elements. That statement does not contradict the present coexistence of two (or several) discontinuous cultural, social, and productive worlds under the same state and the same macroeconomy. On the contrary, it is clearly the case that the traditional sector—often made up of small, family-owned firms, with relatively low productivity—frequently complements the more advanced, modern sector, is supported by it, and is, therefore, not necessarily threatened by it.[34]

Other sociostructural cleavages, which are also largely cultural in nature, are to be found in all these countries on a local and regional basis. One of the most important is the gap, indeed often the abyss, between the highly civilized city and its immediate, backward, rural hinterland—Naples comes quickly to mind. This cleavage has been a fundamental feature of all these societies for many centuries, perhaps millennia.[35] It would therefore be foolish to assume that these varied and practically timeless features of traditional southern cultural anthropology have had little or no effect upon the troubled history of despotism and democracy in Mediterranean Europe. Nor are they likely to change substantially in the near future.[36]

### From Despotism to Pluralist Politics

Two paradoxical developments led the dictatorships of Southern Europe toward a more pluralistic social order and on to an infinitely more democratic situation: first, the exhaustion of traditionalist legitimation via the Fascist ideology and second, the transformation of the structure of the economy produced, to a considerable extent, by the policies of the dictatorships themselves. In turn, the process was made possible by the essentially nontotalitarian nature of the system of class domination.

The stresses and strains brought about by the birth of industrial society—before, during, and after World War I—within the framework of the reactionary structure described earlier, bred a revolutionary opposition rather than a merely radical one. Significant efforts to integrate moderate socialism into the established political system in the end failed under the two-pronged attack of revolutionary movements and reactionary or Fascist repression. Failure was the story from the time of the Turin factory occupations during the *Biennio rosso* (1919–20), which led to the formation of a revolutionary party by Gramsci and his colleagues, to the crushing defeat of Socialists, Communists, and anarchists by the Francoist forces in 1939. Until such time as moderate socialism (either as social democracy or Eurocommunism) was allowed a recognized and assured place in the polity, the dominant regime was quite simply reactionary despotism.

The reactionary regimes of twentieth-century Southern Europe were wedded to the state apparatus in a novel way. They employed the state to complement the weak efforts of private capital in the task of large-scale capital accumulation, massive industrialization, increased urbanization, and so forth. The ruthless methods they used to accomplish these ends are well known and were hinted at earlier in my model of modern despotic regimes. With the partial exception of the "old-fashioned" pre-Keynesian Salazarist economics, the other Mediterranean dictatorships actively engaged in state capitalist expansion and state capitalist monopoly production. Under the aegis of national autarky, Italy and Spain developed vast state industrial holdings, such as, respectively, the Istituto per la Ricostruzione Industriale (IRI, set up in 1933) and the Instituto Nacional de Industria (INI, established in 1941), which subsequent democratic regimes have not attempted to dismantle. The origins of this trend were far from being strictly Fascist or explicitly calculated. In Italy, for example, state industrial holdings can be found in purely remedial public interventions brought about by the dislocations of the 1929 economic crisis.[37] For their part, successive Greek governments have shown strong interventionist tendencies, especially through the banks (whose powers and share of the economy are as great as, if not greater than, Spain) and have included an enormous public investment program. After some early friction and tensions with areas in the private sector, the publicly owned legacy of the defunct Fascist state has easily blended with the new forms of Western advanced capitalism. It functions today, as does state industry elsewhere, as part and parcel of the system. Thus the state may absorb "lame ducks," take over losing but "necessary" industrial, financial, and commercial activities, and sometimes even run profitable public companies, ranging from airlines to civil engineering. After the appearance of massive foreign investment in the 1960s (and even earlier in Italy), spearheaded by multinational enterprise, the role of the state shifted to that of a general coordinator of the economy, guaranteeing its smooth functioning, the easy repatriation of foreign capitals, and its close integration into the capitalist core.

International conditions after Yalta and 1945 entailed the exclusion of Socialist and of state Socialist development in the four countries. That meant that their states, whether dictatorial (Spain, Portugal), parliamentary (Italy), or of the right-wing, anti-Communist, so-called guided democracy type (Greece), had no option other than opening themselves up to foreign capital investment by providing stability and low wages. They sheltered a "liberal" economy within an illiberal polity. Foreign investors did not have to contend with unruly or defiant trade unions and striking workers in the three poorest countries where labor was cheapest. In Greece, stability also meant that Greek diaspora capital could finally be enticed back on a considerable scale, along with other foreign investment. As all these countries entered the 1970s, resistance to foreign capitalist penetration declined to almost nothing. A short-lived exception was the case of Portugal after the Revolution of 1974, which ended with the stabilization plan of 1978 when the economy returned to producing a surplus and international confidence was restored.[38] Greece's entry into the Common Market in 1980 left only the Iberian countries still out. As both Spain and Portugal are now actively engaged in entering it, they have also been engaged in a not always easy process of adjustment (i.e., liberalization) of their economic institutions to the standards prevailing among the Ten, even if, in some cases, that implied dismantling and privatizing certain highly profitable state monopolies.[39]

Exaggerated notions about dependent development and "economic colonialism" in Southern Europe must, however, be avoided. For one thing it is far from clear that all significant national industries and enterprises are or will soon be subordinate to foreign capital. Italy, of course, already has its own important locally based multinationals, and some industries elsewhere in Southern Europe, for instance in Spain, are quite internationally competitive. Furthermore, foreign trade expansion of Spanish and Greek companies (let alone, Italian) is not rare, though its scope is still comparatively limited. Part of this expansion, such as that of the Spanish aircraft industry, tends to be at least partially linked in less visible ways to Northern European firms.[40] Therefore the final entry of the Southern European region into the core areas from the semiperiphery to which they have so far belonged may entail lasting and significant changes in the international division of labor in that zone. For instance, labor migrations from Southern to Northern Europe have declined since 1973 and German, French, American, and other industries have begun to set up factories in the South, where local labor is cheaper, the work force is now sufficiently skilled, and the infrastructure (motorways, telecommunications, etc.) is as good as can be desired.[41] Thus, the "shift to core" has meant not necessarily economic independence, but a much greater subordination to the international corporate economy. The national industrial bourgeoisie, having first seen their power relatively circumscribed by the rise of state economic power, are now rapidly selling many of their industrial possessions to foreign corporate bidders when they are not going into joint ventures with foreign "partners." Under the new circumstances they are rapidly losing the role of economic protagonists they once shared with state enterprise.[42] One of the main consequences of this shift in the heretofore paramount position of the traditional bourgeoisie is the vastly increased importance of new pressure groups, parties, unions, and other organizations linked to different sectors of the economy that were formerly excluded from power. This shift has meant the rise of popular (even populistic) opposition parties with considerable leverage in Parliament and government circles, and also the rise of new corporate groups, such as the technocratic "state bourgeoisie" and financial–industrial conglomerates with their own new interests to foster.

The collapse of the dictatorial ideology, coupled with the changes in the structure of capitalism, has finally opened the gates for a kind of "pluralist" politics which comes much closer to the Northwestern European model, though it is still different in several important ways. Thus, parties of notables, endowed with an eminently syncretic ideology and out to colonize the state, are common on both the political Center and Right.[43] Except for Greece since 1981, they became, in fact, ruling parties. The metamorphosis of the old reactionary political class into a democratic "party" representing Center, Right, and non-Socialist opinion was made possible, as hinted earlier on, by the class composition of the nontotalitarian despotic regimes that came before. This democratization applied equally well to Karamanlis's Nea Demokratia and to Suárez's (and later, Calvo Sotelo's) Unión de Centro Democrático. Their electoral platforms presented noticeable class, factional, and ideological similarities. After a brief period of praetorian-Socialist rule in Portugal, the 1979 and 1980 victories of Sá Carneiro's conservative coalition (later led by Pinto Balsemão) seemed to herald the relative convergence of at least three Mediterranean governments with the formula established in Italy after 1948, which allowed continuous Christian Democratic domination in that country for a long period. Yet events soon took an unexpected turn. The formation of coalition government in Italy including the Socialists and their conquest of the premiership through Bettino Craxi, the triumph of PASOK (Panhellenic Socialist Movement) at the polls in Greece in 1981 and the subsequent Socialist victory in Spain, followed by the rise of Mario Soares to the Portuguese premiership, later indicated that things had profoundly changed in the region. It was now clear that the opposition was finally allowed to govern and reform in peace by conservative forces no longer bent on barring it from power at any cost and by any means at their disposal.[44]

Turkey, of course, followed a different path during the same period. It not only "lagged behind" the other countries in time; its very political dynamics were different, and perhaps unique. After World War II, competitive parliamentary democracy was established, and there was, therefore, a transition from a single-party "authoritarian" rule to unstable pluralism that found some remote parallels only in the Italian transition of the same period. But endemic instability in Turkey led to military coups at roughly ten-year intervals since 1950, so that we should be wary of speaking of "regime breakdowns" in so cyclical a polity. Evren's liberalization of his dictatorship in 1983 and the subsequent premiership of Özal after relatively controlled though significant elections must therefore be treated with circumspection. What is interesting is that, in Turkey, military coups have not been directed against democracy itself (in the sense that General Franco or Benito Mussolini directed their efforts to eradicate it forever) but rather the resumption of democratic politics is nearly always explicitly contemplated by the military and, what is more, does eventually take place. As some observers see it, Turkey often appears as "an embattled democracy with possibilities."[45] This may well be a correct view but, by late 1984, Turkey still looked a strange sort of democracy when viewed from the West: liberal and left-of-center intellectuals were tried by military courts for having distributed a petition to the president demanding greater democracy for the country; Prime Minister Turgut Özal defended the continuation of martial law over more than half of Turkey's provinces, including the main cities; and grave violations of human rights continued.

Nowhere in the countries examined did the transition from dictatorship to a modern democracy occur through revolution. Instead, there has been, in all cases, a significant measure of "democratization from above" even if it was not precisely desired by the dictators themselves, or by many of their successors.[46] In Italy the transition was initiated by a democratic domestic force but was precipitated and made effective by foreign invasion. Allied intervention also dashed the revolutionary aspirations of partisans and left-wingers in the 1948 electoral defeat of the Popular Front. In Spain serious plans for a "democratic rupture" with the dictatorial past, harbored by anti-Franco forces as late as 1977, were rendered inappropriate or unnecessary by certain strategically placed groups within the regime which were inclined to make concessions. These groups were, in turn, helped by the remarkable willingness shown by most outlawed opposition leaders to compromise and embark on consensual politics. A genuinely revolutionary break with the past did not even take place in Portugal, where the initial clamor for justice against the overthrown regime played a prominent role in the 1974 coup and where a Socialist program of reforms was eventually incorporated into the constitution. One of the reasons was that the military coup was conspiratorially prepared and executed only by military officers who themselves were of quite varied political persuasions, and did not initially involve any significant participation by radical civilian political forces.[47] Even though in the early stages the Left, torn between Leninist and majoritarian Socialist tactics, was given a historic opportunity, conservative and moderate forces were allowed to regroup and come back into their own, though this time under constitutional rule by army officers. In Portugal, as three decades earlier in Italy, the international military, political, and economic order of the West would have made any serious attempts at abrupt social or political structural change not only highly costly, in every sense, but ultimately unlikely to succeed.

The narrowness of the choices that have faced all political formations involved at these crucial moments of transition (the government elite, opposition parties—legal and otherwise—army officers, democratic movements, and so on) has led some observers to believe that a "consociational" model of democracy and parliamentarianism ought to emerge, at least in some of these countries. Supposing, for the sake of argument, that consociationalism does exist in some polities such as the Netherlands (a statement also subject to much dispute): it seems rather problematic to me that it will ever happen in Southern Europe. "Consociationalism," or compromise and agreement among the respective elites capable of controlling their respective followers and concerned about establishing a common course of action to avoid polarization, confrontation, and other mutually destructive strategies, can only occur if all are equally free, proportionately rewarded, and equally concerned about safeguarding democracy.[48] In Southern Europe, by contrast, almost all the forces present were obliged to enter into mutual agreements and concessions leading to constitutional rule *under powerful surveillance from above or outside*. In every case certain internal or external arbiters of the situation imposed the limits and conditions of the transition. They did so in a clearly asymmetrical way, in a manner congruent with the existing structures of class, power, and privilege. To assume, therefore, that the transition to democracy in countries such as Spain has been consociational may be mistaken. Rather the contrary could be the case, as Italian politics demonstrate. From the *apertura a sinistra* (liberalization toward the Left) of 1962 to the *compromesso storico* (historic compromise) of 1973, strategies were inspired, one could argue, by a desire to compromise consociationally for the sake of maintaining democratic rule, yet they occurred after, not before, sweeping concessions and mutual guarantees were forced upon all "contracting" actors during the crucial years of 1943 and 1948. Likewise in Greece one party, Karamanlis's New Democracy, imposed the constitution upon the other political forces, without substantial negotiation with them. The Portuguese case, with the military coup of 1974, hardly needs mentioning.

Be that as it may, the result of the transition process has been that—apart from the rise of new political, trade union, and other institutions linked to parliamentary and constitutional democracy—the inherited patterns of class domination and social inequality have been respected by the new system of political praxis.[49] It is, after all, the same system that predominates elsewhere in Western Europe.

## Between Freedom and Corporatism

The final obsolescence and rejection of the dictatorial solution for the political order in Europe's southern region are a particularly significant event, not only because of its intrinsic importance, but also because of the historical moment at which it has occurred. Thus the new European parliamentary democracies have joined not the liberal world of yesteryear, but rather the new postliberal universe of today, based on a technologically advanced, politically competitive, and organizationally corporate society. The corporate society in the West can be characterized on the one hand by a measure of political pluralism, civil rights, and democratic representation, but on the other by the constant growth of large formal organizations at all levels: first and foremost the state, but also trade unions, employers' and professionals' associations, political parties, multinational corporations, financial institutions, welfare agencies, and so forth.[50] It is also a society in which class conflict, market trends, and personal and collective social integration are nearly always mediated by the presence of the all-pervading "corporations": they are redefined, filtered, and governed by them. Political power, market prices, sectional interests, military duties, nationalist movements, working-class demands, even religious beliefs are all mediated by corporate institutions and groups. Such a society cannot therefore be defined only in terms of state intervention in the economy, and much less in terms of any resemblance to the so-called corporate states that once emerged precisely in Southern Europe. Mussolini's and Salazar's "corporatist" orders were shams; their harmonious blueprints hid much harsher and less perfect realities.[51] Therefore they ought not be confused with the new phenomenon.

Southern Europe's entry into the "corporate world" has also occurred when its standards of living, income distribution, levels of urbanization, literacy, health, and many other indicators have either reached Northern European levels or, as is more often the case, are relentlessly approaching them. Is it necessary to give here the familiar data on income per capita, automobiles per 100 inhabitants, and the like? The gulf between Sicily and Franconia is still great, as is the one between Andalusia and the English Midlands, or Thessaly and Jutland, but the significant point is that it is narrowing. What is now being bridged is the gap between the industrialized and developing areas of the South and the corresponding areas in the North, as well as the one that exists between the underdeveloped and poor areas of the South and those that are underdeveloped, depressed, or even undergoing deindustrialization in the North of Europe. By all international criteria, Southern Europe has now ceased to be a part of the periphery, or even of the semiperiphery, of the capitalist world economy.[52]

The acknowledgment of these important facts, however, ought not to lead into simplistic assumptions about the "convergence" between Northern and Southern European societies. For one thing, the historical path followed by the former was by and large grounded on strong and prosperous civil societies. Despite the growth of the state and the recent development of corporate structures their internal equilibrium and order still largely depend on the strong living traditions of their civil societies. In the South, by contrast, civil society was always much weaker. As a consequence, the region as a whole reached the "corporatist order" through a very different historical path, full of strife, stalemates, and confrontations. For another, the "advanced," industrialized, welfare-state capitalist core has been enlarged to cover Southern Europe without absorbing the class structures, local cultures, patronage systems, and other features of the new members into one single wider social system. These features may not have remained intact under recent urbanization and industrialization processes—quite the contrary is the case—but the repercussions have produced structural results that differ widely from those generated in the North. Even the very expansion of the capitalist core farther south has not forced the main centers of political and economic decision-making to shift elsewhere. Societal and geopolitical inequality in participation and influence in such spheres continues unabated. In other words, much integration (even some "convergence") has occurred at the level of corporate organization among European nations, but there has been hardly any at the level of class, community, privilege, and local power. In these areas, the Mediterranean societies of Europe continue to possess their own distinctiveness.[53] So much so that transnational generalizations among southern societies are difficult and often highly problematic. The disparities at this level between, say, Sicily and Andalusia are immense, as are the disparities in overall social structures of each of these countries. Even if they were linked to different stages in the development of capitalism, it would be impossible to plot them along some simple continuum. Italy would certainly appear ahead of the other three, followed by Spain and then perhaps by Greece, with Portugal in last place. But this would be a futile exercise. Thus certain areas of Italy—Calabria, Basilicata—appear to many observers as true enclaves of archaism as do extensive regions of Eastern Anatolia in Turkey. At the opposite pole, we encounter advanced industrial areas in places like Salonika or Setúbal—enclaves of exactly the opposite kind, surrounded still by a large hinterland of simple commodity production, lower acquisitive power, small-scale family business, and so on. Likewise, in at least two countries, Italy and Spain, industry is no longer concentrated upon its traditional regions but far more widely spread. If "enclave" capitalism has long been gone, "enclave" industrialism is now following suit.

The pluralistic corporate societies of the West to which the Southern European countries are now, more than ever, linked, are neither totalitarian nor monolithic. Increasing monopolies and oligopolies in the economic sphere and the constant expansion of the state apparatus and bureaucracy are wedded to a great number of competing parties, political formations, public opinion institutions, and autonomous and semiautonomous bodies. New trends toward further corporateness and bureaucratization can also be detected. They were intensified by the energy crisis and the recession that gripped the Western world after 1973, precisely at the moment when three of the countries discussed here again found their place in its midst as parliamentary democracies. These developments are particularly relevant for the ultimate consequences Socialism may have in the area. By 1983, the entire Mediterranean region, including France, had come under either Socialist-majority governments or under coalition governments headed by a Socialist premier. Yet, they were all treading with varying degrees of care in the implementation of their originally quite radical programs. Some, like the Greek, the French, and the Portuguese Socialists, tried in different ways to live up to the revolutionary promises first made, by implementing at least parts of their programs. Others, having been elected partly on a promise of moderation, found it more expedient to engage in sensible, "nonideological" reformism, such as industrial reconversion, financial restraint, and fiscal soundness. This was the Spaniards' case. The control of public expenditure and fiscal reform was also the chief preoccupation of the Italians, whereas the Portuguese were once more forced to yield to the exigencies of their own economic difficulties. Fortunately, the initial economic setbacks of the French Socialist government had forewarned other Mediterranean Socialists about the costs of structural reforms in times of high unemployment, fiscal penury, and economic stagnation.

There appears to be no reason, however, why Socialism in Southern Europe must be confined to the achievement of minor tasks. In fact, the lingering backwardness of the region affords its supporters a unique opportunity to legitimize their rule and to make a lasting contribution to the prosperity and progress of their countries. In them, administrative and educational reform and regional devolution, for instance, can hardly be considered minor events. The mere consolidation of democracy through the peaceful access to power and effective rule of Socialist governments in all these countries is in itself a unique achievement, and a measure of the extent to which the political world of Southern Europe has changed. However, the shift from the original promises of structural change to a more circumscribed emphasis on the "moralization" and the "modernization" of the inherited world poses interesting questions. What will happen to the Socialist parties when this necessary and preliminary part of their project has been accomplished? For how long can they legitimize their rule on this basis alone?[54]

Here the questions of corporatism—the widespread organization of interest groups of all sorts into large corporate bodies—rears its head once again. In a pluralist corporate society Socialism must come to terms with big business, but also with big labor—the latter often under Communist or non-Socialist control—as well as with a powerful and traditional state machinery. To these, in places like Greece and Spain, the army must be added, and in some senses the church as well.[55] This mix, together with the persistence of regional imbalances and traditional arrangements and institutions of patronage and protection—which in some cases, as in Italy, include criminal networks—confers upon the corporatism of the region its distinctiveness and sets the constraints within which any democratically elected government must operate. Therefore the conglomeration of all these forces is bound to establish notable constraints upon the Socialist effort. At any rate it has already forced a displacement of its immediate goals from revolution to the rationalization and modernization of the existing society. This shift is not only the result of fears of a violent reaction by the right wing opposition and its powerful reactionary allies but is also the consequence of far-reaching changes in the very texture of those societies; a much greater density in the sphere of organized interest representation has brought with it in Southern Europe a world that tends to preclude violent confrontations and ideological maximalism. The institutionalization of the negotiated resolution of conflicts imposed by corporatism represents a final break with the past. The advent of modern times cast those societies into a mold of oppression and fruitless rebellion. Their strife-torn past will not repeat itself. Civil discord and violence, if it comes, will stem from different sources of discontent.

The uncertainties of the Western world as a whole are now also the uncertainties of Southern Europe. Therefore, this exploration into its recent and contemporary political evolution and its cultural and political underpinnings must also end in a note of uncertainty. None of the specific ills of the South can any longer be isolated from the larger whole of which they are now a part. In the same manner that the "dual economy" soon ceased to exist at the national level, the European "dual economy" (North and South) has in a sense also ceased to exist through national, supranational, and international integration and mutual dependence.[56] Vast Northern European (as well as American, Japanese, and Arab) economic interests are now involved in the South—from simple house ownership to large industrial investment. And the weight of the South is not limited to providing a work force for the North, as it seemed it was destined to be during the 1950s and 1960s. Its political and economic strength are already being felt beyond the confines of the European Parliament. Besides increased interdependence, other trends have created a more common framework of problems for all countries, North and South: a sharp drop in productive investment in the 1970s and beyond; the rise of comprehensive welfare programs and their effects on individual competitiveness and trade union strategies; the further development of corporatist interest politics, linked or not to the state; the continued growth of government; the limits to East-West military détente. These harsh facts have pulled all Western European societies together, not apart. They have now thus ceased to be islands if indeed they ever were.

# 3 •

# The Demise of the First Fascist Regime and Italy's Transition to Democracy: 1943–1948

## Gianfranco Pasquino

After almost twenty years of rule, Benito Mussolini was overthrown as head of Fascism and prime minister of the Italian government on 25 July 1943. The political framework of the Italian Republic, as we know it today, was established in the following years and sanctioned in the fateful elections of 18 April 1948, which marked the end of the transition to democracy and the termination of any form of collaboration between the Christian Democrats and the Socialist-Communist coalition. Italian political life has since been dominated by the issue of whether and how an open confrontation or a renewed collaboration of those political forces should take place.

With the benefit of hindsight, many turning points and sharp breaks can be identified during this five-year period. The transition from the authoritarian regime to a democratic Republic was essentially completed by 2 June 1946, but its overall political outcome had not yet been produced. Therefore, in order to understand the dynamics of the transition, attention has to be paid to the events following the instauration of the Republic and the election of a Constituent Assembly and to the results of the first legislative elections of April 1948. As we will see, those results were also the product of some of the same processes and conditions that were involved in the initial transition from Fascism.

Fundamentally there were four phases in the process of transition. The first one started on 25 July 1943 and ended on 8 September 1943. It involved the overthrow of Fascism and the reversal of Italy's position in the war. The second phase, the resistance, went from 9 September 1943 until 25 April 1945, the liberation of Italy. The third phase comprised the creation of the first civilian governments staffed by the parties that participated in the resistance movement, the intensification of political conflicts and struggles, and the breakup in May 1947 of the tripartite ruling coalition composed of the Christian Democrats (DC), the Italian Socialist party, (PSI), and the Italian Communist party (PCI). Finally, the fourth phase was characterized by the full impact of the cold war on the Italian domestic situation and led to the polarization of the political alignments and the formation of a Popular Front (Socialists and

Co..munists) which was severely defeated in the April 1948 elections. All these phases are important for a full understanding of the process of transition and also reveal the nature of both the authoritarian regime that collapsed and the democratic regime that was established.

## The Demise of Fascism

The formal demise of Fascism was the product of a vote taken by the Fascist Grand Council "calling for royal leadership and the rehabilitation of moribund state institutions."[1] This vote (by nineteen out of twenty-eight members) created the conditions under which the king could dismiss Mussolini as prime minister of Italy. Historically responsible for having appointed Mussolini in 1922, the king assumed responsibility for his dismissal as well. No single institution opposed the king's action and the immediate reaction of the population was one of enthusiasm as well as preoccupation: enthusiasm for the fall of Fascism, preoccupation regarding the continuation of the war.

Many issues were raised by this bloodless breakdown of a twenty-year-old regime and by the lack of organized reaction and opposition to it. The two most important ones are, of course, the nature of the regime (and its apparent weakness) and the determinants of its demise. The two are related, and their analysis will yield the elements necessary to explain the process of breakdown and to understand the subsequent transition to a democratic regime.

It has rightly been pointed out that the Fascist attempt to integrate Italian society into the state in a totalitarian way did not succeed.[2] Italian Fascism can thus be characterized as a failed totalitarian experiment; it allowed the persistence of a degree of limited pluralism which has been singled out as an important characteristic of authoritarian regimes.[3] The presence of the monarchy created what Mussolini dubbed "the tragedy of the diarchy," whereby it was impossible for the Duce completely to "fascistize" the state.[4] The Italian form of limited pluralism was evident on the one hand in the existence of the monarchy and the preservation of its constitutional powers; the persistence of an army whose loyalty went to the king rather than to Mussolini or to Fascism; the continuity of a state apparatus already bureaucratic and authoritarian, but fragile and cumbersome; and on the other hand, in the inability of Fascism to create viable institutions of its own to replace or supersede the traditional institutions. The House of Corporations never really took hold (while the Royal Senate remained a respected body); the National Fascist party became more and more a bureaucratic organization, overstaffed and largely passive.[5] Ironically, the only body that could exercise real power and play an active role, the Fascist Grand Council, was the one that took the initiative in the ousting of Mussolini and, consequently, in the demise of Fascism (a connection of which most of its members were well aware).[6]

Not even in civil society had Fascism achieved hegemony. Landowners and industrialists acquired and enjoyed a free hand; protected from a working class deprived of its organizations, they made large profits both in peacetime and in wartime. Most important of all, through the concordat signed by Mussolini and the Lateran Pacts, the church was able to reacquire a legally sanctioned role in civil society. While the church never became an anti-Fascist institution, and in some instances was deeply compromised with the regime, it prevented Fascism from achieving full hegemony over the minds of many Italians.[7]

Does this mean that Fascism never had the consent of the Italian population? On this point the debate is still rampant, and acrimonious. According to the influential, but also controversial, interpretation by Renzo De Felice, Mussolini and his regime did enjoy consensual support from most social strata after the agreement with the church (11 February 1929) and probably until the creation of the empire in May 1936, following the conquest of Abyssinia. The issue, of course, is whether that consent was a purely passive acquiescence to the existence of a regime that granted security and internal peace to most of its citizens, or whether it involved active support for the choices and the policies made and implemented by that regime.[8]

In order to arrive at a balanced assessment of the quantity and quality of consent Fascism received, one cannot refrain from pointing to one historical fact. Despite the persistence of anti-Fascist activities throughout the *ventennio* (twenty-year reign), the great majority of the population "did not demonstrate a willingness to consider the regime as a mortal enemy which had to be overthrown at any cost or, even less, to run serious risks in order to achieve such a goal."[9] On the other hand, it is also true that Fascism never engaged in massive mobilization efforts after its phase of initial consolidation and, therefore, potential conflicts were largely avoided (with few exceptions such as a clash with the church and Catholic associations in 1931).

Expressions of support became, as in other authoritarian regimes, fundamentally ritualistic and symbolic, and oppositional activities never enjoyed widespread support. In a distorted way, Mussolini was aware of the underlying component of his consensus: "To speak the truth, I have not even been a dictator, because my power to command coincided perfectly with the will to obey of the Italian people."[10]

Briefly, the most important conclusion to emerge so far is that Fascism never enjoyed full control over the Italian political system and its members. It was unable and unwilling to destroy and reshape all political and bureaucratic institutions (there was no *Gleichschaltung* as in Nazi Germany) and therefore was compelled to share power with the fundamentally monarchist state apparatus and with the church. It was unsuccessful in the creation of its own institutions, for example, the House of Corporations, the National Fascist party, the Fascist Syndicates. It exploited adroitly a pervasive climate of authoritarianism in Europe and the imperfect democratization of the previous Italian regime, but it proved unable to build large-scale support for its aims and goals. However, one should be cautious in concluding that Fascism was consequently and certainly doomed. Indeed, the debate on the determinants of the fall of Fascism remains lively and unresolved, for good reasons.

In this debate are two easily identifiable extreme positions. According to the first one, the crisis that led to the demise of Fascism was the product of personal and dynastic motivations, by those "patriotic" Fascist members of the Grand Council and by the king and his close advisers. It was the final attempt by the monarchy to dissociate its responsibilities from those of the regime and to save itself institutionally. According to the second position, the crisis was rather the product of political events, of class contradictions, of socioeconomic problems, and clashes of interests. Here emphasis is placed on the changing orientations of major financial and industrial groups and on the strikes of March 1943 in northern factories.[11]

All these elements were important as accelerators of the decision taken by the Grand Council and by the king and were instrumental in shaping the further evolution of the transition, yet there is no doubt that "the cleavage between the regime and the people was the product of the war and its tragic failure."[12] The war and the invasion of Italy by the Allies detonated the internal contradictions and ideological and structural deficiencies of the regime. With them came the fundamental revelation that Mussolini did not represent the will of the Italian people in any way, that Fascist institutions were hollow, and that the penetration of the Fascist "mentality" was quite limited.

With these factors in the background, one element deserves additional consideration. The decision to overthrow Mussolini must be placed in the context of the dynamics of the war as well as the nature and evolution of Italo-German relationships. In particular, some attempts had already been made in the winter of 1942–43 either to obtain better equipment and more resources from the Germans or to disengage Italy from the war altogether. When both options proved to be impossible, the conspirators realized that Mussolini himself was the obstacle to a separate peace. Hence, the decision to get rid of him.

Two groups were working to achieve fundamentally the same goals. One group, representing the old, pre-Fascist, political class, which the king called contemptuously the *revenants*, was led by Ivanoe Bonomi. The other was a group drawn from the Fascist political class and given some cohesion and much strength by Dino Grandi, former minister of foreign affairs and Speaker of the House. Both groups intended to achieve the same goals: Mussolini's replacement and Italy's disengagement from the war. The king and his entourage, the military advisers included, were to play the role of arbiter.

Grandi asked the Grand Council to approve his resolution to end the dictatorship "because it has compromised the vital interests of the nation; it has led Italy on the brink of military defeat; it has eroded and worn the trunk of revolution and of Fascism itself."[13] Grandi's aim was to prevent "any solution of continuity in our constitutional life." Understandably, he bitterly resented and denounced the behavior of those military leaders who had decided to transform a constitutional act into a coup d'état characteristic of "a Balkan or South American country," and had proved unable to free Italy of the responsibilities for the war.[14]

Mussolini's overthrow and his subsequent immediate arrest and short imprisonment signaled the end of the authoritarian regime, but by no means the return to a democratic regime, albeit of limited democracy. The transformation of the Italian authoritarian regime partook of two strategies: on the one hand, it was a transfer of power made possible by the existence of the monarchy; on the other, it was a surrender of power made advisable because the war was still going on.[15] Grandi himself might have led the transition, but decided not to in order clearly to mark the return to constitutional government and also because he wanted to play the role of negotiator with the Allies. In the end, given the "withering away" of Fascism and its leaders, the king felt entitled to play the decisive role, however indecisively.

Two issues had to be tackled immediately: the selection of a prime minister and a new government and the terms for concluding the war. It is not clear how much chance the pre-Fascist political class really had to provide the prime minister and the personnel for the first post-Fascist government. Grandi pressed for a solution of this kind, but the king decided to follow the route of a "monarchist restoration," as Deakin puts it.[16] An aged and rather discredited marshal, Pietro Badoglio, formed a goverment composed of military men and civil servants. The message was clear: the king wanted to stress the continuity of the state and its apparatus, and, in all likelihood, to turn the clock back to 1922 (a concrete implementation of the thesis that Fascism had only been a "parenthesis" in the history of Italy). With varying nuances, the reactions of the opponents of Fascism were negative. Still, a chance was given to Badoglio because of the difficult circumstances: "We will forgive Badoglio his past dealings, if he reverses the Italian situation by declaring void the treaties with the Axis and stating immediately that we are at war with Germany."[17]

Indecision, opportunism, and inability correctly to identify the options and to evaluate the costs and benefits have variously been imputed to the proclamation by Badoglio that "the war continues." However, according to some scholars, there is more to it than sheer incompetence and lack of courage. On the one hand, he feared that the Germans might occupy Rome and, on the other, was preoccupied with the conditions the Allies were imposing for an armistice with Italy: that is, unconditional surrender. In the forty-five days between Mussolini's fall and the signing of the armistice with the Allies on 8 September 1943, however, no preparation was made for withstanding the likely German reaction. Thus, "the escape from Rome and the lack of orders to the army [were] intended to secure for the king and his entourage the exclusive representation of the Italian people vis-à-vis the Anglo-Americans and, at the same time, to prevent or at least to delay the anti-German struggle."[18]

At the closing of the first phase, some aspects of the Italian experience deserve to be stressed in a comparative perspective. First, the impulse toward the transition came fundamentally from within the configuration of forces that made up the Fascist regime or gravitated around it. Second, the war created rather than simply accelerated the conditions for the demise of Fascism. In its wake, the regime was unable to maintain its grip over the country because (1) it was deemed responsible for entering the war and suffering a series of crushing defeats; (2) the internal situation revealed the emergence or reemergence of some sociopolitical opposition (e.g., the northern workers' strikes of March 1943); (3) some "reserve" institutions existed and indeed had preserved some autonomy and some legitimacy of their own (above all the monarchy, but in a different way and in a different sphere the church as well). The last point also suggests or makes clear Mussolini's failure to "fascistize" Italian institutions and social life; at the same time, it shows the resilience of traditional political institutions and social forces (as well as the old political class).

A combination of factors related to the aftermath of World War I—the polarization of opinions in a supposedly prerevolutionary climate, the transition from a limited to a mass democracy, and the incomplete democratization and differential rates of democratization of various institutions and Italian political life—made the rise and consolidation of Fascism possible. A similar configuration of factors, namely, the disruptive impact of World War II, changed the attitudes of state institutions and of political and social forces toward Fascism, and played a decisive role in its demise.

A profoundly different outcome from the historical one, namely, the total collapse of the regime, was unlikely because of the survival not only of institutions not fully identified with Fascism, but also of large sectors of the moderate-conservative pre-Fascist political class. In the light of the experience of other Mediterranean countries of Europe, one might speculate on why the Italian armed forces did not play a more active role. They lacked any tradition of an active and independent involvement in politics, were hampered by the imminent military defeat, and lacked truly charismatic personality, an outstanding *condottiere*, even though they were backed by the monarchy and perhaps also because they were loyal to it and perceived their prestige and their future tied to the monarchy. A military dictatorship was ruled out at the beginning of the transition process: institutionally unviable, politically unprecedented, diplomatically counterproductive. The option was not even entertained.

It is likely that had Badoglio immediately surrendered to the Allies the transition might have been halted for some time, with a less than democratic outcome; some liberalization might have ensued, but the process of democratization would have been seriously delayed. The monarchy would have acquired a respectable face, but the most important features and certainly the major institutions would not have changed significantly. A minor broadening of the political arena would have been necessary, but the struggle for the establishment of a democratic regime would have been hindered more than helped by the recognition that, after all, the king and Badoglio had brought peace to Italy. The vacillations of the royal entourage and various attempts at playing shrewd games prevented a development of this kind and so produced a more complex and prolonged transition to a more democratic regime.

**The Resistance Movement**

The armed resistance movement which was launched in the northern part of German-occupied Italy represented not only the climax of two decades of anti-Fascist propaganda and activities, but also the start of a new political organization: the Committees of National Liberation (CLN). These committees were the product both of the clandestine struggle of some old parties and of the new circumstances. Staffed and strengthened by the return of some famous exiles and by the release from prison of many anti-Fascists, the CLN were rejuvenated by the influx of a large number of young Italians. While military actions in the Center and North of Italy were and remained of utmost importance, the resistance movement consistently attempted to create the foundations for a new, democratic, and republican state in the various zones it succeeded in liberating from the Germans.

A new constellation of actors emerged side by side with the old actors, the monarchy and the state apparatus. It was composed of, first of all, the Allied commanders in Italy and, second, the Committees of National Liberation and their representatives. The most important issue on which they clashed was the relationship between Badoglio's government and the anti-Fascist parties. It is from the development of the many facets of this issue that one can proceed to an analysis of the preconditions for the transition to a democratic regime. Up to the appearance of the new actors, in fact, Badoglio's government represented more than anything else monarchist continuity and was in no way related to anti-Fascist public opinion.

It is easy to understand why the king resisted all pressures to dismiss his new prime minister or, for that matter, to abdicate. He hoped to save the monarchy and to be able to legitimate or, better, to relegitimate *his own* position by accomplishing a smooth transition to a new regime of limited democracy. If worst came to worst, he might abdicate in favor of his son, Humbert. The constellation of forces supporting the king's determination was, of course, represented by all those who wanted to avoid "a leap in the dark," that is, all those groups who strove to preserve the continuity of the state and to prevent the emergence of an institutional vacuum. In essence, the monarchy was the remaining rallying point for all Italian conservative forces, and they behaved accordingly.

The Allies, too, had to take sides on this issue. "Washington and London differed substantially in their attitudes toward the abstract merit of kingship. Churchill, whose opinion usually counted most in the Mediterranean, intended unquestionably to uphold the royal binomial of Victor Emmanuel and Badoglio."[19] The British prime minister feared that any politico-institutional change at this stage might impair the war effort. Foremost among his motivations, however, was his concern for the political future of Italy. Churchill wanted to prevent, or at least to postpone, any increase in the influence of the Left. He operated accordingly and thus became a staunch supporter of the Italian king.

In the meantime, the representatives of six parties had created the Committees of National Liberation in Naples under the leadership of Ivanoe Bonomi. The so-called hexpartite included representatives of the Liberal party, Labor Democracy, Christian Democracy, Action party, Socialist party, and Communist party. None of them favored the existing institutional arrangement. The spectrum of preferences went from the representative of the Liberal party, the famous philosopher Benedetto Croce, to the Socialists and the representatives of the Action party. Whereas the latter were fervently pro-Republican and unwilling to collaborate at all with the king and his prime minister, Croce remained a monarchist but asked for the abdication of the king in favor of his six-year-old grandson. The adamant pro-Republican sentiment was dominant among the leaders and members of the Northern Committee of National Liberation located in Milan; in fact, it was unquestioned.

All these events were taking place while Italy was divided into two halves, both, though in a very different way, occupied by foreign powers. Moreover, in the northern part of Italy, Mussolini's puppet Social Republic (Repubblica Sociale Italiana, RSI), buttressed by the Germans, had provoked a lively resistance movement in which leftist, republican elements played a major role. In the South, the relationships among the parties and between the CLN and the government had reached an impasse. Preceded by the recognition of Badoglio's government by the Soviet Union and by the exchange of diplomatic representatives, the return of the leader of the Communist party, Palmiro Togliatti, after almost two decades of exile, the latter part in the Soviet Union, set into motion a solution to the political stalemate.

The *"svolta di Salerno"* (31 March–1 April 1944) is not simply one of the most controversial historical decisions of this or any other period of Italian history. It is also a turning point in the dynamics of the transition and it certainly affected it in multiple ways. Briefly, the Communist leader abruptly put an end to months of bickering among the representatives of the six parties by indicating that he was willing to collaborate with Premier Badoglio whether or not Victor Emmanuel stayed on the throne.[20]

It would be comforting to find *the* official and authoritative Communist interpretation of that momentous decision. At the time that the *svolta* was communicated to the leaders and members of the PCI, disagreements and differences of opinion immediately appeared (later to be subdued), but even today Communist historians and political leaders have not come to a uniform appraisal. Indeed, since the party is currently undergoing a process of critical assessment of its own past, there is reason to believe that the *svolta* will soon be criticized, particularly in the light of its consequences.

From the point of view of the evolution of the international system and its swift restructuring, there is no doubt that Togliatti's initiative was specifically based on a sober and perhaps pessimistic evaluation of the prospects for change in international politics.[21] With reference to the conflicts taking place in the Italian situation, some historians claim that Togliatti introduced into the relationships of power among the various forces "an autonomous and original inspiration."[22] Other Communist historians have stressed "the lesson of the revolutionary method" which Togliatti taught to the members of the CLN.[23] Many of these members, in fact, considered Togliatti's line either, at best, a mistake or, at worst, an unscrupulous move to strengthen the PCI, if not an outright betrayal of the republican position.

On balance, it is appropriate to conclude that "in the *svolta* of Salerno, international motives—of the USSR, of Stalin—are combined with national motives—the wish of the PCI, to achieve its 'insertion' into the country and, even more, into the mechanisms of the state. After the *svolta* the formulation and the construction of the *partito nuovo* began. After the *svolta* the costs of inserting the party [into Italian politics] began to mount, for the country as well as, and indeed more than, for the party."[24]

The immediate outcome was the king's retirement and the appointment of Prince Humbert as lieutenant general of the realm, with the actual transfer of power to take place when the Allied troops entered Rome. Having dropped the institutional *pregiudiziale*, the CLN parties were now free to accept positions in the cabinet led by Badoglio. They immediately did so and created the preconditions for Badoglio's replacement. After the liberation of Rome on 4 June 1944, the conditions had been met for the formation of a new cabinet. "For sure, the hypothesis of the monarchist-representative state was still alive, only the institutional referendum would be entrusted to dissolve it, not without difficulties, in June 1946; but the hypothesis of the monarchist-administrative state, which had been at the roots of the ruinous experience of the forty-five days, was definitively defeated and filed away by the '*svolta* of Salerno.' "[25]

It is difficult to underestimate the impact of the *svolta*, particularly its long-term effects. For better or for worse, Togliatti put the Communist party at the service of the national cause; the war of national liberation took precedence in his strategy over the goals of sociopolitical reforms. The Communists were then asked and are today still inclined to justify that decision not on the basis of an irreconcilable contrast between national and class interests, but on the basis of a temporary postponement of the latter. The justification was that without the achievement of the liberation of Italy, it would have been impossible to struggle for social reforms. The so-called theory of the two speeds (*due tempi*) was of course immediately criticized within as well as outside the party.

Moreover, while Togliatti explained his line in terms of the importance and, in practice, the supremacy of national interests over any others, his strategy did indeed serve interests that were not at all national. Paradoxically, but certainly not without his previous knowledge, the line implemented with the *svolta* served Soviet interests, or what the Italian Communist leader perceived them to be. But most important of all, the line launched at Salerno was intended to serve the interests of the Italian Communist party. To some extent, the PCI needed to present itself as a responsible party willing to collaborate in the liberation of Italy without resorting to maximalist demands. All the more so in domestic affairs, in so far as the party remained, or was obliged to be, identified with the Soviet Union.

The success encountered by Togliatti's line is indicative, not so much, as many Communist writers put it, of its "correctness," but of many other important factors. First of all, objectively speaking, Togliatti's line introduced the least amount of change in the politico-institutional framework. And those changes deemed indispensable followed smoothly and without the pressure of popular demands. The constellation of moderate and conservative forces which had supported Badoglio's government and defended the monarchy, if not the king himself, were obviously strengthened and heartened by Togliatti's decision. To some extent, they were even justified a posteriori in their resistance to the changes advocated by the Socialists and by the Action party. Needless to say, the institutional question was to burden the Italian political system for two more years.

As for the other parties' perception of the PCI and the Communist image, there is no doubt that the reservations concerning the "duplicity" of the Communist strategy found their starting point in the *svolta* of Salerno. The unscrupulousness of the Communist leader, his almost complete disregard for the positions of the other parties of the Left, and the demonstration of unity and discipline of the PCI following such a momentous decision alarmed the other parties and many sectors of the emerging Italian political class.

Finally, Togliatti and his collaborators were fond of pointing to the *svolta* of Salerno as a turning point in the conception of the Communist party as the living instrument of the revolution. From that moment, they have claimed, the very idea of the *partito nuovo* was born, a mass party that addresses its appeal to all sectors of the population, a mass party that is more than a class party, a truly national party. This element is certainly correct, yet there is another, more disturbing implication of the way the *svolta* of Salerno was decided upon, communicated, "explained," and later quickly accepted by the Communists, especially those working in the Northern Committee of National Liberation and in principle more opposed to it. Giorgio Amendola has put it in honest and concise terms. The expressions of dissent to Togliatti's policy were rapidly blocked by Togliatti himself: it was "the end of a regime of more open discussion. This regime had had some difficulties, but it had accustomed us to so frank a relationship that we would not easily have recovered."[26]

In sum, the *svolta* of Salerno had positive consequences for all those who, in the domestic situation as well as with regard to the international balance of power, thought, hoped, and acted with the aim of achieving a stable political and institutional outcome—that is, for those who strove to keep the political struggle confined to the various existing institutional actors: the monarchy, the Allied military government, the Soviet Union, the hexpartite government, the church, and the top echelons of the different parties, the PCI included. The influence of the masses remained, for the time being, suppressed.

It was in the armed resistance movement that this influence continued to be felt. Unfortunately, for geopolitical reasons, the war of liberation could be conducted only in Central and Northern Italy. Therefore, it had no political impact on those areas where it was most needed to stimulate political awareness and political mobilization and to break the chains of subordination to traditional authorities of all kinds (the old local notables and the Mafia, the Fascist representatives, the priests, and the new local notables). To the well-known cleavage between North and South in economic terms, was added in these two fateful years a sociopolitical cleavage—a cleavage based on political perceptions and experiences which has yet to be mended.

If politics had to remain institutional politics, then it is easy to understand why the war of national liberation was not encouraged by the Allies, especially Churchill. The misguided proclamation by General Harold H. R. G. Alexander to the partisans "to halt large-scale military operations" because of the impending winter (13 November 1944) was interpreted by many as an attempt to disband the resistance movement and as such sternly rejected by the partisans. Notwithstanding Alexander's motivations, there seems to be little doubt that the partisans were seen as a destabilizing force; even more so after the Communist-inspired uprising in Athens in December 1944.

As for the political maneuverings, two issues became paramount. The first had to do with the purging of all those involved in the Fascist regime from positions of responsibility. The second concerned the role, present and future, of the Committees of National Liberation. Both issues were, of course, extremely important for the shaping of the new regime and were recognized as such by the participants.

Once more, in this phase, Churchill played an influential role. First, he vetoed the ascent to the office of prime minister of one of Italy's most prominent and capable statesmen, Count Carlo Sforza. Bonomi's second cabinet was therefore weakened from the beginning because the Socialists and the Action party stayed away from it. Sforza was appointed high commissioner of expurgation, but he soon resigned in order to defend himself against Churchill's personal attacks. The result was that "the purge program ground to a near halt by the year's [1944] end. The conservatives had triumphed; the purge machinery ceased to be a political weapon and was turned over to the jurists who, understandably, were reluctant to apply ex post facto legislation."[27]

It is fair to add that, while the conservatives clearly understood the political advantage of becoming a rallying point for all those who were thus saved from expurgation (and there were many, since, after all, Fascism had enjoyed at least a mass passive acceptance, and a somewhat active consent among bureaucrats and numerous groups of government employees and middle sectors), the representatives of the left-wing party underestimated the problem. At best, they believed they would be able to sweep away all the remnants of Fascism once they came to power.

For different reasons, and from different perspectives, the Communists and the Socialists shared this approach, while Action party leaders refused to compromise and took a more adamant stance against Fascist influences.

There is no doubt that the Socialists believed that in postwar Italy power would fall into the hands of the Left. When that happened, a new political class would inevitably emerge. Their idealist expectation vanished slowly. On the other hand, at the rank-and-file level many Communists shared the Socialist position (something that made collaboration at this level rather easy), but at the top, Togliatti in particular showed his realism (or the pessimism of the intelligence, as Antonio Gramsci would have put it) by accepting as a fact of life that no full purge was possible. In the war of attrition he foresaw for postwar Italy, even repentant Fascists should not automatically be compelled to join the ranks of conservative parties (this policy was immediately applied to party recruitment).

The lack of a severe, rigorous process of political expurgation was especially evident in three sectors: the top ministerial bureaucracy, the prefects, the armed forces. Only 403 high-level bureaucrats were retired or suspended from their office. As for the prefects (the real backbone of the Italian state),

> the conservative request to repeal the prefects appointed by the CLN was motivated by the need to avail oneself of "impartial" functionaries, in view of the forthcoming elections: only very few of the men appointed by the CLN accepted the government's offer to transform themselves into career functionaries, and the [parties of the] Left aimed at the possibility of keeping open the prospect of the institutional transformation of the state, sacrificing the renewal of the personnel of one of the most decisive nerves of the Italian state apparatus.[28]

As for the armed forces, the issue of their renewal had two aspects: on the one hand, the expurgation of the officers compromised with the Fascist regime and, even worse, with the Italian Social Republic. "The expurgation was never completed notwithstanding the fact that the Minister of War Jacini declared in August 1945 that as many as 688 generals and 83 colonels had been retired. To tell the truth, the selection had been made in a rather chaotic way which did not affect the officers compromised with the past regime."[29] On the other hand, partisans had the legally sanctioned opportunity to become members of the armed forces, retaining the rank they had acquired during the resistance struggle. Few partisans, however, took advantage of this opportunity; most of those who decided to opt for an army career were discriminated against so that by the end of 1947 the Italian armed forces had been reconstituted as an instrument of the government rather than of the new republican state.

Behind all these phenomena lay the dispute on the nature and the role of the CLN. In the North of Italy especially, these committees might have transformed themselves into genuine ruling organizations, creating a democracy of a new type largely supported by the mobilized sector of the population and wholly outside the traditional channels of political influence. Once more, it was the division within the leftist camp that prevented this solution from being implemented. Once more, the line of division passed between the Action party, which was in favor of a full and immediate transformation of the

CLN into governing bodies, and the Communists, who pleaded the case for the participation of the large masses organized by the major parties.

The controversy was critical. It involved three major aspects: the timing of the sociopolitical changes; the nature of the forces entitled to introduce those changes; and the very quality of the changes. Empirically related to one another, these aspects have to be kept analytically distinct in order to appreciate the differences of opinion (and behavior) among the parties of the Left.

With regard to the timing of the changes, the Communist position fundamentally meant the subordination of all reforms to the liberation of Italy and effectively discouraged any attempt in northern areas to introduce irreversible political changes as well as changes in the ownership of the industrial companies. The Socialists and the Action party, in contrast, were in favor of creating situations that would anticipate a new structure of the state: republican, democratic, decentralized, with rigorous limits on private property. The Christian Democrats were content to take advantage of the differences of opinion within the Left. Their positions, therefore, were not challenged and the past involvement of the church in legitimizing the Fascist regime was not called into question. Moreover, the postponement of any change after the liberation of Italy had a practical effect only in the North where the parties represented in the CLN were subject to pressures from the grass roots and the struggle against the Fascists and the Germans had opened up new political spaces. In the Center and the South of Italy, one can speak of a rapidly achieved consolidation in terms of power relationships and, above all, in terms of the restoration of the socioeconomic fabric of the system.

By far the most important aspect of the post-1943, and especially the post-1945, situation was the mobilization of large popular sectors into politics. Two new parties were so to speak obliged to mobilize large masses of Italians: the PCI and the DC. The Socialist party was also a mass party, whereas the Action party, especially strong among intellectuals and influential because of its innovativeness, remained a small elite movement. Because the Communists perceived that political competition in postwar Italy would entail struggle among organized groups, their attention was addressed primarily to the Christian Democrats and the Catholic church. Their efforts were directed at maintaining a good relationship, close ties, and a working agreement with the representatives of the DC whose strength among popular *and progressive* sectors they did not underestimate. What the PCI overestimated or misjudged was the willingness of the majority of these sectors to accept, let alone to implement, incisive reforms.

The logical consequence of the Communist policy of collaboration among mass parties, of the primacy given to political considerations (and not to the dynamics of the social movements), and of the cool appreciation of international realities led Togliatti to accept the replacement of the Action party leader Ferruccio Parri as the first prime minister appointed after the liberation. Parri had been a political and military commander of the resistance in Northern Italy and was a direct expression of the CLN. Once more, for better or worse, Togliatti preferred a simplification of the political game by allowing DC leader Alcide De Gasperi to become prime minister. The date 10 December 1945 inaugurated the era of De Gasperi government, an era that lasted until 28 July 1953, and of DC hegemony over all successive cabinets until the present. More than that, Parri's overthrow signaled the deflection of the "wind of the North"—that is, of the more radical aspirations for social change nourished by the resistance fighters and their supporters—in favor of the prudence that characterized the activities of the parties' representatives in Rome.[30]

Finally, the creation of the De Gasperi government decisively barred the way to any expectation of transforming the CLN into autonomous governing organizations. From then on, politics would largely be institutional politics. It would have to pass through well-defined institutional channels without yielding to extrainstitutional pressures or utilizing external channels of communication and mobilization. To this end, a formal pact of collaboration was signed among the three major trade union movements (Catholic, Socialist, and Communist), which effectively blocked the more radical demands of some groups of northern industrial workers. The very quality of the changes to be introduced into the Italian sociopolitical and economic system was affected by the policy of moderation pursued at this stage in a very disciplined way by the PCI.

In synthesis, the resistance must be understood as a transitional phase in the progress toward a democratic regime, an interlude rich in implications and potentialities. In about eighteen months, the amount of political activity and mobilization that took place showed that Fascism had not succeeded in destroying Italian civil society and wiping out all organizational networks, as some authoritarian regimes in Latin America have tried to do.

It is not simply that many members of the pre-Fascist Italian political class survived the *ventennio*—the moderate opponents such as Croce, De Nicola, Bonomi, De Gasperi himself living in the country and retaining some prestige and visibility, the most outspoken enemies of the regime such as Salvemini, Sforza, Sturzo, Nenni, Togliatti, and Saragat working in exile for its delegitimation and demise. It is also the case that during the frequently criticized period of Giolitian democracy (1900–14), a number of Italian political organizations, parties, and unions of the Left, as well as those belonging to the Catholic world, had been able to root themselves, to acquire the allegiance and the support of many newly politicized groups. Organizationally and socially, and perhaps also culturally, they were fairly well established in 1919. Only through a massive use of force, and subsequent repression, could Fascism produce the retrenchment of this associational network and the apparent atomization of society. (It is astonishing to notice, however, that the electoral implantation of the Socialists and the Communists in 1946 is closely patterned upon their electoral strength of 1919 and 1921, with the Communists having, of course, made inroads into many Socialist strongholds. As to the Christian Democrats, in addition to taking over the areas of traditional Catholic implantation, they absorbed the votes of the many southern notables and of the divided right wing.) Thus, one must stress not only the importance of anti-Fascist activities, which continued throughout the twenty-year rule—witness the incessant operation of Fascist special tribunals—to keep alive the loyalty and the memories of the Left, but also the role of the Catholic church which, enjoying a relatively free hand in the social and cultural sectors, educated practically all those Catholics who were to make up the Italian ruling class after 1945.

The persistence of partisan identification is an obvious element of strength in the Italian case. To this factor one must add the impact of the resistance. Although the consequences of the mobilization it produced were geographically limited, its political and symbolic impact was indeed pervasive. On the one hand, it was rightly perceived as a rehabilitation for Italy and showed that Fascism had not corrupted all consciences. It was also considered a continuation of the Risorgimento and its culmination, particularly in terms of the radically democratic socioeconomic demands it promoted. Politically, the very existence and diffusion of the war of national liberation made it at first inconceivable and later impossible to proceed to the creation of a semiauthoritarian regime or to the restoration of a regime of limited democracy.

Moreover, the resistance also constituted or functioned as a relatively large-scale experiment of accelerated political socialization and recruitment of cadres for the parties of the Left, establishing and molding the necessary links between top national leaders and rank-and-file followers and sympathizers. Finally, these eighteen months in which the Italian government enjoyed limited sovereignty, plus those few additional months during which the Anglo-American tutelage was still evident and influential, allowed the leaders of the different parties enough time to get to know each other well, obliged them to act within some ill-defined but real boundaries and to solve their conflicts by taking advantage of a sort of safety net, that is, without risking a breakdown because irreconcilable differences of opinion might have activated the intervention of the Allies.

From many points of view, therefore, the resistance was a substantially positive interlude, along the path of transition to a democratic regime, from the cleansing of the Fascist experience to the apprenticeship of political leaders who had to learn to live together. Its importance for the subsequent stability of the democratic regime and its exeptionality should not be underrated.

## From the Liberation to the Breakup of the Tripartite Collaboration

The period that runs from 25 April 1945 to May 1947 was characterized by major changes in the domestic as well as in the international situation, by shifts in the number and quality of the relevant political actors and by a dynamic pace of events. All these elements were closely intertwined. The various international factors impinged upon the Italian situation particularly through the interpretation given to them by the different Italian political actors. There were exceptions, however. Let us start with a brief identification of the changes in the international scene and their impact on Italy.

I have already mentioned that the defeated Communist attempt to take power in Greece was given an interpretation by Togliatti that excluded any insurrectionary effort in Italy. The "Greek prospect" was not simply a lesson drawn from those events, it was also a calculation made on the basis of the power relationships at the international as well as domestic level and with reference to the presence of Allied troops on Italian territory until the end of 1945 (and to the ease with which they might reenter Italy). This observation is not tantamount to saying that Togliatti had already renounced the prospect of seizing power, but simply to state that he was perfectly well aware of international constraints and therefore unwilling to use any means that might jeopardize his longer-term perspective on the struggle for power. In his mind, the insurrectionary way was barred from the very beginning, even though the "comrades" were never (in that period) openly and explicitly told so—another instance of "duplicity" on his part.[31]

Chronologically, the second important event that influenced Italian political life was the United States replacement of Great Britain as the decisive power in the period from the end of 1945 up to the elections of 1948 (and, of course, well beyond that year). Churchill had played an active and incisive role in buttressing the monarchy, in defending Badoglio and the continuity of the state apparatus, in downplaying the resistance contributions to the liberation of Italy, in opposing the transformation of the CLN into governing bodies. With the electoral victory of the Labour party in England and with declining British interest in Italian affairs, the influence of the Americans over Italian politics replaced that of Britain. But, contrary to Churchill's stubborn determination, the Americans did not have a specific policy for Italy, or any clearcut design for the shaping of the Italian political system. Therefore, at least from the end of 1945 until May 1947, it is likely that autonomous Italian initiatives might have been successful.[32]

The Communists were blocked by their allegiance to Moscow (and by the hope that the collaboration between the USSR and the Allies would continue) and, hence, remained cautious in order not to rock the boat (and the Socialists had to follow suit, compelled to do so by their "Unity of Action" pact with the PCI, already resented by some internal groups), and so the Christian Democrats quickly exploited the emerging international alignments. There were limits, of course, to a dynamic policy, but between a complete subordination to the U.S.A., which American policy-makers did not demand at the time, and a neutralist stance, there potentially remained enough space for leftist forces to find a more favorable position. They might have thus saved their own domestic reform program.

When the cold war started, the Italian Left found itself utterly unprepared to face its development and consequences. The immediate outcome was its exclusion from the government in May 1947. From then on the Christian Democrats and the Catholic church were able to present the political struggle in Italy as a choice between civilizations. This polarization not only led to the resounding defeat of the Popular Front in the elections of 1948, but to an insistent propaganda and a thorough process of delegitimation of the Communist party ("the puppet," the "ally," the "representative of the Soviet Union") whose effects are still felt today.

Perhaps there was no alternative to the close identification of the PCI with the Soviet Union once the cold war started. Many scholars maintain, however, that what was not inevitable was an almost complete reliance on the United States on the part of the Christian Democrats and, consequently, the referral of many important decisions in the field of economic reconstruction to American preferences. Once more, it is not that the U.S.A. *dictated* policy choices, but that the dominant forces in Italian politics and economy opted for a capitalist reconstruction in order to obtain some advantages from their allegiance to the United States.[33]

The advantages deriving from this kind of dependence were clear at the time and have retained their validity up to now. It was not simply the possibility of participating in the European Recovery Program and, therefore, of rebuilding the Italian economy along a purely capitalist pattern (while the Left had, of course, pressed for some nationalization, and the workers had for a short period managed some occupied factories in the North). This was an important aspect. But more important, and in the eyes of the dominant groups in the Italian political system decisive for throwing their support behind the United States (in spite of the reservations some Catholic groups harbored regarding the "American way of life"), was the clear perception that the United States would protect their political power, would act as a shield against the eventuality of Communist subversion.

I have probably overstressed the clarity of the conservative design and the determination with which it was pursued. Indeed, one ought to attribute the success of the moderate forces as much to their more "natural" homogeneity (without ignoring that the Catholics-turned-Christian Democrats were not fully integrated with the Italian capitalist class) as to the mistakes and the heterogeneity of the leftist forces. Probably, a sober assessment of the dynamics of the Italian situation would point to differences of opinion and fluctuations both in the domestic alignment of Italian moderate forces and among U.S. policy-makers. The Left was unable to exploit the opportunities for political initiatives that were open, while the Italian moderates and U.S. policy-makers quickly understood the importance and the necessity of an agreement as soon as the first winds of the cold war started blowing.

If international events and constraints shaped the framework within which Italian political actors had to implement their strategies, one should not forget that important changes had occurred in the Italian domestic situation. The first was the disappearance from Italian politics of the Action party. With the benefits of hindsight, one can attribute the dissolution of this party to the coming to an end of most of the principles the party had fought for and to a realignment of its actual and potential electoral and political basis.

The Action party had taken an intransigent, republican stance (which would be vindicated by the results of the institutional referendum of June 1946). It had advocated the transformation of the Italian state on the basis of the structures of the CLN, conceived as popular and revolutionary bodies. It had stressed the importance of creating workers' councils and the need for political decentralization and had supported the unity of leftist forces. The political basis of the party was to be found among the middle strata and its leadership in the progressive intellectual bourgeoisie. Its position in the party spectrum, or better, its ambition, was to occupy the center of that spectrum.

As long as Parri remained in office as prime minister, the Action party could, indeed, present itself as central in the Italian political alignment. When Parri was ousted, all the contradictions came to the fore. It became clear that "without the support of the Communist party, the reform program of the Action party could not be implemented," as Leo Valiani, then political leader and later historian of the party, appropriately noted. By the beginning of 1946 it was evident that its most ambitious proposals for the reform of the state were already doomed. Finally, not only had the Christian Democrats succeeded in occupying the center of the political alignment, pushing the Action party to the left and therefore into competition with the Socialists and the Communists, but they were undermining its electoral basis as well. In the process of the political radicalization that was occurring, Italian middle strata were increasingly torn between the DC and the Socialist-Communist alliance, and so no space for the Action party remained. One might even question the feasibility of a strategy founded on the expectation that, in a country such as Italy after twenty years of Fascism, a party would find enough support for a reform program among those very middle strata, a large majority of whom had represented the backbone of the previous regime.

For all these reasons, the disappearance of the Action party following its convention in February 1946, and its poor showing in the municipal elections of March 1946, seemed inevitable. Its political goals appeared out of reach and its social basis was evanescent. The eruption of mass parties into the Italian political scene and the nature of the two major Italian parties made the hypothesis of a political struggle based on an idealized British pattern far-fetched and rendered the Action party which had cherished it irrelevant. Its members and leaders joined either the Socialist or the Republican parties and retained an important role in Italian politics (e.g., Ugo La Malfa, Francesco De Martino, Riccardo Lombardi, Emilio Lussu, Tristano Codignola).[34]

Until the beginning of 1946, the parties belonging to the CLN had collaborated on the basis of "parity," that is, an equal allocation of ministerial positions, although, in a few instances, some parties had not joined the government; the Socialists and the Action party, for example, remained outside the second government led by Bonomi. Moreover, in many cases local administrations had remained in the hands of the traditional local leaders, even if most of the Fascist *podestà* (appointed mayors) had been quickly removed by the Allies.[35]

The timing and the sequence of the first free elections in post-Fascist Italy were, of course, a matter of controversy. The Left was in favor of early political elections, that is, the election of a Constituent Assembly endowed with legislative powers as well. The Christian Democrats and the small rightist groups favored a different sequence: first municipal elections, then Constituent Assembly elections, in the hope of utilizing the power thus acquired at the local level (where many nonpolitical factors might play into the hands of the "traditional" dominant figures and against the Left) in order to influence the outcome of the elections for the Constituent Assembly. De Gasperi succeeded in securing the support of Alexander Kirk, the American ambassador, and municipal elections preceded national elections. The two parties of the Left nonetheless did very well, perhaps too well, producing some fear in the moderate sectors of the population. The DC also polled a large number of votes, strengthening the Communist inclination to consider it as representative of all those sectors the PCI could not reach.

The institutional issue also had to be solved through an electoral consultation. In a last-minute effort, Victor Emmanuel abdicated in favor of his son, trying to save the monarchy by removing his person. However, it was the institution itself that was considered responsible for many unconstitutional deviations and, as even this belated abdication showed, played the role of rallying point for all moderate and conservative forces. Humbert II was given the nickname of "King of May." On 2 June 1946 the dynasty of Savoy, whose historical contribution had been the unification of Italy, was ousted by a popular vote (12,718,641, that is 54.26 percent against the monarchy, 10,718,502, 45.72 percent in favor). The results of the vote showed not only widespread support for conservative ideas but that, particularly in the South, the republican and democratic "wind of the North" had not arrived.

At the same time, the Constituent Assembly was elected. Party fragmentation was high: fifty-one lists received votes, but only nine obtained seats. The Christian Democrats came out on top (35.12 percent) followed by the Socialists (20.72 percent) and the Communists (18.96 percent). The combined leftist vote was therefore higher than that of the Christian Democrats. The latter, however, occupied the central position in the political alignment, retained the office of prime minister, and were quickly becoming the major object of support for the Catholic church, the Italian bourgeoisie, and the United States. A new historical bloc was well into the making: the Christian Democrats had already succeeded in producing a realignment of all moderate and Conservative forces around themselves and were in the process of giving them cohesion and a sociopolitical project based on anti-Communism and support for capitalist reconstruction.

A final blow was dealt to the reforming hopes of some sectors of the Left. The Constituent Assembly was not given legislative powers: the government retained them and the Constituent Assembly could only play the role of control over its acts, at the same time performing the task of drafting the constitution. This task was important indeed and its fulfillment, according to most commentators, proved to be not only lasting, but a true political monument to some of the demands that had emerged from the resistance movement. As a famous professor of law, and a member of the Action party, Piero Calamandrei, put it, the republican constitution was "a promised revolution in exchange for a revolution *manquée.*" Approved at the end of 1947 and enacted on 1 January 1948, the constitution represented the final act of the uneasy collaboration between the Christian Democrats and the Socialist-Communist group in the Assembly. So important was that period of collaboration, and so celebrated were its results, that to this day the Communists have stressed that they have little in common with the Christian Democrats, except for the fact that they drafted the constitution together.[36]

For international as well as domestic reasons, the Left was losing its momentum. At the beginning of 1947, those Socialists who opposed the "Unity of Action" pact with the Communists split from the PSI and created what would become the Social Democratic party (PSDI). By May 1947 all the international and domestic conditions conducive to an easy ousting of the Left from De Gasperi's government had been created. The cold war was rampant. Its effects were already felt in France where a Socialist prime minister had obligated the Communists to leave his government. The Americans gave their approval to De Gasperi's decision and, more than that, promised their financial and "ideological" backing. The era of the tripartite arrangement was over and the seeds of *centrismo*, of centrist governments with Liberals, Christian Democrats, Republicans, and Social Democrats, were planted. This coalitional formula would dominate Italian political life until the early 1960s.[37]

In this climate, the elections of 18 April 1948 only sanctioned a *fait accompli.* They did it with the high visibility and the great reliability that only hard electoral data can provide. For the first and so far only time in the history of the Italian Republic, one party, the DC, polled enough votes to secure an absolute majority of seats in the House of Deputies (elected according to proportional representation). United in a Popular Front list, heavily damaged by the Communist coup d'état in February in Prague, the Socialists and the Communists lost more than 7 percent of their 1946 combined votes. Not only had the founding coalition of the Republic come to an end, but two of the most important participants were now relegated to the role of secondary actors.[38]

What was accomplished by the Christian Democrats in this period is fundamentally the reorganization and consolidation of a powerful center. In the South, including the city of Rome, and in the various state branches, the bureaucracy, the judiciary, the armed forces, the Center-Right had not been challenged and enjoyed a head start. Togliatti's acknowledgment that De Gasperi was indeed entitled to form the government in his capacity as representative of the party of relative majority was a boost for the entire Center-Right alignment which found, if not a spokesman, certainly a powerful point of reference. On the other hand, the Left showed itself to be divided on some important issues (the institutional questions, the politics of alliances, governmental collaboration). Divided it would remain on many other issues (the insertion of the Lateran Pacts into the Italian Constitution, the Concordat with the church, the relationship with the trade union movement). Moreover, it underwent a process of political fragmentation with the decline and disappearance of the Action party first and with the Social Democratic split in January 1947, which deprived the PSI of at least one-quarter of its votes and members and helped to lay the foundations for the splitting of the labor movement.

Uppermost in Togliatti's mind, however, was the search for a credible and powerful interlocutor empowered to speak for the interests of the Catholics and of large sectors of the popular classes as well as the petty bourgeoisie (the ghost of fascism loomed large in Togliatti's mind). This strategy might have prevented a bloody showdown with the supporters of a right-wing turn and avoided a sharp limitation of democratic rights and electoral competition, but it certainly underestimated and did not anticipate the regrouping of the interests of the landowning classes and the industrial bourgeoisie around the DC.

Moreover, since Togliatti openly supported the efforts of Communist trade unionists to take full control of the unified trade union movement, at the same time disavowing and discouraging those workers' groups that wanted to expropriate some factories, his strategy remained confined within more or less defined, but contradictory, institutional boundaries. Yet it was widely perceived as a purely opportunistic strategy. Certainly, the PCI resorted to more militant tactics of mobilization at the end of 1947 and in late 1948, when national political power seemed out of reach. The net result was then to increase the fears and hostilities of the Center-Right without obtaining significant social or institutional advantages.

Throughout this period, the hardening of the relationships between the U.S.A. and the USSR reduced the possibilities for the Left to be perceived as a viable and safe political alternative. One might even speculate that, because of the international climate, Togliatti would have preferred the continuation of the tripartite coalition to a thin electoral majority for the Left. He was painfully aware that the Popular Front would have been unable to govern if confronted with the hostility of the Americans, the lack of cooperation of the state apparatus, and the outright opposition of the DC and the church. However, the abrupt end of the tripartite arrangement, the electoral defeat, and the split of the labor movement obliged the Communist leader to follow the inclination of many militants and to resort to an aggressive opposition, in Parliament as well as in the squares.

## A Successful Transition? "Ció che è stato conquistato non è perduto"[39]

A balanced assessment of a transition from authoritarianism to democracy is always a difficult task, not only because it requires precise analytical standards but also because the protagonists and the scholars are the bearers of wide political and ideological differences as to the desirability and the feasibility of specific outcomes. One ought to avoid oversimplifications, especially those deceptively simple dichotomies (e.g., restoration vs. revolution, but also authoritarianism vs. democracy), yet the Italian debate has taken some time to go beyond this stage. Some remnants of easy definitions and misguided accusations are still present in the debate among and between scholars and politicians. I will try to avoid them and offer instead some considerations in comparative perspective.

There can be no doubt that in Italy the transition from an authoritarian regime to a democratic one was accomplished and that it was essentially the work of domestic forces. There is widespread, almost universal, agreement concerning the success achieved by democratic groups in defeating those representatives of the past regime in their attempts to prevent the democratization process, both by hindering the mobilization of new political forces and by retaining the monarchist institutional arrangement. The very emergence of mass parties, out of the resistance struggle as well as of the efforts of Communist and Catholic organizers (the Socialists were already a mass party before Fascism) provided the opportunity for expanded electoral and political participation. This is the most novel component of the Italian political system and at the same time the most important in explaining the persistence of the republican regime in spite of the many difficulties encountered and created by the Italian democracy.

Differences of opinion exist and disagreements persist on the evaluation to be placed on the defeat of the Popular Front's bid for power in the 1948 elections. It might sound "impolitic" to say so, but it is likely that the democratic regime was saved by the defeat of the Popular Front—I would not go so far as saying "by the victory of the Christian Democrats," since other outcomes in the distribution of votes were conceivable. Because of the international situation, in the light of the strength of domestic forces opposing "Communism," and, to be sure, if one takes into account the tactical and strategic postures of the PCI itself, a left-wing coalition would have found it extremely difficult to govern. Under tremendous internal and external pressures, a coalition dominated by the PCI, at that time loyal to the Soviet Union and organizationally centralized and politically "extremist," might have resorted to undemocratic deviations, further polarizing the domestic situation; perhaps, *malgré lui*, and probably against the intentions of most Socialist and Communist leaders.

The consideration that the left-wing path was the most difficult to follow leads to a brief evaluation of the overall results of the transition accomplished in Italy. Two extreme positions have been taken, on the one hand, by those who speak of the "resistance betrayed" and, on the other, by those who stress that the outcome achieved in 1948 was, if not the best possible outcome, certainly one of the best and anyway, in the circumstances, almost predetermined (though more in its limits than in its configuration).[40]

In the abstract, of course, it is clear that not all the ideals of leftist groups active during the resistance have been put into practice. The obsession of the Communists with a continued collaboration with the Christian Democrats, with their strategy of political and social alliances, entailed a high price in terms of socioeconomic reforms. These reforms, for example, more control by the workers over the production process in their own companies, better protection over working conditions, decentralized bargaining, were postponed or renounced until it was too late.

In between the restoration of a capitalist system and the revolution and the creation of a Socialist system lie many more or less satisfactory options. The time and the ground for a revolution were not available, but the opportunities for the restructuring of the Italian socioeconomic system were not exploited with determination and foresight. In particular, the Communists utilized their working-class support to buttress political goals, essentially their governmental role, and not to pursue the establishment of better conditions for the workers in many local areas and industrial companies.[41] Defeated at the national level, and ousted from the government, they found themselves with poor leverage in the industrial sector—that is, powerful in their opposition, but powerless in their capacity to introduce changes. Thus, most of their energies had to go to the defense of positions, at the level of socioeconomic democracy, that had not been institutionalized when it was possible and which were easily rejected because of the new power relations—the 1950s represented the worst period since the war for the organized working class as well as for the many migrant workers.

The Italian political system was fully liberalized, if by this statement we mean the creation of a parliamentary democracy based on free elections, a reasonable protection of civil rights, due process of law. But it was not democratized, if we refer to a process of expansion of democratic procedures in the socioeconomic field and in the workings of the state apparatus. Indeed, some pre-Fascist or even Fascist features were reacquired or retained. Thus, one can speak of limited democratization, a process subject to reversals but also to gains, but also of a limited democracy, at least formally—the PCI was considered for a long period of time an unviable political alternative.

What was not gained reflects as much the strength of the conservative forces as the limits of approach and analysis of the Left to the problems of democratization. Fundamentally, the Left proved unable to go beyond two major formulas: the first one based on the idea of political decentralization and of workers' councils (in more modern terms, autogestion or self-management) and the second defined as "progressive democracy." But it was not even united in the pursuit of these two goals.

The first formula was put forward by the Action party and was therefore doomed as soon as the party disappeared, but probably even before then. The Socialists and the Communists were largely in favor of a centralized state; moreover, because of their control over the organized working class and their overall strategy concerning the role of the trade unions, they remained essentially opposed to any proposal that might increase the decision-making power of the workers regardless of their union affiliation. The Action party formula appeared to be on the one hand too modern, on the other lacking the necessary support of the workers, encapsulated by the Socialists and the Communists or tied to a somewhat anachronistic Catholic doctrine of "solidarity."

The Communist formula of "a progressive democracy" was vague and obscure, particularly in institutional terms. That is, either the Communists had in mind something resembling a "proletarian democracy" or a "popular democracy," which would alarm most potential partners, or they simply envisaged a regime characterized by the powerful presence of the masses organized by the Communist party, the *partito nuovo*. But then, the institutional shell would appear to be, with some ambiguities, still a representative regime. This was in fact the definition they gave the emergent system during the electoral campaign of 1946: "a democratic republic of manual and intellectual workers ruled by a representative parliamentary regime."[42]

It is somewhat surprising, therefore, that the actual text of the constitution also contains, in addition to some traditional features (a bicameral Parliament, a Constitutional Court), many provisions dealing with the social aspects of private property, and with citizens' rights and not only duties; a constitution that is, as Calamandrei stressed, projected in the future, providing a framework that accommodates political struggles and makes room for progressive changes.[43]

Having marked the various novelties of the Italian Republic, however, one must be aware that considerable continuities with the past persisted. The state apparatus, in its multiple components, was largely able to survive and to thrive. So much so that it has revealed itself as the major stumbling block against which all reform proposals have run aground. It might therefore be appropriate to quote the sad words of a disillusioned protagonist of the resistance:

> After the insurrection, a new state might have been built in which De Gasperi would have remained in the opposition. The Socialists and the Communists, who would have to be the most important leaders, did not believe in it. One might also have restored the old pre-Fascist state, provided the political class were renewed. De Gasperi believed in it. One could not do what the Socialists and the Communists believed—to keep indefinitely the interregnum of a weak state, always ready to yield to the pressures of the organized masses. De Gasperi put himself at work to restore the old state and was successful with the forced consent of the Socialists and the Communists themselves. He wanted to rejuvenate the political class and was successful, gradually dividing almost one-half of the Socialists from the Communists and absorbing the former into the state of the restoration.[44]

## Concluding Remarks

Italy partakes of Northern Europe and of Southern Europe in its geography, in its socioeconomic structure, in its political dynamics. Even the transition process to a democratic regime provides an instance of the difficulty of locating the Italian case among other Southern European cases. The authoritarian regime lasted for a shorter time than the Portuguese and the Spanish equivalents; political instability and the role of the military have loomed much less than in the Greek case.

In the Italian case the factors conducive to the demise of Fascism have generally been more favorable than in other Southern European cases and in Latin America. Specifically, Italy could count on a democratic past, the traditions and the organizations associated with it, a supportive international climate (in the last, decisive phase). Also important was the relentless struggle against Fascism by its opponents in Italy and in exile. Finally, the resistance movement, the accelerated politicization of a new generation, the experiences and the memories of a profound moral renewal constituted one additional, probably unrepeatable phenomenon.

These aspects explain why it was possible to overthrow the Fascist regime and to start a process of transition to a democratic one. The democratic outcome was not, however, predetermined—certainly not in the very first phase, when it was harshly resisted by forces other than those associated with Fascism, by the king and his military-civilian entourage, which hoped to stalemate the process. The decisive blow to this hope was dealt by the emergence and reemergence of organized political parties. Relevant, too, in a comparative perspective, the armed forces had not been the ruling group, lacked any tradition of political involvement, were without a charismatic leader, were discredited by their defeat in war. Institutionally, the moderate and conservative forces did not offer a united, cohesive front. Moreover, they could not hope to be able to create one around a discredited monarchy, without the support of a well-organized party. When it became clear that, even with some ambiguities, the Christian Democrats were unwilling to play the role of unifying center for them, the majority of the conservatives still decided, tactically, to support the DC. This support helped to solidify the conservative front at the same time that it isolated the reactionary elements.

The organization and reorganization of social, political, and economic groups were facilitated by the relative lack of success Fascism had enjoyed in trying to destroy or to wipe out civil society or to accomplish a *Gleichschaltung*. Where successful as in Germany, democracy subsequently had to be imported. Moreover, the decisive impulse to a complete political reorganization came from the resistance movement. This period, a productive interlude between the demise of the authoritarian regime and the inauguration of the democratic one, acquires even more relevance if one assesses all its positive contributions. In particular, it created and strengthened a core of central values common to the major political forces, most of which found an almost immediate translation into the constitution.

A final, important factor of the Italian transition is represented by the constitution itself. Its profoundly democratic character, its progressive potentialities, the very manner in which it was drafted and enacted gave the major political forces a sense of involvement which cemented the democratic fabric of the country. One can maintain, with specific reference to the constitution, but also in more general terms, that in this founding period political leaders of all parties were shown to be much more advanced and farsighted than some socioeconomic institutions and groups, such as the church and Confindustria

(Confederation of Italian Industrialists), largely dominated by conservative spokesmen whose supremacy might have produced intolerable tensions and strains within the system, and whose power certainly delayed further democratic gains.

Perhaps the most important element of all was that the transition was piloted by the three major political groups and, at the same time, countervailing powers remained dominant in their respective arenas: the church in the socioreligious sector, Confindustria in the economic sector. The state of relative equilibrium, the uncertainty of the various competing groups about the quantity and quality of resources in the hands of the other groups, the probable risks to be encountered in an open, head-on confrontation produced a situation of restraint in success (the DC, the church, Confindustria) and of confidence in defeat (the PCI and the PSI, the unions, the leftist intelligentsia). Therefore, it was not so much the defeat of the Left that assured a successful inauguration of the democratic regime and its institutionalization, but the conviction that the outcome of the process was after all acceptable (and binding), that it allowed the Left to enjoy positions of power in the many local municipalities and among many social and political organizations, chiefly the trade unions, and that it offered the prospects for significant changes and major improvements. The cards were not fixed.

Finally, Italy's regional position in the international system obviously acted as a constraint on the dynamics of the domestic political struggle. It set clear limits to socioeconomic transformations; it worked to the advantage of the forces locating themselves, more or less opportunistically, on the side of the "West." But it also, in the very first phase, worked to the advantage of those who intended to consolidate a democratic regime. If there is a lesson here, it is that the international climate can provide the impetus for the transition, but it cannot produce a successful democratic outcome unless many other conditions are simultaneously present. The best foreseeable outcome remains the one that creates a situation of relative uncertainty for all political forces and of clear risks for those forces trying to subvert the process of democratization. It is like walking on a tightrope, and those who do the walking are as important as those who may shake the tightrope or shout and hinder them.

# 4 ·

# Political Change in Spain and the Prospects for Democracy

José María Maravall and Julián Santamaría

## Introduction

This chapter deals with the processes of transition to, and consolidation of, Spanish democracy. In the mid-1970s Spain was still ruled by a repressive and exclusive authoritarian regime which arose from the 1936–39 Civil War. In the early 1980s a constitutional and politically responsible government was established in the country, several elections were celebrated, the protection of human and civil rights was guaranteed, and a competitive political party system existed. In other words, the old authoritarian regime was replaced by a different, democratic one.

Obviously, the new regime could be described as a "fragile" or "difficult" democracy. Furthermore, the presence of certain elements of continuity could give rise to speculation as to whether the change in regime had been complete or not. But there could be no doubt whatsoever that the configuration of political institutions in force in 1980 was not the same as that which had existed in 1974. To prove this transformation, it is sufficient to differentiate, at least analytically, between the processes of transition and of consolidation which are involved in all changes of political regime. On the one hand, by a process of substitution, the previous regime is dismantled and another set of political forces takes its place. On the other hand, by a process of development, the new regime differentiates itself from its predecessor and crystallizes its institutional structure.

The latter aspect of regime consolidation was dealt with—albeit vaguely—in the studies on democratization that abounded in the 1950s and 1960s under the influence of the functionalist paradigm. This approach was logical inasmuch as the problem then under discussion was not so much how to emerge from dictatorship as how to preserve democracy and, from this perspective, a series of variables associated with existing and apparently stable democracies, such as a high degree of economic development and social modernization, public consent, civic culture or coherence between the political system's models of authority and those dominant within other social groups, were considered as preconditions for democratic viability everywhere.[1]

Critics of this form of reasoning pointed out that it was impossible, either logically or historically, to prove the existence of a prior and necessary causal

71

relationship between those variables and democratic stability. Consequently, it was fallacious to consider them as prerequisites for its implantation. In order to counter the ahistorical nature of the functionalist approach, Dankwart Rustow proposed an alternative genetic approach to the study of political transitions.[2] In order to counter mechanistic assumptions, Robert Dahl advocated a probabilistic approach to the problem.[3]

Rustow suggested an examination of the different phases of the process of regime change and the influencé of each on the following phase; Dahl specified the particular combinations of socioeconomic and political variables that might make the beginning of a transition probable and those that might favor the consolidation of a new democratic regime. Both authors restored attention to the important role attributed to social conflict and political action by classical political theory, from Hobbes to Marx, on the one hand, and from Machiavelli to Tocqueville, on the other.

Both approaches, that of Rustow explicitly and that of Dahl tendentially, also coincide in their emphasis on compromise and gradualism as explanatory elements in the origins and bases of new democracies. However, they were conscious that history has seldom followed the same track. The transition from absolutism to a representative regime took place in England and France by means of a revolution. The transitions to democracy in Germany, Japan, and Italy took place after military defeat under the auspices of an occupying power. More recently, a military defeat and a coup d'état gave rise to the regime change in Greece and Portugal.

Consequently both approaches should be complemented by stressing the sequential dimension of change.[4] The examples we have mentioned clearly show that the transition from an autocratic authoritarian regime to a pluralistic democratic one arises from a crisis of the former. This crisis may derive from the regime's inability to resolve its own problem of reproduction, or from its inability to adapt itself to rapidly changing and unexpected circumstances.[5] It is usually expressed by a manifest decline in the regime's internal cohesion and/or by a loss of its capacity to repress conflicts and prevent the emergence of any type of alternative mode of governance.

The specific content of the crisis may vary greatly from one case to another. The regime may react at an early or late phase of the crisis, something that significantly conditions the relation of forces between itself and its opposition. Whether the transition takes place through a self-transformation of the regime, that is, through a series of pacts between different political actors, or through a rupture brought about by the growing strength of opposition forces, depends upon the extension and intensity of the crisis and, consequently, on the relationships between the coalition sustaining the regime and the alternative coalitions in existence. In other words, the degree to which ideological, institutional, repressive, and personal resources are exhausted will determine the dimensions of the crisis, and this depletion, in turn, will condition the specific pattern of transition.

Whatever the form or type, the transition is initiated by the crisis of the existing regime and concludes with the setting up of a new regime, putting an end to the intermediate stage of provisional governments, overlapping and contradictory principles and regulations, political and legal uncertainties. Normally the transition's conclusion is signaled by the approval of a new constitution drafted by an elected assembly, or with the election of a parliament once the constitution has been restored. That is to say, consolidation begins once the basic institutions of the new political order are organized and begin to work and to interact according to new rules of the game.

Regime transition is, therefore, terminated by legal-formal institutionalization. Consolidation is the process that, eventually, leads to political-material institutionalization.[6] Briefly defined, consolidation includes the processes by which the emergent regime eliminates, reduces to a minimum, or incorporates its initial ideological and institutional inconsistencies; establishes its autonomy in the face of pre-existing established powers within the country, especially the armed forces; mobilizes civil society into political forms of expression; and develops and maintains a structured and relatively stable party system, capable of guaranteeing popularly accountable government. Obviously, these objectives may be aided or impeded by a mass of internal and external factors: that is, by a whole series of contextual and systematic elements. The specific mode of transition is of no less importance than these new contingencies. Nevertheless, the degree of continuity in basic legislation, juridical-legal instruments, criteria of legitimation, symbolic ideological forms, and repressive capabilities during the transition can influence the outcome.

In light of the above, we propose to take a sequential approach in the specific case of Spain: to analyze, in the first place, the factors that led to the crisis of Franco's regime and the dimensions of that crisis; in the second place, the peculiarities of the transition itself; and finally, the contextual and systemic circumstances that have influenced the consolidation process.

## Origins, Dimensions, and Scope of the Crisis

The transition from authoritarian rule to democracy took place in Spain not by means of a radical break with the previous regime, or through a process of self-transformation by the regime itself.[7] It was rather the product of a series of pacts and negotiations in which several political actors were the key protagonists. The Spanish terms *ruptura pactada* and *reforma pactada* are expressive of this ambiguity. The former underlines the lack of political continuity between the two regime types and the principles of legitimation that support them, and the latter emphasizes the element of legal continuity through which the change was put into practice, with a high degree of formal respect for the legality of Franco's political system. In any case, both formulas emphasize the significance of agreement, consent, or compromise during the political operation that permitted the substitution of one regime for another.

The reasons that favored this particular mode of transition and made it possible must be sought in the nature and dimensions of the crisis suffered by the Franco regime—a crisis that began in the mid-1960s and finally came to a head with the assassination of Carrero Blanco in December 1973. This crisis cannot be entirely explained either by the structural transformations undergone by Spanish society since the late 1950s or by the political changes and contradictions experienced within the state organization from the 1960s onward. It is rather in the coincidence and interaction of both types of transformation that we should look for a more adequate explanation.

When the profound economic crisis of the late 1950s demonstrated the exhaustion of the economic model introduced after the Civil War, and the fragility of the grounds on which the regime was based, the existing policies of economic self-sufficiency were replaced by a new development strategy for survival.[8] These policies were directed toward rapid industrialization and modernization of the economy by encouraging the import of foreign capital on a massive scale, persuading unemployed manpower, particularly from the agricultural sector, to emigrate either to the EEC (European Economic Community) nations or to the industrial areas of the country, and financing the overall project with international loans and aid, revenue from the tourist sector, and the emigrant remittances in foreign currency. Indiscriminate protectionism was abandoned; liberalizing measures were adopted; the Spanish economy was opened to competition; and the Spanish market was linked to international markets.

The revised economic strategy produced some spectacular results. Between 1960 and 1970 the industrial sector of the economy grew at an average yearly rate of 15 percent; the gross national product (GNP) and real salaries doubled; and productivity rose by an annual average of 7 percent. This rapid growth made it possible for the regime to preserve the passive consent of large segments of society at a safe level. These unprecedentedly explosive rates of change, however, also had some unintended consequences, which made it much more difficult for the regime to confine other social groups within the conservative patterns that had characterized the previous two decades.

First of all, rapid industrialization imposed more drastic changes upon the occupational and territorial distribution of the population than had been experienced in the first half of the century. For example, by 1950 about half the population was occupied in agriculture—a level unchanged since 1940. By 1970 less than a quarter of the population still remained in that sector. The industrial population rose from less than 25 percent in 1950 to over 37 percent in 1970, and approximately the same occurred in the service sector.

The redistribution of the working population brought with it massive migratory movements from the countryside to urban areas, giving a dramatic boost to the transfer of manpower that had begun in the 1950s. The figures are eloquent enough. In 1950 about 70 percent of Spaniards lived in towns and villages with fewer than 50,000 inhabitants. In 1970, only 55 percent still resided in them. In short, within an extremely brief period a predominantly agrarian and rural society had become a predominantly industrial and urban one, with a solid industrial working class and a renewed middle class on its way to consolidation.

Second, the liberalization and modernization of the economy could not have been achieved without a certain liberalization of industrial relations. Collective bargaining was legalized; a certain flexibility was introduced in the mechanisms of representation within the official syndicates; and penalties for strikers were reduced, although the right to strike was not acknowledged. This liberalization of industrial relations, coupled with the sudden economic expansion, the social mobilization, the imbalanced distribution of the social product, both at regional and at individual levels, the rising expectations prompted by the general atmosphere of economic euphoria, led to widespread collective bargaining and a dramatic increase in industrial conflict.

Third, these changes in the "economic market" had a clear impact on the "political market," particularly in some working-class enclaves, the universities, and the historically autonomous regions such as Catalonia and the Basque country, where the democratic political organizations of the prewar years had managed to survive or where a number of new political organizations had emerged by the end of the 1950s. In the early 1960s, these organizations began openly to challenge the legitimacy of the regime, both internally and externally. The Munich Convention in 1962, to which most of the opposition groups gathered, can be considered as the symbolic starting point for the reorganization of the regime's democratic opposition.

Fourth, this process of change greatly affected the structure of the Spanish ruling class and the nature of its political problems. The economic and political weakness of the bourgeoisie has long been an important issue in the history of modern Spain. Spanish economic development and industrialization under the dictatorship resembled the "Prussian model" of economic growth. The "financial aristocracy" and the state were largely responsible for this growth. The former was involved in an increasing symbiosis between banks and large industrial enterprises and the control of industry by financial capital. Thus, in 1956, 5 banks controlled 51 percent of the country's capital. In the 1960s, when there were 112 banks in Spain, 7 managed 70 percent of all foreign resources, granted 60 percent of all loans, held 90 percent of all private assets, and exercised direct control over a quarter of the country's 200 largest concerns. This concentrated banking group played a crucial role in the creation of national industry. A process of mutual understanding between the financial bourgeoisie and the aristocracy had begun with the liberal disentailment of the mid-nineteenth century and gave rise to a "national ruling class." The political significance of this class was obvious because of its contribution to the financing of Franco's insurrection. The financial aristocracy exercised great influence in the Bank of Spain through its board of directors from 1875 until 1962, when the bank was nationalized, and played an important role in the creation of national industry. Subsequently, the Spanish state under Franco played a decisive role in the accumulation of capital and helped directly to create a new industrial infrastructure through the National Industrial Institute (INI). It was, therefore, a close collaborator of the financial aristocracy in reconstructing the national economy after 1939.

The new "Prussian" style of economic development, which originated in the late 1950s and was partially promoted by the national ruling class, gave rise to a new industrial bourgeosie and to a wave of "new directors" in the government banking system and industry. From 1965 to 1968, the number of professionals within the economically active population rose by 66 percent, businessmen and managers by 45 percent, service sector personnel by 51 percent, and employees by 49 percent. At the same time, there was an increasing spread of more liberal political views, generally connected with monarchist loyalties, within the financial aristocracy itself. For example, of the ninety-one members in the Count of Barcelona's Private Council (the Count of Barcelona was the successor to the deposed King Alphonse XIII and father of the present King Juan Carlos; he was known to have liberal sympathies), eighty-one belonged to the financial aristocracy and thirty-nine were associated with the seven big banks. Thus, the ruling upper class became more fragmented and the middle classes gained strength.

The traditional political weakness of the bourgeoisie, however, was made manifest by its difficulties in setting up political organizations. Under Franco, interest representation or organization did not exist outside the state itself. Moreover, the democratic ventures of the bourgeoisie under Franco were individual rather than collective and sporadic rather than continuous actions. In a word they were carried out "a-legally," rather than illegally, to use Juan Linz's terminology.[9] The relative political disarticulation and predominantly conservative orientation of the bourgeoisie subsequently posed serious problems for the transition from dictatorship to democracy.

Finally, and paradoxical as it may seem, the relative success of development policies during the 1960s weakened rather than strengthened the regime's internal cohesion. Franco closed the breach opened between Catholic and Falangist groups in the mid-1950s by simultaneously rejecting both the former's moderately "liberal" projects and the latter's attempts to increase the influence of the authoritarian movement within the state, although the conflict was to remain more or less latent and to resurface repeatedly during the 1960s and 1970s. A new group, the technocrats of the Opus Dei (a semisecret religious society of lay Catholics) entered the political scene as the main protagonists of the new economic policy. Beginning with the economic ministries that they first occupied in 1957, they gradually invaded other areas of government previously reserved for the exclusive influence of the Catholic or Falangist groups. The old coalitional equilibrium was thus broken and tensions among the regime factions increased. What was at stake from the mid-1960s was the hegemony within the coalition. These internal conflicts acquired a new dimension as Franco aged and each faction approached the succession problem with different perspectives and conflicting interests.[10] The disintegration of the coalition became more acute as the working classes grew more politically active and organized, and the democratic opposition began to reorganize itself. Thus, in spite of uninterrupted economic growth and unprecedented prosperity, the period from 1965 to 1975 was characterized by a gradual erosion of the regime's suppressive capabilities, a progressive narrowing of its social support, and a continued disintegration of the internal balance and consistency of the ruling coalition. However short a period of time it may seem, three distinct phases can be defined in that process of deterioration and decay.

The first covers the period from 1965 to 1968. It was marked above all by a qualitative jump in the combativeness of the working-class organizations that had emerged or reemerged at the beginning of the 1960s. If we take the number of working hours lost through strikes as an indication of working-class pressure, these rose from 1.5 million hours in 1966 to 8.7 million in 1970 and then to 14.5 million in 1975. This conflict was widely discussed by the recently liberalized press and it had a serious political impact. But at the same time, and in a more specific way, the working-class movement took on a political dimension. From 1963 to 1967 political demands had made up only 4 percent of all strike demands; after 1967 they escalated to 45 percent.[11]

This first phase was also marked by a more persistent and open conflict than before among the regime's factions. This conflict was linked to opposing views about the economic role of the state and the institutionalization of the regime, and was politically expressed in connection with issues raised by the Ley Orgánica del Estado (Basic Law of the State) approved by referendum in December 1966. The main issues involved the future of the Falangist movement as an organization and the succession problem. They were the cause of a serious confrontation between the technocrats of the Opus Dei and the bureaucrats of the Falange. The former proposed the dissolution of the movement into a loose, ideological framework, allowing political differentiation among the regime's factions and favoring immediate restoration of the monarchy and even the transfer of power from Franco to Juan Carlos so that the general could preside over the initial years of succession. The Falangists favored the postponement of any decision on this matter until Franco's death and demanded a tighter institutionalization of the movement within the structure of the state. In his memoirs, Manuel Fraga Iribarne located the "beginning of the great confrontations" in this period, more specifically in 1967.

The outcome of the confrontation was a stalemate. The Falangists achieved their goal of strengthening the role of the movement, while the technocrats managed to impose the nomination of Prince Juan Carlos as Franco's successor. The harsh struggle within the regime, however, hindered the development of the political "liberalization" inaugurated in 1966 with the Law of the Press. It also prevented the implementation of a strategy intended to divert the working-class movement by reforming trade union legislation, as had been planned. Finally, it made the continued coexistence of opposed factions within the cabinet almost impossible. In the summer of 1969, two cabinet members uncovered the biggest financial scandal in the history of the regime, in which several ministers and officers of the Opus Dei were implicated. Franco dismissed his cabinet in October 1969.

The second phase runs from 1969 to 1973. It was administered by an Opus Dei "mono-color" government under the leading figure of Admiral Carrero Blanco and was characterized by an increase in repressive policies aimed at undercutting working-class advances and undermining the democratic opposition.

During these years, at least 500 union leaders were arrested (in January and February 1974 alone, 24,818 workers were laid off and 4,379 fired for political activities). Some 2,000 worker representatives lost their jobs and three states of emergency were decreed. The repression was not only intensified, but also extended to other sectors. The university was permanently occupied by the police and a number of professors and students were confined to remote villages in the countryside, arrested, or dismissed from their positions. Opposition groups became a prime target for the police and the Tribunal de Orden Público (a special court for political crimes). In January 1970 alone, this court dictated 100 sentences in trials for "crimes of association and propaganda." The press suffered frequent attacks. Almost 700 sanctions were imposed on it, according to official statistics, between 1968 and April 1972, ranging from fines of 10,000 pesetas to the confiscation of offending newspapers, their temporary or permanent suspension. The sermons of certain priests were censored and the political activities of others led to imprisonment.

Although the intensified repression from 1968 to 1973 succeeded in containing the working-class movement, it was much less effective in controlling the mounting terrorist activities of ETA (Euskadi Ta Askatasuna-Basque Homeland and Freedom) and other groups. Moreover, it led to a spread of the political "contagion" to larger groups of students and university professors, indignant at the indiscriminate and brutal actions of the police and the paralysis of the universities. Repression and censorship also failed to prevent the hardest-hit newspapers from continuing daily to print the vindictive political cartoons that caustically caricatured the regime's unchanging and anachronistic attitude.

The greater internal solidarity within the "mono-color" cabinet, and its blocking of the "liberal" legislation that had been designed in the late 1960s to reestablish the coherence of the dictatorship, narrowed the bases of its social support and proved ineffective in neutralizing the regime's internal conflicts. Even more important, these conflicts were no longer confined to the cabinet. Confrontation set the government against the Falangist movement, while generational and tactical differences surfaced at all levels and in all institutional settings. The Catholic church, which had been distancing itself from the regime since the mid-1960s, finally broke its politically legitimizing ties. This action became publicly explicit when it published a document in 1971 acknowledging its error in taking sides in the Civil War.

The mounting evidence that immobilism and repression were as inadequate as they were ineffective led to a growing discontent within the economic elite, the higher levels of the public administration, and the middle classes. A serious political crisis—especially a collapse—would have resulted in social and economic catastrophe for them. For this reason, informal groups, frequently associated with a newspaper or magazine, arose; they questioned the viability of the system and put forward proposals for democratic reform based on legal continuity. The withdrawal of their support was a clear indication of the deep erosion of the regime's social bases. The survival of the regime was closely linked to the continuance in power of Carrero Blanco as a temporary guarantor of continuity.

His assassination by ETA in 1973 dashed this last hope. As López Rodo, his faithful adviser, put it: "His death meant the end of Franco's regime." From that moment, the regime went into an open crisis. The efforts of Carrero's successor, President Arias Navarro, to reconstruct the social bases of Franco's political system by giving new impulse to the "liberalizing" policies of the previous decade and by preparing the Statute for Political Associations failed dramatically. His strategy of liberalization (*apertura*) exacerbated the opposition of Franco's extremist supporters, the so-called Bunker, but did not attract moderate sectors of the democratic opposition. Nor did it isolate or divide the Left, which reacted by taking advantage of the increased freedom to give a final impulse to its reconstitution as a political force.

The extremists were able to rally Franco's support and succeeded in neutralizing the government's strategy of liberalization. They forced the minister responsible for freeing the press to resign and defeated the president in the debate on the Statute for Political Associations. Their success was seen as a clear indication of the regime's inability to adapt. The expectations generated by the liberalization policies were completely frustrated. Several groups belonging to the so called civilized right wing emerged with the aim of backing some politically known figure who might lead the country toward an eventual pluralist or semipluralist outcome.

On the Left, by 1973, clandestine workers' organizations were regaining their momentum. Strikes in 1973 increased by 84 percent over 1972, and in 1974 by an additional 62 percent. During these two years Workers' Commissions (CCOO) began to recover from their repression, particularly in Madrid where they had been hardest hit. The Unión General de Trabajadores (UGT, the Socialist trade union) also gained considerable strength with the transfer of the leadership from groups in exile to groups inside the country. The resurgence of the Socialist party (PSOE) from 1972 onward added to this recovery. During the summer of 1974, the Junta Democrática, led by the Communist party and including the CCOO, the Popular Socialist party (PSP) led by Tierno Galvan, several small parties, and some independent personalities, was established in Paris with correspondents in each provincial capital in Spain. One year later, the Plataforma de Convergencia Democrática including the Socialists, Social Democrats, Christian Democrats, the Basque Nationalist party, and some other smaller parties was formed. In spite of the fact that the democratic opposition remained divided from that moment, it had become a "credible alternative."

When Franco died in November 1975, the political pillars of the regime were already crumbling. The church had withdrawn its valuable support. The old political factions within the regime were deeply fragmented because of their differing views on a strategy for survival. Large sectors of the new industrial bourgeoisie saw the dictatorship as fully dispensable, considering it a political impediment to Spanish integration into the European Common Market. For their part, large sectors of the middle classes set their hopes on democracy. Most of the surveys conducted during this period demonstrated increasing support for democracy, particularly among the middle classes and educated people.

On the other hand, the regime's values no longer corresponded to those of a largely secularized society.[12] Its institutions lacked all authority and credibility. The regime's authorities were largely discredited because of their inability to counter terrorism effectively or to face the economic challenges, their complicity in brutal repressive practices, or their participation in the financial scandals that had come to light in the last few years, and which extended even to some members of the dictator's immediate family and entourage.

Nevertheless, faced with a divided opposition, and short of financial and organizational resources as well as of a solid social following, the remaining segments of the ruling coalition still retained their monopoly of the repressive apparatus, controlled the largest portion of the ideological apparatus, and could rely on a large part of the civil bureaucracy, as well as on an army recruited during the Civil War that was suspicious of democracy and firmly loyal to Franco's memory. It was this unequal and unstable equilibrium between democratic and antidemocratic elements that initially framed the transitional process in Spain.

### The Type and Direction of Transition

We have underlined the extent to which the regime's crisis was related to its inability to cope with the consequences of the economic and social change it itself had induced. This crisis of policy adaptation was deepened by the crisis of leadership succession. In purely legal terms, as Franco once said, "Everything was tied up and well tied up." When Franco died, Prince Juan Carlos was to succeed him as the head of state, with the title of king. The king would enjoy greater powers than any parliamentary monarch. He would be under the tutelary advice of several institutions to which he was expected to be accountable. An example of these was the Consejo del Reino, in which the aristocracy of extremist Franco supporters remained entrenched. Therefore, King Juan Carlos was supposed to have only limited capacities to engineer an overt transformation of the old regime.

The succession could not be reduced, however, to the mere substitution of the head of state. First of all, there was the intricate problem of finding a substitute for the defunct charismatic leader. Second, there was the touchy question of restoring the monarchy. It was particularly difficult to imagine how a "new prince," lacking any charismatic, historical, or democratic legitimacy, and deprived of the "exceptional" powers of his predecessor, could ensure the continuity of a regime in crisis whose principal beneficiaries were not monarchists at all. It seemed rather doubtful that this newly restored and weak monarchy could gain in strength and legitimacy by linking its fate to that of a decaying and largely delegitimized dictatorship. The examples of Spain in 1931, of Italy in 1946, and, more recently, of Greece in 1974 raised additional doubts on this score.

Within the regime itself, some readily understood that, under such conditions, the monarchy would not have much chance of achieving a solid institutionalization. Some sort of popular legitimation was needed. The plebiscite on the monarchy advocated by some parties of the Left was not even considered. The recent experience in Greece was only one of the reasons for discarding that option. Instead, the idea that the institutionalizing of the monarchy required a democratic transformation gained ground among reformist sectors within the regime. One of its speakers openly proposed that the king use all his inherited powers to act as a dictator for a short time in order to achieve a long, peaceful reign as a constitutional monarch.[13] Cardinal Tarançon, representing the official church view, explicitly linked the reestablishment of the monarchy to the restoration of democracy. The king himself expressed a similar view before the Cortes when he accepted the crown in December 1975.

In retrospect, the logic of this exchange looks transparent and compelling. It is quite clear, however, that it did not automatically and immediately impose itself. Neither the transitional process nor the specific form it finally assumed can be interpreted exclusively or fundamentally in the light of the dilemmas arising from the succession crisis. Rather, the period between December 1975 and July 1976 must be seen as the culmination of the "preparatory phase," to use Rustow's terminology. The decision to restore democracy and the decision to initiate for that purpose a process of negotiation, reciprocal guarantees, and pacts were not taken by the Suárez cabinet until July 1976— and only after the earlier attempt by the Arias government to impose a sort of "limited democracy" from above, a "démocratie à l'espagnole" as it was wrongly called, had failed. Those decisions were only accepted by the democratic opposition forces once they realized that their lack of resources made it impossible to force a sudden change in regime type.

In fact, Prime Minister Arias Navarro never accepted the idea of transforming the inherited regime into a pluralist democracy. He reshuffled his cabinet to include some supposedly reformist figures, tried to divide the opposition with a policy of selective repression designed mainly to isolate the leftist parties, cautiously enlarged the margins of tolerance, and promised a project to introduce some type of controlled or limited democracy. His government never got off the ground. The opposition took the initiative during the crucial, post-Franco months, putting into practice a most effective strategy of "pressure from below." In the early months of 1976, the workers' movement showed unprecedented strength and combativeness. In 1976, the number of working hours lost through strikes reached 150 million (as compared to 14.5 million in 1975). The struggles and mobilizations were especially intense in the first three months of the year. In that period alone there were 17,731 strikes; whereas, in 1975, the year of the most widespread working-class militancy under Franco, there had been only 3,156.

The worker mobilization was coupled with the fusion of the Junta Democrática and the Plataforma de Convergencia into a single organization, Coordinación Democrática (CD), which expressed the common purpose of all democratic parties to force a transformation in the nature of the regime. CD included liberals, a fraction of the Christian-Democrats, Social Democrats, Socialists, Communists, Maoists, and the illegal trade unions. They resisted the divisive and isolating tactics of the government. Instead, they took advantage of the new margins of tolerance. In response to the persistently repressive actions taken by the government, every arrest of a leader, every abuse or provocation was used as an occasion for joint actions and massive demonstrations. The government responded with a spiral of repression and concessions, with moments of dramatic violence. In order to appease the "Bunker" at the end of April, Arias Navarro finally disclosed his "reformist" project, as well as his firm refusal to negotiate with the opposition.[14]

Only a few weeks later, the king himself confirmed his unease with that program. Before the United States Congress, he made explicit his desire for Spain to move toward a parliamentary democracy. On the other hand, in the Spanish Cortes, the immobile sectors of the "Bunker" struck the government a fatal blow by rejecting a bill that partially facilitated the legalization of some parties.

Arias Navarro resigned. The main difficulty facing the government formed by Adolfo Suárez at the beginning of July was that of finding a way out of the impasse produced by the previous government. His declaration of program aimed at doing so. In it, he proclaimed the principle of popular sovereignty and his government's intention to work for the "establishment of a democratic political system." He also announced the granting of a political amnesty and he promised to submit to the nation, by way of a referendum, a project of constitutional reform which would include the celebration of general elections before 30 June 1977. The declaration thus fixed the government's objectives and the process intended to carry them out. This "legal" process respected the demands and conditions set by existing institutions and established powers (poderes de hecho), in clear opposition to the formula of ruptura pactada, advocated by the opposition. Nevertheless, this strategy basically coincided with the opposition's expressed aims and was in open conflict with the aspirations for continuity of important sectors within the regime. Thus, the government recovered the initiative and situated itself in an intermediate position between those in favor of rupture and those in favor of continuity.

The declaration also expressed the government's willingness to start talks with the most important groups in the regime and the opposition; informal contacts were initiated at once. But the cabinet's mediating and conciliatory strategy was, in the first phase, directed toward negotiating with the right wing. The church had already declared its support for the installation of a democratic system in December 1975. During the spring and summer, Suárez obtained the support of the financial aristocracy by assuring them that the reform would not jeopardize the foundations of the capitalist system. In September, with the king's backing, Suárez managed to coax consent out of the top military command by guaranteeing that the authorities within the armed forces and the civil administration would remain untouched, that the established legality would be scrupulously respected in putting the reform in practice, and that the Spanish Communist party would be excluded. The last impediments were the Consejo Nacional del Movimiento (National Council of the Movement), which was supposed to decree the projected Law for Reform into being, and the Cortes, still packed with Franco appointees, which was to approve it before submitting it to referendum.

Both institutions were already somewhat conditioned in their response by the backing the government had obtained from the established powers and by the relatively favorable public response to the project. However, the government had to offer better guarantees in order to persuade the Francoist "political class" to go along. First, there were guarantees of personal continuity. Of the 500 Procuradores in the Cortes, some 80 reappeared in 1977 as deputies or senators. Detailed information on the composition of the boards of directors of public bodies between 1977 and 1982 is not available, but a study of these would probably be most revealing. Second, the government deleted the preamble to the project, which increased the margins of uncertainty about its final aim.[15] Whether or not the Cortes members would become "constituents" was left to the results of the subsequent election. In addition, certain amendments were admitted to the electoral system outlined in the project, which reinforced the possibilities for the electoral success of the conservative forces. The project was finally approved by the Cortes with 426 votes in favor, 59 against, and 13 abstentions. On 15 December 1976 it was ratified by referendum. The turnout was 78 percent; 94 percent of the voters approved the transition to democracy.

The successful outcome of the referendum considerably strengthened Suárez's position. He could interpret the favorable results as a sign of his own popular backing. The symbolic legitimacy of the democratic opposition groups was seriously damaged when they failed in their attempt to persuade the electorate not to vote. It was in this context that Suárez moved to negotiate with the Left, whose participation in the projected "founding" election was obviously essential. The opposition was represented by a Committee of Nine, ranging from liberal monarchists to Maoists and including Basque and Catalan nationalists. Suárez rapidly agreed to some of their basic demands. Among these were the extension of political amnesty, a proportional electoral law, legalization of the parties extended to cover the PCE (the Spanish Communist party), and the dissolution of the Movimiento (the single party created by

Franco) and the Sindicatos Verticales (the state corporatist interest associations for workers and capitalists). The last was, however, the only reform directly affecting the political apparatus and personnel of the Franco regime. Even then, the syndicate bureaucrats were merely recycled into the regular state administration. The opposition groups were, in turn, compelled to make some important concessions. The idea of a government including both opposition and reformist groups was abandoned. In the same vein, the opposition groups had to renounce any policy of prosecution and punishment of those politically responsible authorities and officials involved in repressive activities under Francoism. The regionalist parties accepted a postponement of the process of territorial devolution until after the elections. The Left parties were unable to extract more progressive economic policies. They had to withdraw their republicanism and to admit to certain national symbols, as well as to a series of correctives to the proportionality of the electoral system that openly favored the conservative parties.

That the opposition made more concessions than necessary or showed more moderation than was needed are questions open to discussion. However the heterogeneity of the Committee of Nine made its survival as a "pressure block" unlikely, particularly when some of the moderate conservative groups represented in it were negotiating at the same time for the formation of the union (UCD). The concessions were also conditioned by the persistent threats against democratic reform that hovered over the transitional period, leading to periods of extreme violence and tension, such as the "Black Week" in Madrid (23–28 January 1977) when two students, five Communist lawyers, and five policemen were murdered. Although the pressures from the working-class movement remained intense until the June 1977 elections, they did not entail the mobilization of other sectors of society and were, therefore, insufficient to compel the government to yield to leftist claims. Finally, faced with the pending electoral challenge, the opposition parties had to consider the political and ideological predispositions of their presumed constituencies and not be misled by the views of their more active militants. In fact, popular attitudes were quite moderate. On an ideological scale of 1 to 10, over 40 percent of the population placed itself in the middle (positions 5 and 6). The average position was 5.47. Even the bulk of the working class proved rather moderate in its general political views.

From a different perspective, Suárez had considerable success in subduing the resistance of the continuist "hard-line" groups and in leading the democratic opposition to accept limitations, and the content and procedures of "legal reformism." His success made him the natural leader of a coalition of moderate parties—Liberal, Christian Democrats, populists, and Social Democrats—that he subsequently put together. These groups provided him with some form of democratic legitimacy, while he contributed his personal popularity and authority to make of the resultant UCD (Union of Democratic Center) a political party that was widely accepted and initially viable.

*Elections and Pacts*

The second phase of the transition began with the general elections of 15 June 1977. The result of these elections would determine whether the new Cortes would meet as a Constituent Assembly and, if so, whether the new constitution it drafted would be more or less progressive and whether it could count on wider or narrower political support.

The elections produced three important results. In the first place, and in sharp contrast to the 1930s, the number of politically active cleavages expressed in the electoral arena was considerably reduced. Neither the religious cleavage (clerical-anticlerical) nor the institutional cleavage (monarchist-republican) appeared at all. Political competition was built around two dimensions. At the national level, the dominant one was formed by an ideologically polarized, class-based Left-Right division. To this was added, in Catalonia and the Basque country, a center-periphery, nationalism-centralism line of conflict. The emergence of "insoluble" problems at the regional level was limited by the deep penetration of nationally based political parties within Catalonia and Basque country. In the second place, the results confirmed the moderation of the electorate and its desire for democratic change. The insignificant electoral support for the extreme Left (3.1 percent) and Right (0.6 percent) denied both parliamentary representation. Even those elements of the Right linked to Franco and identified with the AP (Alianza Popular), received only 8.5 percent of the vote, less than the PCE, which obtained 9.3 percent. Their prospects for holding back the democratic process were severely deflated. The new Cortes would meet as a Constituent Assembly, which was agreed to at the first session. In the third place, the results established a clear electoral balance between Right and Left. The electorate was divided almost evenly between them. Only about 6 percent of the vote went to the regional parties. Within both Left and Right, the predominance of the centrist formations was clearly established. On the one side, the Socialists gained 34 percent of the votes (29.4 percent for the PSOE and 4.5 percent for the PSP). On the other side, the UCD alone gained 34.8 percent. The prospect that a constitution would be either imposed by force or impregnated with a marked ideological bias was greatly diminished.

The inherent (and deliberate) misrepresentation and malapportionment in the electoral system converted the UCD's 35 percent of the vote into 47 percent of the seats. Neither UCD nor the PSOE supported the PCE's thesis of constituting a "concentration" or "grand coalition" government along the lines of the provisional governments of France and Italy from 1945 to 1948. A coalition between UCD and AP was unacceptable to everyone, in view of the differences between these parties and the reluctance of the latter to accept democratic change. Finally, a UCD/PSOE coalition would have generated bilateral opposition from both extremes in the style of the Weimar Republic and deprived the system of any viable alternation in power. Consequently

Adolfo Suárez chose to form a quasi-majority party government based on his UCD that, from its strategic position in the center, could be backed by the Right or the Left alternately in the management of ordinary policy matters. Moreover, such a formula enabled the government to exploit consociational techniques in facing the three main problems: (1) the establishment of the constitution, (2) the struggle against the economic crisis, and (3) the institutionalization of regional autonomies. In other words, the electoral results of 1977 implied an extension and renovation of the strategy of compromise and pact-making.

Another series of factors also favored the adoption of this consociational formula. In the first place, the experience of the 1930s taught actors to avoid block action and majoritarian principles in making basic decisions about political institutions. In the second place, the willingness of the democratic component of the regime to compromise was reinforced by pressures from established powers, such as the armed forces, and the threat of terrorism from the extreme Right and the extreme Left. Finally, the consociational formula was made more acceptable by the existence of a wide personal communication network, which had been established between many of the UCD and Left party leaders since the years of opposition to Franco, and further reinforced in the initial phase of transition.

The first of these major efforts at compromise was aimed at reaching a social pact to face the economic crisis that began in 1973. The final Franco governments had lacked the authority to face it, and the first of the transition governments, concentrating their efforts on the solution of political problems, paid little attention to it. As a result, the deficit in the balance of foreign trade reached a record figure in the summer of 1977, while unemployment rose to 7.5 percent of the active population and inflation was running at a rate of nearly 30 percent. In order to deal with this situation it was necessary to apply a policy of austerity and reform which required the support of all partisan and trade union forces. The agreement took shape in September 1977 and was called the Pact of Moncloa. It was signed by the government, parliamentary parties, and trade unions, giving the government authority to freeze salaries, reduce public spending, restrict credit, and increase fiscal pressure. In exchange, the government promised to carry out a progressive tax reform, to make the social security system more efficient, to reorganize the financial system, and to put into practice a series of urgent political reforms.

The strategy of pacts had as its second objective the resolution of the regional problem. This problem has been a permanent issue in Spanish history for the last 150 years, raised primarily by Basque and Catalonian claims for a devolution of governing powers. It was the cause of three civil wars in the nineteenth century, had contributed decisively to the crisis and breakdown of the liberal Restoration (1875–1923), and had frequently overshadowed the short life of the Second Republic (1931–36).[16] That Republic, however, had for the first time attempted a conciliatory answer to the problem. Catalonia received its Statute of Autonomy in 1932 and the Basque country in 1936.

These were later abrogated by Franco, who went as far as to forbid the use of the Basque and Catalonian languages.

The humiliation of the old-established "nationalities" during the Franco era provoked even deeper resentment against central authority and simultaneously helped to consolidate and extend a feeling of distinct national identity within these areas. Since the 1960s, this resentment had resulted in the active or passive support given by large sectors of Basque society to the violent actions of ETA and also produced a coalition of all Catalan opposition groups in the Assemblea de Catalunya. Basque and Catalan demands for devolution were pressed throughout 1976 and became particularly intense after the 1977 election. A much less intense, but widely spread, claim for similar measures of home rule was voiced by other regions in Spain, as a reaction to what was seen as the privileged position enjoyed by Catalonia and the Basque country.

The regional question posed a serious dilemma to the government. Because of its historical significance, it could not be ignored. However, it also raised great suspicions and resentment within the armed forces, extremely zealous in their role as guardians of territorial unity and incapable of distinguishing between "regional devolution" and "separatism." A general agreement that included the majority of the parties concerned was thus essential to legitimate whatever solution was found for this problem. The initial response was gradual and tentative. After the elections, the political amnesty was once again extended to Basque nationalists. At the same time, conversations were held with Josep Tarradellas to bring him back from exile as president of a provisional government in Catalonia, invested initially with symbolic rather than real powers.

However, the Basque and Catalonian statutes granted in the 1930s were not restored as demanded by the nationalists in both regions. They were forced to wait until the constitution had defined the terms of the new territorial distribution of power within the Spanish state. In fact, the basis for a general agreement on the issue was eventually found in the general application of the statutory formula to all regions, instead of restricting it to the Basque country and Catalonia. This choice of a mixed type of "federal-regional" state calmed the impatience of the other regions to a certain extent, and established a common ground for a compromise among nationalist, leftist, and conservative parties, although each was motivated by different, and even opposing, views. Some nationalist parties saw the generalization of the statutes as an expedient measure to dilute the armed forces' persistent suspicions regarding Basque and Catalonian ambitions in particular, while they pressed in favor of special statutes for the two "historical" regions. In contrast, the rightist parties tried to put all regions on the same level, thereby reducing the degree of political autonomy granted to Catalonia and the Basque country. Finally, the decentralization of political power was seen by the leftist parties as an effective tool for making the administration more democratic and for dismantling arbitrary and authoritarian elements within the state bureaucracy.

The constitutional agreements were the third and most pivotal of the pacts reached at this stage of the transition process. They included, on the one hand, compromises between Left and Right and a set of guarantees conceded to established powers. Briefly, the rightist parties wanted a short constitution, institutionalizing the monarchy and protecting it against any threat of change by means of an extremely rigid procedure of constitutional amendment. They also insisted on explicit recognition of a free market economy and a strong, stable cabinet with clear supremacy over parliament. The leftist parties doubly conditioned their backing of the monarchy: (1) it should be a "parliamentary" monarchy with limited, well-defined powers; and (2) the rigidity of the amendment procedure should be extended to cover all possible revisions of a progressive and detailed bill of rights that was to preface the constitution. They accepted the principle of a market economy in exchange for recognition of the state's powers of economic initiative and its right to intervene in the economy. They accepted the principle of reinforced governmental stability within the framework of a greater equilibrium between government and parliament, in exchange for the insertion of proportionality within the constitution as the basis of any future electoral law.

These constitutional pacts could not overlook the significance of the established powers. Therefore, in addition to the guarantees provided for the existence of a capitalist economy, they recognized the special position of the Catholic church and the armed forces within the Spanish state. Although the constitution consecrated the secular character of the state, it also guaranteed the Catholic church's freedom to teach, to found educational institutions (not only schools), and to receive state subsidies to run them.

The constitution referred to the armed forces in its preliminary title as a symbol of the recognition and importance of their political role. They were charged with ensuring the sovereignty, independence, and territorial integrity of Spain. To this charge was added an explicit role as defenders of the constitutional order. Though the last clause was subject to some ambiguous interpretation, it was clear, in the light of other sections of the constitution, that the armed forces had not been elevated into what Carl Schmitt used to call the "defenders of the Constitution."[17] It rather stressed their submission to the basic law, while their constitutional duty of defending the territorial integrity of Spain helped to calm any possible unrest caused by the institutionalization of the "federal-regional" structure of the state. They were also put under the direct command of the king himself, an arrangement that satisfied some military claims without granting to the armed forces full corporate autonomy. The determination of the military policies and the administration were unequivocally assigned to the national executive.

The constitution was not only elaborated by compromise and consensus. It was passed almost unanimously by the Cortes. Only some of the AP's deputies voted against it, whereas the National Basque party abstained, as a protest against the refusal of the main parties to accept an amendment to the text concerning recognition of the "historical" territorial privileges of the Basque country. The constitution was ratified by a referendum in which 87.8 percent of the voters approved, with a rather considerable 32.3 percent of those eligible abstaining. After the parliamentary and municipal elections in the spring of 1979, the new regime was installed. The composition, organization, and functioning of its basic institutions, as well as the relations among them, conformed to the patterns established by the newly agreed-upon rules of the game. Transition, as we have defined it, was practically at an end. The problem now was consolidation.

### Problems of Consolidation

The consolidation of democracy means guaranteeing the necessary conditions for the regime's regular functioning, its autonomy, and its reproduction. It requires the institutionalization of the regime's norms and structures, the extension of its legitimacy, and the removal of the obstacles that, in its initial phases, made its establishment difficult.[18] It is a prolonged process, and in some cases may last an entire generation. It is during the initial phases of the new regime, however, that problems are most acute, since these are the moments when democracy is usually most fragile. Its principles and values still have to be converted into norms and practices. Its institutions have not yet been completely developed. The regime may still exhibit a certain lack of coherence, while the incipient democratic legality must continue to coexist with important elements of the authoritarian legality which contradict it. These inconsistencies are likely to occur within certain institutions. Their suppression, the fixing of priorities, and the solution of the basic problems are a logical cause of division within the main political formations and institutions at a time when it is most probable that those sectors sympathizing with the previous regime have not yet totally transferred their loyalties to the new one and have not yet resigned themselves to accepting the change. If, in addition, some of those groups have retained strategic positions within the newly inaugurated regime, the difficulties for consolidation are likely to be greater.

As has been suggested already, the initial prospects for a successful consolidation seem to depend on three variables: first, the type of transition, which may reduce or exacerbate some of the already mentioned difficulties; second, the external and internal context within which the regime change takes place, which determines the number, nature, intensity, and importance of the main problems to be solved, or, to use a different term, the "confining conditions" that the new regime must remove if it is to ensure its viability; third, the party system that emerges and which affects the extent of agreement or disagreement in fixing priority objectives, the efficiency of government, the restriction of political conflict to the parliamentary arena, the possibility of alternation in power, and the viability of peaceful resolution of conflicts. Let us examine each of these variables in turn, with respect to the problems of Spanish consolidation.

As far as consolidation processes are concerned, the way in which the transition from authoritarian rule was effected had an ambivalent impact for a certain period. The power imbalance from which it arose, together with the symbolic continuity represented by the king, made possible a high degree of material and personal continuity with those groups previously identified with the Franco regime and occupying key positions in its state apparatus, such as the armed forces, the judiciary, the intelligence services, the police, the various national bureaucracies, the municipal and provincial governments. The peaceful and law-abiding nature of the transition did not imply—nor could it ever imply—that the legitimacy of the old regime had been transferred and, thereby, reinforced the new regime since the latter was clearly inspired by contrary values and purposes. It did, however, permit the legitimation of the monarchy to remain beyond dispute. The guarantees offered to the Francoist political class and the established powers resulted in a fragmentary and partial transfer of loyalties from one regime to the other. One sector of the previous ruling group integrated itself with the new regime through the AP and UCD in particular. Another stayed out of the fray, weakened and incapable of causing serious harassment. Only the so-called Bunker maintained a position of open hostility, giving rise to extreme right-wing terrorism and support for several conspiracies aimed at a coup. The case of the armed forces was more complex. It is practically impossible to detect the degree of unity or diversity within their ranks, although it seems in retrospect obvious that the diversity was greater than was popularly thought at the time. Their acceptance of the new regime seems to have been cautious and conditional, limited in any case by their loyalty to the king as commander of the armed forces. The continued monopoly of the military high command by officers appointed during the Civil War aroused suspicion, whether justified or not, about their commitment to democracy. Various incidents demonstrated the persistence of hostile military sectors. Hence, during the early years, the consolidation was overshadowed by a permanent threat of impending coup d'état.

In order to counteract the menace of these factors, a political annex was included in the Moncloa Pacts, in which the government promised to carry out a series of reforms directed at modernizing the military, civil, and legal administrations, and replacing or modifying important parts of previous legislation. The UCD governments were reticent about fulfilling these commitments and the left-wing parties lacked the strength to impose them. The persistence of those elements of continuity constituted a considerable obstacle for the consolidation of the new regime, and was proof of its fragility from 1979 to 1982.

Otherwise, the comprehensive, inclusive nature of the new regime, together with its strategy of consensus-building among the main political parties during the second phase of the transition, partially counteracted the intrinsic fragility. First, as has been mentioned, it made possible solid parliamentary and popular support for the constitution. Second, the consensual method and practices were highly instrumental for the reciprocal legitimation of parties and their leaders.[19] Third, the new habits of democratic compromise and negotiation were signs of a new pragmatism, substituting old cultural patterns of intolerance, exclusiveness, and rigidity. Finally, these very facts, together with the common dangers experienced by most parties as a consequence of the double threat represented by terrorism or coup, clearly contributed to setting up both an encompassing network of political communication among parties, leaders, government, and opposition, and to reducing any temptation to resort to a pattern of adversarial politics with the debilitating effects it would have produced during the early stages of consolidation.

The second set of variables conditioning the success of the process of consolidation refers to the environmental context. No external factor seems to have had a negative influence in this respect. The initiation of the transition was entirely unconnected with any external stimulus, in contrast to the transitions of Portugal and Greece. The international atmosphere was, on the contrary, quite favorably disposed toward the new regime. There were no hostile political systems in the Western world as in the 1930s. The new, strategic importance of the Mediterranean, following the oil crisis and the conflict in the Middle East, reinforced the "commitment of West European governments and that of the United States to democratic stability in the region."[20] As far as the Eastern countries were concerned, Spanish democracy did not imply any change in the balance of power between the two blocs, and the normalization of diplomatic and commercial relations that would follow could only be seen as advantageous.

The main difficulties were, however, related to the internal environment. The territorial reform of state power, the political violence, and the economic crisis presented important challenges to the rather weak UCD governments at a time when poor government performance was easily attributable to the inadequacy or inefficiency of the regime.

The regional problem reemerged with force from the very beginning of the transition. In 1976 it made unification of the democratic opposition groups particularly difficult. Early in 1977, Basque and Catalonian representatives formed part of the Committee of Nine that negotiated with Suárez. As a result, they reached several agreements of principle regarding possible constitutional responses to the problem. Neither they nor the three successive political amnesties granted between 1976 and 1977 sufficed to reduce the pressures and demands coming from Catalan and, especially, Basque nationalists. In 1978 discussions on the problem were particularly sharp and hostile within the Constituent Assembly, under crosscutting pressures from nationalists and the military establishment. The solution provided by the constitution introduced a complex scheme full of ambiguities. It did not initially allow actors to decipher exactly what would be the final structure of the Spanish state after its territorial reformulation was completed. Nor did it tell them when and how it would happen. Neither the government nor the nationalists were clear in spelling out the ultimate logical and temporal limits to the process. Lingering negotiations between them led frequently during 1979 to changing strategies, alternating and "unnatural" alliances, blackmail, deadlock, and confusion. Thus, the development of a general constitutional formula and the specific drafting and enactment of the Basque, Catalonian, and Galician regional statutes occasioned a deep conflict over rules among the new political elites. Moreover, the regional problem, which had historically been confined to the Basque country and Catalonia, took on a national dimension as newly formed regional parties artificially activated the issue in other regions. For example, in the case of the Socialist Andalusian party (PSA) in Andalusia, the government was forced to call a referendum on the autonomy issue, put a virtually unintelligible question to the electorate, and then recommended that it not vote! The regional question, in other words, gained rapidly in saliency, intensity, and visibility throughout that period.

The preferential attention given to this issue by the political elites, in contrast with their postponement of crucial economic issues, was an additional source of irritation, mistrust, and disillusionment in most Spanish regions, and their inability to reach a satisfactory agreement added to the climate of political violence in the Basque country and Madrid.

Political violence was, indeed, a critical challenge—both before and after the approval of the constitution. From 1976 to 1982, ETA wounded 540 people and murdered 345, including among the latter some 30 high-ranking military officers. Terrorism also increased throughout these years. Sixty-eight people were killed in the Basque country in 1977, 70 in 1978, and 130 in 1980. At the same time extreme right-wing violence also increased, particularly after 1978, producing 40 deaths and 128 wounded in the Basque country alone, as well as a long list of assaults and deaths in Madrid and other big cities. This considerable level of violence was mainly connected with nationalism and with the regionalization of the state. It was also connected with the general process of democratization since it reflected in some cases opposition to the reform of certain institutions, including the security forces, and the persistent toleration of an underground rightist plot (*trama negra*) which involved top military officers and former ministers from the Franco period.

Additional difficulties stemmed from the prevailing economic crisis. By the summer of 1977, the figures for unemployment, inflation, and the trade imbalance had grown to previously unknown proportions. In large part, the crisis was a legacy of the Franco regime, whose late governments had been weak and lacking in authority as well as unwilling to face the aftermath of the oil crisis and to enact needed fiscal reform that would have permitted a counteracting budgetary policy. In 1977 inflation rose to 30 percent. The Moncloa Pacts were the main instrument chosen to curb these tendencies. Inflation subsequently went down to 16 percent in 1979 and to 14.2 percent by 1981. But in spite of this drop, inflation continued to obstruct economic recovery. The unemployment figures continued their ascending trend, reaching more than a 3-percent rate of annual growth in 1980 and directly affecting 13 percent of the economically active population in 1981 and 17 percent in 1982. Meanwhile, the GNP grew at around only 1 percent in contrast with the 4.5 percent needed by the Spanish economy to absorb unemployment.

As in the 1930s, the initiation of democracy coincided with an international economic crisis which badly affected the Spanish economy after a long period of prosperity associated with the outgoing authoritarian regime. Whether the perceived inefficiency of the government in dealing with the crisis did or did not have a delegitimizing effect is open to discussion. Survey data suggest that most people blamed the international crisis rather than the government or the regime. The general view that democracy "in the abstract" was a good system did not seem to be eroded. About 80 percent of the population believed that elections were the best method for the choice of a government. Favorable expectations of democracy as a problem-solving instrument fell, however, from 35 percent to 25 percent during 1980. Moreover, the perception of the country's economic performance became increasingly negative. Whereas in 1975 evaluations of the economic situation divided Spanish society into two halves, in 1980 only 2 percent of the population considered the situation to be good, as opposed to the 66 percent that judged it bad. In 1976 over 20 percent thought that the economy had improved in the preceding year and almost 60 percent expected it to improve in the following year. Only 8 percent and 25 percent respectively shared those views in 1981.[21] No more than 10 percent of those interviewed in 1981 trusted the government as a good administrator of public money and 55 percent believed that the government used its power for the benefit of the few.

Of course, these contrasting figures lend themselves to divergent interpretations. One might argue that in spite of frustrated expectations, mistrust in government, and political cynicism, democratic legitimacy or widespread diffused support remained almost intact or one might argue that it affected the government but did not focus on the regime itself. One might also argue that, whatever was the extent of democratic support, its intensity had dramatically declined. This intermediary situation has been aptly described as one of "dealignment." It was not caused solely by a disappointing economic performance in the face of a worsening situation. Increased political violence, unchecked by effective government measures, and a sense of disenchantment with the hesitant, erratic, inconclusive, and complex policies related to the regional issues, were also sources of public frustration. In addition, the recourse to "invisible politics" during the constituent period, the growing monopolization of political life by party elites, the reorientation of political conflict toward the parliamentary arena, and the general demobilization that followed the 1977 elections may have proved highly instrumental in reaching and implementing a policy of pacts and compromises, but this strategy also had negative side effects. Party affiliation stagnated or diminished. The rates of electoral abstention increased alarmingly. Political pessimism became rampant from 1979 on. Moreover, these attitudes were not confined to the mass public. Intellectuals and columnists daily voiced their frustration and disenchantment (*desencanto*) with the restrictions imposed by compromised democracy. Antidemocratic groups increased their harassment of the regime. Undoubtedly, this rarified atmosphere favored the attempted military coup of 23 February 1981.

## Competition and Performance: Some Notes on the Party System

Faced with these serious problems, the new Spanish democracy needed a government with sufficient popular and parliamentary support to carry out a program of economic, social, and political reforms that would break the log-jam and counteract the twin challenges of terrorism and right-wing subversion.

Yet one of the new democracy's greatest weaknesses was the difficulty of forming a strong government—with a solid, stable majority. The process of transition and the reestablishment of the party system after forty years both contributed to this difficulty. We shall discuss two aspects of the problem of governability in the early years of the Spanish democracy: on the one hand, the support enjoyed by each of the principal political options in Spain, and on the other, the patterns of party competition and polarization.

The political option provided by the Right was the Unión del Centro Democrático (the UCD), formed shortly before the 1977 elections as an electoral coalition of fourteen small parties based on local notables. It suffered from its own ideological and organizational difficulties, and these were seriously aggravated after the 1979 and 1980 general and regional elections. The coalition included fractions of Christian Democrats, liberals, Social Democrats, populists, together with some independent reformists with a Francoist past, thus embracing what in some European countries would be the entire political spectrum.[22] From its origins it was divided between those groups who tried to maintain their own independence within the coalition and those who tried to transform the coalition into a unified party. As compared to the conservative and centrist parties of Italy or France in the 1940s, the UCD lacked a unifying negative criterion for legitimation that could serve as an ideological cement (as with "anti-Fascism," "resistance," and so on). Instead it was the state that cemented the coalition together and made it into a relatively unified (though internally strained) governing party.

This particular characteristic of the party explains why the UCD conceived the state as its own territory and why it hesitated to reform the structures of public administration. The UCD's reluctance to relinquish control over RTVE (Spanish Radio and Television) or its policy of colonizing state and parastate agencies provide two good illustrations of its dependence on patronage in the public administration, which was also reflected in the party's policy with regard to local government. The UCD postponed municipal elections which might have provided an organizational base for the Left from 1977 to 1979 while, at the same time, leaving important sectors of Francoism still firmly rooted in public enterprises, banks, and the armed forces.

After the UCD had defeated its rightist competitors in 1977 it became the sole representative of the moderate Right. This status was clearly confirmed in 1979 when Alianza Popular (AP) was reduced to 5.9 percent of the vote and lost half of its seats in Parliament. The UCD strengthened its position, particularly in the big cities, and improved its results in Aragon, Catalonia, Asturias, and Castile-Mancha, although it lost ground to the PSOE in rural areas. Increased abstentionism did not seem to damage the party much, although it reached a high level in Galicia, one of the UCD's strongholds. Nor did the extension of the franchise to the eighteen–twenty-one age group appear to have negative effects for the UCD. A good proportion of this segment of the electorate abstained, while the rest tended to follow the votes of their parents. In fact, UCD captured all but 1.5 million of the right-wing vote.[23]

Throughout 1980, the UCD electorate became much less stable than in the 1979 legislative and municipal elections. After a dramatic loss of votes in the Basque and Catalonian parliamentary elections and in the partial elections for the Senate in Sevilla and Almería, the UCD's electoral future began to be questioned. These doubts were intensified following its overwhelming defeat in the October 1981 regional elections in Galicia, one of its electoral strongholds. These electoral results produced considerable internal tensions. Different sectors of the party gave them conflicting interpretations. The most conservative faction pointed out that the UCD was losing its "natural" right-wing electorate and argued that its policies had not been acceptable to growing sectors of the population because of UCD's "leftist" inspiration. The progressive wing argued in turn that UCD could not move to the Right without running the risk of losing the reformist vote which was crucial from the electoral point of view. They therefore blamed the government for leaning to the Right.

The political instability of the UCD and its internal difficulties are better explained by its heterogeneity as a party than by any supposed conflict between its positions and the interests of its electorate. This heterogeneity is due to the party's origins as a coalition of political factions and elites with different identities that never entirely fused. The UCD has often been seen as a syndicate of interests rather than as a unified party. In this sense the electoral reverses of 1980 and onward and the prospect of an additional defeat at the general elections that would force the party out of office embittered the internal disputes and led the UCD toward irreversible disintegration. The process initiated in 1980 produced three cabinet reshuffles in that year, forced Suárez's resignation in early 1981, and gathered momentum by the end of the year, with the Social Democrats splitting off and the departure of some individuals in the direction of the AP. The climax came after the party experienced a setback in the May 1982 parliamentary elections in Andalusia, where it lost over three-fifths of its 1979 electorate whereas the PSOE increased its vote by 50 percent. During that summer, with the prospect of a general election looming, two additional groups split away. The right-wing Christian Democrats formed the PDP (Popular Democratic party) to join an electoral coalition with the rising AP led by Fraga. At the other end of the UCD's ideological spectrum, Suárez and his followers moved out of the party to create a Center-Left formation, the CDS (Social and Democratic Center). In view of the likely victory of the Socialists, the CDS had from the outset the aim of being a pivotal grouping.

On the Left, the political options were dominated by the PSOE. Its electoral support rose slightly between 1977 and 1979 from 29.4 percent to 30.8 percent. After the municipal elections of 1979, twenty-one provincial capitals, including Madrid, Barcelona, Valencia, Zaragoza, and Malaga had Socialist mayors and the PSOE won 1,100 municipalities. During this period the PSOE gained reinforcement in areas where it had formerly been at its weakest, for example, in ten out of the thirty-six districts where UCD had won a plurality in 1977. One of the PSOE's campaigning objectives was to win votes in conservative rural areas, and led to Socialist advances in Extremadura, the two Castiles, and Galicia. There is an important correlation (r: 0.50) between areas with low population density and the advance of the Socialist vote.

On the other hand, the PSOE maintained its influence in most of its strongholds: Catalonia, Valencia, Murcia, Asturias, and in the big cities. Nevertheless, the party suffered important losses to the nationalists in Andalusia and the Basque country. It was also hurt by increasing abstentionism, particularly in the Basque country, where nonvoting was high among industrial workers. In Bilbao it may have reached as much as 42 percent. In the 1980 elections to the Basque and Catalonian parliaments, the PSOE again lost votes to the nationalist parties and to abstention. However, in the same year the PSOE regained its position in Andalusia at the expense of UCD and the PSA, winning by a large plurality the partial elections to the Senate in Sevilla and Almería. It confirmed those results in the 1982 elections to the Andalusian Parliament by badly defeating both the UCD and PSA, winning an absolute majority.

In general, the Socialist party faced three problems concerning its social and electoral support. First, in the Basque country and Catalonia its political-cultural support for nationalism did not express the class demands of its Socialist supporters. Nationalism and autonomy were not easily compatible with a class-based appeal largely directed at an immigrant population. The representation of working-class interests and the construction of a democratic and dispersed system, two of the PSOE's principal aims, seemed difficult to reconcile electorally. Thus, in the Basque country, the votes of a working class with a long tradition of Socialist loyalty turned into abstentions, while in the Catalonian parliamentary elections, abstention increased, particularly among the immigrant sectors in Barcelona.

A second problem was posed in rural areas by the PSOE's progression. In spite of advances, no changes in the Left/Right balance of power in these areas seemed likely within the foreseeable future. The roots of rural conservatism would take a long time to disappear. This impression was reinforced by results in the regional elections in Galicia where the PSOE advanced by three points, but hardly reached 20 percent of the vote.

The strength of the UCD within the politically uncommitted mobile section of the electorate was a third problem, and one that has been a tradition throughout Southern Europe. The undecided and "pseudo-centrist" electorate usually leans to the Right and is sensitive to arguments based on fear, such as those used by Suárez in his 1979 electoral campaign.

The position of the Communist party (PCE) proved more unfavorable than had been frequently foreseen in the final decade of the dictatorship. The outcome of the 1977 elections could still be taken as provisional, but the results in 1979 had to be considered evidence of a fairly stable distribution of preferences within the Left. In that year support for the PCE rose by 1.6 percent while that for the PSOE increased by 1.4 percent. The additional 241,325 votes for the PCE were distributed among thirty-four provinces, but the Communist vote went down in eight crucial districts, most of them in Catalonia and the Basque country. On the other hand, the increase in the Communist vote did not occur in areas where either the Workers' Commissions or the PSOE had influence. In 1981, the PCE suffered important losses of membership with some relevant leaders leaving the party and with severe organizational strains in the Basque country (where the majority of the Basque Communist party [EPK-PCE] split away), Galicia, Andalusia, and Catalonia (where the Stalinist wing of the Partit Socialista Unifical de Catalunya [PSUC] split).

The distribution of Spanish political opinion between Left and Right was rendered more complex by the presence of the nationalist parties. In no other country of Southern Europe does regional nationalism have such importance. Its growing influence was confirmed in 1980. In Catalonia the nationalist parties obtained 21.7 percent of the vote in 1977. Three years later they gained 37 percent in the elections to the autonomous Parliament, obtaining control of the government of the Generalitat. In the Basque country, nationalism increased spectacularly throughout the transition, from 39.6 percent of the vote in 1977 to 64.5 percent in autonomous parliamentary elections of 1980. The PNV (National Basque party) was thus able to form a single party government. It is true that partial elections in Sevilla and Almería in 1980 and elections in the regional Parliament in Galicia in 1981 showed a decline in the political support for nationalism. It is also true that in the Spanish parliamentary elections the nationwide parties were much stronger than in elections for the autonomous regional parliaments. Nevertheless, in 1980 Spain faced special difficulties because of the distribution of the power centers, not between Right and Left, but between the nationwide parties dominating the Spanish Parliament and the nationalist parties controlling autonomous parliaments and the regional administrations.

The coexistence of "nationalist" and class cleavages has resulted in a rather electorally fragmented party system. In spite of the restrictive barriers of the electoral law, the party system was also fragmented at the parliamentary level, with some four to five nationwide parties and some two to three regionally based parties. Thus the difficulty of building a "federo-regional" state and simultaneously consolidating democracy has been compounded by the obstacles hindering the formation of a homogeneous, solid, majoritarian government. There was no dominant party nor did any party approach an electoral majority. The electoral system, though extremely favorable to the biggest party, particularly if it is of a conservative nature (UCD with 35 percent of the vote in 1979 came to 48 percent of the seats) cannot, on its own, produce a parliamentary majority.

Coalition-building, however, has not been easy. A huge coalition integrating all democratic parties in the transition years in the vein of the French or Italian governments after World War II was not viable given the impact veto of the strategic elites toward the PCE. A big coalition of UCD and the PSOE was hard to conceive except in the case of an extreme political emergency because of the ideological differences between the two parties and the danger that such a coalition would weaken support for both parties and generate centrifugal tendencies. Alternative unipolar coalitions (AP and UCD or PSOE and PCE) were unlikely. The AP was seen as a "semiloyal" party and therefore the first formula would have aroused social antagonism, induced polarization, and probably deprived the UCD of its image of moderate reformism. The second formula, in addition to being insufficient in parliamentary terms, was politically unviable. A coalition of UCD with the Catalan and Basque minorities was out of the question given the harsh competition between them in Catalonia and the Basque country, together with the wide distances separating them on the "autonomy" issue. Finally, though a Socialist majority could not be dismissed as a possibility, it was severely hindered by the electoral system. A low number of seats (350) must be distributed among the high number of districts (50) of very different sizes, with the provision that each district, whatever its population, must receive a minimum of three seats. Thus the conservativism that is so highly concentrated in the least populated areas becomes extremely overrepresented.

Patterns of electoral competition make coalition-building even more complicated. Interparty competition has tended to be bilateral rather than unilateral. Bilateral competition is a common trait of party systems with more than two or three parties aligned along a single or dominant dimension, since voters usually choose among close ideological options. What is special about the Spanish case is the intensity and extent of this type of electoral competition, which are due to several factors. First has been the low level of party identification. As a rule about 50 percent of the electorate did not feel close to any party. Second, the internal fragmentation of the Left and Right blocs and the relative proximity of electorates within each bloc rewarded *expansive* rather than *defensive* competition.[24] The same strategies were fostered by the concentration of a great part of the voters in between the two blocs of Left and Right, and by the positions of the predominant parties within each bloc, PSOE and UCD, close to each other in the competition for these segments of the vote. Each of the main parties had therefore two flanks to cover and two avenues for expansion. This picture is again complicated by the existence of a second dimension of competition related to the center-periphery cleavage. On the one hand, we should underline the almost perfect overlapping in the Left-Right ideological scale of the UCD's and PNV's electorates in the Basque country, of those of the UCD and CiU (Convergence and Union) in Catalonia, and of the PSOE and PSA electorates in Andalusia. Finally, the "nationalist" vote is also internally fragmented along class lines in Galicia, Catalonia, and particularly in the Basque country. That altogether these four regions concentrate one-half of the Spanish electorate helps explain the width and intensity of bilateral competition in Spain.

Bilateral competition should not be identified with bilateral opposition.[25] The former notion refers to a type of electoral interaction between parties, the latter to a type of parliamentary interaction between government and oppositions. This latter concept is better applied to situations in which the cabinet finds itself under crossfire from negative oppositions, usually made up of antisystem parties that are critically delegitimizing but unable to provide an alternative majority since they stand at the left and right ends of the ideological spectrum. This has not been the case in Spain. In fact, rather, the UCD's cabinets found themselves in the opposite position. Based on a quasi-majority they could draw support from their right flank when attacked from the Left and vice versa, just as they could get support from the "nationalists" when attacked by the nationwide parties and vice versa. The initial strategy of consensus and the moderation of all parties set the ground for this possibility and made it plausible for the UCD's minority cabinets to impose packages of moderate reforms in spite of opposition from the Right (like the fiscal reform or the Law on Divorce) together with conservative packages of legislation in spite of opposition from the Left. Nevertheless, the inability to form stable coalitions and the continued resort to conjunctural, ad hoc, and ever-changing alliances in Parliament greatly weakened governmental authority. It also confused an electorate hardly familiar with parliamentary practices and it probably contributed to political "cynicism" and distrust of politicians.

On the other hand, Spanish politics have proved somewhat less polarized than Southern European politics in general. Thus, on a scale of 10 points, in France the distance between the Communist party and Giscard's government coalition was 4.9 points whereas the latter was 3.3 points away from the Socialist party. In Italy, the distance between the Communists and the governing Christian Democrats is 3.4 points. In Portugal, the Communists were over 5 points from the governmental coalition and the Socialists were 2.6 points away. In Greece, 6.6 points separated the Communists from New Democracy, whereas the latter was 3.8 points from PASOK (Panhellenic Socialist Movement). In Spain, on the other hand, the distances between PCE and UCD and between PSOE and UCD respectively were 3.2 and 2 points. It is precisely this lesser polarization and greater convergence between parties that explains the bilateral and expansive character of electoral competition in Spain. These data are confirmed by the political moderation shown by Spanish society at large. At their best, the extreme Right parties only captured a tiny 2 percent of the votes, the electoral ratio between the PSOE and the PCE is 3 to 1, and moreover, the PCE is not only the weakest in electoral terms but also the most moderate one in the South of Europe.[26]

Thus, in contrast with the critical experience of the Second Spanish Republic (1931–36), the fragility of democracy in Spain was not linked to the existence of deep multiple self-reinforcing cleavages, sudden massive mobilizations, extreme polarization, and radicalization. It was rather connected with low mobilization of support for the parties, weak consolidation, extreme competition, and segmented fragmentation of the party system, making it difficult to form strong government and to institutionalize a party government capable of removing the remaining vestiges of Francoism, or of meeting the challenges of the economic crisis, terrorism, and the need to reconstruct the state.

## The 1982 Elections and the Prospects for Democracy

The 1982 general elections were a milestone in Europe's electoral history. Abstention fell by thirteen points. Between six and eight out of every ten voters (depending on the calculations used) showed a different behavior pattern from that of 1979. The electoral and parliamentary map was completely changed. The preexisting Left-Right balance was substantially modified, and what is more, the distribution of forces within each bloc was also substantially altered. Extremist formations on both Right and Left were eliminated from the political scene. Except in Catalonia and the Basque country, where nationalist parties consolidated their positions, in the rest of the autonomous areas, the regional formations—whose advance had been the most significant aspect of the previous elections—obtained no parliamentary representation. Finally, the UCD, which had been governing on its own since 1977 and had almost achieved a parliamentary majority, was electorally crushed, whereas the PSOE virtually doubled its electoral strength, almost winning an absolute majority of votes and obtaining an overwhelming parliamentary majority in both chambers of Parliament.

It is understandable that observers find it difficult to classify elections of this type. Some consider that they belong to the category of so-called critical elections, that is to say, those elections whose results decisively modify the lines of division between parties and produce a lasting realignment of electoral preferences and of party loyalties. Jean Blondel points out in this connection that there are at least five different reasons, each of which alone would justify this classification. For others, on the other hand, these elections were, rather, exceptional or, as Mario Caciagli states, cataclysmic.[27] These are elections that have acted as an earthquake on the electorate, and at the same time have shown a degree of voting fluidity which makes it impossible to make a clear statement regarding the crystallization of voting habits. Instead they reflect the influence of circumstantial factors and reflect a low level of party identification. Similarly, and apart from whether the new structure of the party system arising from the 1982 elections is more or less stable, it is of great importance to understand the consequences of this new structure for interparty competition.

Another aspect requiring special attention concerns the importance of the 1982 elections in the context of regime consolidation. Did the growth in participation strengthen the legitimacy of the system? Did the alternation in power guarantee regime continuity and validate its institutions and constitutional mechanisms? Did the plebiscitary triumph of the Socialist Workers' party serve to overcome the uncertainty and instability that had prevailed during the transition period? Did it widen or narrow the margin of autonomy of Spain's democratic institutions? We discuss these matters first, and then consider the structural changes in the party system and its dynamics.

Between 1979 and 1982, the social bases of democracy seem to have been weakened. The lack of a government majority, difficulties in forming a relatively united coalition, and divisions within the governing party all deprived the cabinet of sufficient authority effectively to combat the economic crisis, or to free itself from the double harassment of terrorist attacks and the threat of a coup d'état, or to define and give shape to the model of state described in the constitutional text. Governmental inefficiency and the use of electoral contrivances to block the emergence of an alternative majority created an atmosphere of disappointment and disenchantment which helps explain the increase in voter abstention.

A young regime, with a weak, minority government, sustained by a party that was internally split and had declining support, offered a precarious image in the face of de facto powers. Thus there were widespread doubts as to its own viability, especially given shrinkage of the resources necessary to ensure its independent authority. Consequently, the 1982 electoral results had an exceptional or even historical significance.

In the first place, the high electoral participation renewed the legitimacy of the system. It is true that the relationship between participation and legitimacy is one of the most debatable points of the empirical theory of democracy. It is especially difficult to demonstrate that a considerable fall in participation implies, of necessity, a corresponding reduction in the system's diffuse support. Nor, inversely, does a high rate of participation necessarily express a high degree of system identification. Historical, cultural, circumstantial, and institutional factors, peculiar to each society and moment, affect the significance of turnout and of the behavior patterns of the electorate.

In the case of Spain, however, the increase in abstention after 1977 had been unanimously interpreted as a sign of disenchantment with the regime. Although it is clear that no precise study was carried out to form a basis for this hypothesis, simple diffusion contributed to weaken the identification of certain, strategic sectors with the new regime and, probably, to stimulate the frustrated coup attempt of 23 February 1981.

Given this atmosphere, the spectacular increase in participation in 1982 (which reached 80 percent as opposed to less than 68 percent in 1979) was perceived as a real plebiscite in support of democracy, inverting the previous situation, and providing a key contribution to democratic relegitimation. Political observers were unanimous in this respect. And it would seem that public opinion was of the same view, as suggested by several studies carried out in 1983 and 1984. A nationwide poll, carried out in mid-1983, showed that, of those Spaniards who held an opinion, three out of four considered that democracy was more stable than a year before and almost nine out of ten evaluated it more positively than previously. At the end of 1984, only one in every ten Spaniards holding an opinion preferred any other regime to democracy, and four out of every five regarded it as preferable to any other form of government. This proportion rose to more than 95 percent in certain collectivities of special significance such as civil servants, judges, and teachers.

In the second place, democratic legitimacy was likewise strengthened as a result of the alternation in power brought about by the election. The first succession crisis of the democratic period was handled normally. It is true that the results were inexorable. But, in any case, they were accepted without question. The coup, planned for the eve of elections, was prevented in time by the UCD government. Neither they nor the other parties nor any other group questioned the legitimacy of the PSOE's triumph or its right to take over the government. The transmission of powers was effected in a relaxed atmosphere characterized by understanding and collaboration between the outgoing and the incoming parties. The alternation underlined that the rules of the game were in force and indicated the system's ability to generate alternatives. Finally, with the formation of the new cabinet, any remaining reservations about the Socialists and their relations with the crown disappeared. The routine coexistence of the two reinforced the credibility of the party system and the viability of democratic institutions.

In the third place, the scale of the Socialist triumph led to a notable widening of the margin of independent initiative available to the political system's democratic components. The PSOE came to government with four million more votes than the UCD in 1979 and with 202 seats in Congress out of a total 350. It was the winning party in fifteen of the seventeen autonomous communities and the second party in the other two. It won in forty-four of the fifty-two electoral districts. It achieved an absolute majority in eighteen of them, and was on the point of doing so in another four. Such a strong social backing was, on its own, an important factor of dissuasion for the remaining conspirators who still favored a coup and for the pretensions to autonomy professed by the so-called neutral powers. Regarding the former, it is important that when the sentences on the members of the army implicated in the coup of 23 February 1981 came up for revision the terms of imprisonment imposed on those most responsible were considerably increased. A second aspect was that, at last, it became possible to apply a policy of compensated modernization to the armed forces, the basic pillars of which were to be, on the one hand, a reduction in size, a redistribution in its territorial patterns, and the reorganization of the command structure. This policy package was aimed at ensuring the unequivocal subordination of the military to civilian control, with objective standards for promotion. On the other hand came a salary adjustment making military and civil earnings more similar, a convergence with NATO standards and practices, and an increase in defense spending for the modernization of weaponry and other equipment. These changes appear to have been noted by public opinion. Thus, at the close of 1984, opinion polls revealed that almost 70 percent of Spaniards expressing an opinion on the matter considered that the possibilities of a coup d'état had diminished over the previous two years, with 64 percent maintaining that, over the same period, the military establishment had lost political influence.

Fourth, the existence of a single-party government, backed by a solid parliamentary majority, paved the way for greater efficiency in the system and for a greater capacity to meet the double challenge of, on the one hand, removing the factors that threatened its stability and, on the other, removing obstacles to the economic, political, and cultural modernization of Spanish society. New possibilities arose to intensify the antiterrorist struggle, to counteract the pretensions of certain regional governments, and to reorganize and rationalize the process of regional devolution. There were also new opportunities to develop a rigorous economic policy directed toward bringing the sectors in crisis back to economic health and the reindustrialization of the country, to reform civil, legal, and military administration, to secularize and modernize health and education systems, and to develop the constitutional rights and liberties of individuals and groups.

In all, the election results of 1982 introduced a triple injection of legitimacy, autonomy, and efficiency, widening the possibilities for consolidation of the new regime. Furthermore, they confirmed what two earlier elections had already indicated concerning the fundamental dynamics of the party system, even though unanimous agreement had not been reached on its specific features. There was discussion as to whether the number of parties justified the term "limited" pluralism and whether the type and scale of party competition, and the degree of political polarization, merited description as "moderate," "polarized," or "segmented" pluralism, or indeed some intermediate classification. Other observers, perhaps thinking more of the eventual evolution of the system rather than its initial nature, described it as a two-party regime, or at least, as an "imperfect two-party system."[28]

What seems, at least provisionally, to have emerged from the 1982 elections is a shift toward a predominant party system, with the relevant parties at national level being reduced to two: the PSOE and the CP (Popular Coalition). The relevant formations at regional level have also been reduced to two: CiU (Convergence and Union—Catalonia) and the PNV (National Basque party).[29] Thanks to the electoral downfall of UCD and the thinning out of political options in the Center, the PSOE, occupying practically the whole political left-wing space, obtained an advantage of more than twenty points over the second party.

The dynamics of party competition underwent a basic alteration. In the first place, although the population as a whole maintained its previous ideological positions, the redistribution of political space and, in particular, the displacement of a wide sector of the moderate vote toward the Right brought with it a considerable increase in polarization measured in terms of ideological distance between the two main parties. On a scale from 1 to 10, those who voted for the PSOE and those who voted for AP (Popular Alliance) were at a three-point distance as opposed to the two-point difference that separated those who voted for the PSOE and UCD in 1979. However, these figures should be analyzed carefully. First, the distance between the PSOE and the AP electorates fell by almost one point between 1979 and 1982. Second, in 1979, both AP and the PCE (Communist party), had to be taken into consideration in measuring ideological distance. The distance was much greater between those two parties than that which now separates the two main parties. Finally, such ideological distance is still less than that which separates Socialists from Giscard supporters in France, the Christian Democrats from the Communists in Italy, the Socialists from the Social Democratic Centrists in Portugal, or PASOK and Nova Democratia in Greece.

In the second place, even though the party system never presented bilateral "oppositions," from 1977 onward it was subjected to the influence of a strong bilateral "competition." Thus, while AP and PCE were in competition with UCD and PSOE respectively, they were also competing, defensively, with the extraparliamentary forces located on the extreme Right and extreme Left. In the same way, the UCD and the PSOE were forced to compete among themselves, as well as with the AP and the PCE respectively. The tensions created by this type of expansive and defensive competition have been greatly reduced by the disappearance of the UCD and the extremist parties, by the transformation of the PCE into an irrelevant party, and by the bipolar configuration of the new party system. An additional change follows. The central space is no longer occupied by one party, a fact that discourages centrifugal tendencies and encourages even more centripetal competition.

Two additional factors should be mentioned. On the one hand, the CP (Popular Coalition) now occupies all the space to the Right, including its extreme. Its only possibility for expansion is therefore toward the Center. The CP could successfully make use of the advantages conferred on large, conservative formations by the electoral system only by directing its strategy in that direction. On the other hand, the presence of the PDP in the Popular Coalition along with AP should also favor that tendency, counteracting the inclination of certain sectors of AP toward "outbidding" on the Right and engaging in irresponsible opposition of a type that would put in doubt the efforts of AP leaders to integrate the party within the system and dilute the party's image as a semiloyal party, to use the terminology of Juan Linz.

A predominant party system, with relative polarization, without bilateral oppositions or clearly antisystemic parties, with centripetal competition and a limited number of parties, is, in principle, a viable system. What are its chances of consolidation? In order to arrive at an answer it is necessary to consider, at the same time, the degree of crystallization of electoral preferences and the probable outcome of competition for the centrist vote.

Regarding the first point, an extremely low volatility percentage between 1977 and 1979 was the main indicator persuading numerous observers that the party system arising from the first elections adequately expressed the lines dividing Spanish society and so was destined to take root. In contrast, the extremely high volatility rate between 1979 and 1982 (it reached more than 42 percent) reopened debate over the problems of electoral cleavages. Consequently, the question arises whether the flow of votes between the last two elections is explicable in structural or circumstantial terms, or whether it reflected a persistent state of availability among the voters, or whether the change of behavior was prompted, with special intensity, by other coincidental changes.

The first thing to note is the low degree of party identification. Although, in a recent poll, one in every twenty-five adults acknowledged a current party affiliation and one in every ten admitted to having been affiliated in the past, the numbers of members given by the parties themselves are much lower. Furthermore, more than half the adult population stated, in the same poll, that they did not feel close to any particular party. The degree of party identification did not fall between 1979 and 1982. Consequently, this fact alone cannot explain the high volatility shown in the elections of 28 October. It may have served as a necessary condition, but is insufficient in view of the exceptional viscosity observed in 1979.

On the other hand, the format of the party system may explain part of the variation. Neither the extremist parties nor the myriad minor candidates existing in 1979 reappeared in the 1982 elections. The UCD ran under the same initials, but it was not the same party after the splitting away of the Social Democrats, Christian Democrats, and Suárez supporters. The first group fused into the PSOE. The second aligned itself with AP. The Suárez supporters created their own party, the Centro Democrático y Social (CDS), which contested seats for the first time in 1982. These alterations in format are, however, probably insufficient to explain the scale of the electoral volatility. It can only be understood in view of another set of circumstantial variables. In particular, the crisis of the PCE and UCD and the urgent need for a strong government capable of responding to the atmosphere of instability, uncertainty, and provisionality generated by the 1981 coup attempt converted the elections into a plebiscite to decide whether the PSOE was or was not to be the party to set up such a government. Data on the evolution of voting intentions between December 1979 and October 1982 clearly show the rise of PSOE support from the spring of 1981 and its crystallization in the summer of 1982. The leftist vote shifted massively in favor of this option, while the Right underwent a dramatic restructuring after the virtual disintegration of UCD.

This interpretation also allows us to put the exceptional rise in the volatility index in a different perspective and to examine the transfer of votes that took place within both the right- and left-wing electorates and between the two. The flow of votes between the two blocs was quite small—about 6 percent. In the regional elections of 1983 it was even smaller. In the regions where the party subsystem coincided with the state system, it was minimal—less than 3.5 percent in Castille and Extremadura, 2.8 percent in Asturias, 2.4 percent in Mancha, and about 1.5 percent in Madrid and Valencia. Within the Left, volatility reached about 14.75 percent, a figure that, although high, was only a little more than half the one that occurred on the Right. In both spaces, the shift of votes was less in the regional elections of 1983. Both in 1982 and in 1983, however, the same patterns were reproduced. That is to say, there was a much larger shift of votes within the Right than within the Left.

Three conclusions are possible. In the first place, the heightened volatility of 1982 does not mean that the entire electorate was "disrupted" and "available." It reflected the dismantling and restructuring of the party system before the elections, together with a series of environmental changes. In the second place, a certain rigidity was observed as far as the exchange of votes between Right and Left is concerned, and suggests the existence of an important grouping of the electorate around these two poles. Finally, the lesser volatility within the Left revealed a certain degree of crystallization of party preferences pertaining on that side, a process subsequently accentuated by the PCE's continuing crisis. In contrast, Center and right-wing voters show a high level of receptivity toward the range of political groupings that compete for their vote with some degree of electoral credibility.

This analysis leads on to the second issue indicated above: that is, how the competitive dynamics of the Center may influence the consolidation or modification of the present party system. Here we face a historical problem which curiously retains all its relevance today, in spite of the profound social, economic, political, and cultural transformations that Spain has undergone during recent years. This is the problem of political articulation on the Spanish Right, a problem that first arose in the years of the Republic. It was considered unnecessary to seek a solution under Franco and then it reappeared, surprising a quite disorganized spectrum of conservative opinion at the beginning of the transition to democracy. Since then the question has appeared in the following terms: first, "Is it possible to mobilize all the forces to the right of the Socialists in a single party?;" second, "In any case, which is the best position for competition and alliance within the Right?;" finally, "In view of the new party structure that has emerged since 1982, which type of competitive strategy would produce maximum benefits?"

In order to answer these questions it is necessary to ask how politically and socially united this sector of the electorate may be. Opinion polls suggest that, for the majority of Spaniards, the social composition of the Center party vote is clearly differentiated from that of the right wing. On the political plane, several indications of attitude reveal notable differences in crucial aspects such as tolerance, the type of state, rights and liberties, and the role of the state in society. The point of convergence that most stands out among the Center and right-wing supporters is their religiosity, which is virtually identical in both cases. However, it would appear that this is no longer a strong enough uniting factor to integrate the conservative vote into a single confessional party. To do so it would be necessary to reactivate a dividing line that, nowadays, lacks its former salience, especially because almost 75 percent of the Left and almost 60 percent of the Right are against any ecclesiastical interference in the political debate.

The political and ideological differences separating the social strata occupying the conservative position represent a basic hindrance to their uniting in one party. They caused the failure of the UCD's attempts at integration between 1977 and 1982. More important still, the appearance of these divergencies brought out the existence of two opposed strategic conceptions within the UCD which contributed as much to the party split within the coalition as the ideological tensions. On the one hand, there were those who attempted to intensify competition on the Right, at the risk of losing part of its support from the Center-Left to the PSOE. On the other hand, there were groups insisting on the need to compete with the Socialists, even at the risk of ceding some space on the Right.

For its part, the Popular Coalition (CP) has, since 1982, unequivocally supported the first of these alternatives, absorbing the votes of its competitors on the extreme Right and of a substantial part of the more conservative electorate in the conservative area, but with considerably less electoral strength than that which the centrist coalition had held up to then. A strategy of expansion toward the Center does not seem to have prospered; this observation is understandable if we bear in mind the ideological differences that separate the Right from the Center. It is important to remember that, in spite of the UCD's disintegration, about 10 or 12 percent of the electorate remained faithful to centrist options in 1982, showing great reluctance to join the Right. This factor explains the emergence of new parties, such as the Partido Reformista Democrático (PRD), and the persistence of others, such as the CDS, which are prepared to fight the CP for the Center ground.

So, the results of the confrontation for the Center will determine the evolution of the system. The various political leaders within the conservative spectrum seem to have rejected the idea of integrating this whole electoral segment in a single party. Instead they foresee a dual grouping of Center and right-wing opinion. Whether the ascendancy of the latter over the former will be maintained, or whether both tendencies will reach a balance, or indeed whether the Center can recuperate its former dominance probably constitutes the most interesting aspect of the elections expected in 1986. It is obvious, in this regard, that parties such as the CDS and the PRD are located much nearer to the majority of their joint electorate on an ideological plane than is the Popular Coalition. But it is also evident that these centrist parties possess a much lower degree of electoral credibility than the CP, which can present itself as a coalition capable of uniting the useful vote.

One additional variable should also be taken into account, namely, the interaction between general elections and regional elections in some autonomous communities such as Andalusia and Galicia, and especially Catalonia and the Basque country. There are hardly any studies on this aspect, which would require special attention.

In Galicia and Andalusia, the general elections of 1981 and 1982 clearly brought about the collapse of the UCD as the polls anticipated. Apart from this, Galicia witnessed the rise of the AP to displace the UCD as the main force on the Right. In Andalusia, the tendency of the PSOE to monopolize representation on the Left became clear. In this respect, it would be interesting to analyze the degree to which the results in both these regions were a straightforward forerunner of the inclinations of the national electorate and to what degree they contributed to sway the vote in the direction anticipated by regional elections. As far as the Basque country and, above all, Catalonia are concerned, the problem becomes even more interesting. The reciprocal influence of the party subsystems and the national system of parties is, as yet, to be studied. When electoral circumstances vary at a regional level, to what degree, for example, and on what basis does voting behavior differ?; in what measure does the consolidation of the national parties in the regional ambit depend on or affect their electoral possibilities in a general election, or vice versa?; in what way does the association of the great nationalist parties, such as the PNV and CiU, with parties of national relevance contribute, or not, to their electoral appeal within their respective regional communities?

The public opinion data upon which the preceding statements are based was culled from surveys conducted by the Centro de Investigaciones Sociológicas. Some have been published in *Informe-Síntesis de los Barómetros de Opinión Pública* (June 1979–November 1981); others have appeared in *Revista Española de Investigaciones Sociológicas* (especially no. 28 [October–December 1984]) or are contained in the CIS, *Banco de Datos* and in the *Estudio* series (especially July 1983 and November 1984).

# 5 •

# Regime Overthrow and the Prospects for Democratic Transition in Portugal

## Kenneth Maxwell

### Liberation by Military Intervention

The immediate origins of the coup of 25 April 1974 lay as much in Africa as in Europe. Portugal had been struggling for over a decade to contain a spreading guerrilla war in its overseas colonies. Violence had erupted first in Angola in 1961, and rapidly spread to Portuguese Guinea in West Africa and then to Mozambique in East Africa. Portugal had possessed the first and oldest of Europe's colonial empires. In 1974 it possessed the last. As other European powers had been obliged to divest themselves of overseas territories during the 1950s and 1960s, Portugal had, with embarrassing tenacity, remained, surviving even the preeminence of Europe itself in world affairs.

The burdens of the African campaigns on a small, poor nation with limited natural resources and severely retarded economic and social infrastructures proved unsustainable. The burden was especially onerous on those called to fight the battle: the Portuguese army. The single most important fact about the Portuguese Revolution is so obvious that its significance is often overlooked. It is that no mass movement brought the old regime down, and that the participation of the clandestine political parties of the Left was negligible. The dictatorship was toppled by the army, not by Communists or anyone else.

The coup d'état of 25 April 1974 was carried out by a small group of junior and middle-rank officers, all of them influenced by their extensive experience in the colonial wars, most of them believing that the military should play a major role in the political process. The action of the Portuguese military and its many factions was a central and unique element in the Portuguese situation. The multitudes that assembled in the streets of Lisbon and Oporto in the hours and weeks that followed the coup made the army's action irreversible. Popular mobilization followed the coup; it did not cause it.

The Armed Forces Movement (MFA) originated in response to professional grievances and concerns with status and privilege.[1] The dissension within the officer corps, however, was a reflection of a much deeper malaise which grew out of the scale, composition, and organization of the Portuguese armed forces, all of which in turn was a consequence of the seemingly endless military commitment in Africa.

In 1974, out of a population of a little over eight million, one in four men of military age was in the armed forces. The army alone contained at least 170,000 men, of which 135,000 were in Africa. The air force had 16,000, the navy 18,000, the units of the Republican Guard (GNR) 10,000, and the paramilitary security police (PSP) 15,000. The armed forces represented (at a low estimate) a proportion per 1,000 of the population (30.83) exceeded only by Israel (40.09), and North and South Vietnam (respectively 31.66, 55.36); five times that of the United Kingdom, three times that of the United States or Spain. The military budget represented at least 7 percent of the gross national product (GNP), more than that of the United States. With a per capita income of just over $1,000, Portugal spent a minimum per capita on military expenditure of $63.27, and this amount despite abysmal pay for officers and troops. It was an army with almost no totally professional units.

After the fighting began in Angola, there had been a rapid falloff in the number of applicants to the Military Academy and, as a result, a chronic manpower shortage in the middle ranks. This aggravated a problem that had begun in the 1950s when the government shifted its recruiting policies, providing free tuition at the Military Academy in 1958, and offering a monthly stipend to cadets in 1969. By the mid-1970s, the recruiting policies had produced a marked social cleavage within the professional officer corps at the rank of lieutenant colonel, and an extraordinary tangle of jealousy and dissension. Standards for admission to the service academies also fell after 1958, except in the engineering course. The number of applicants continued to decline nevertheless. By 1969 they were down 80 percent from 1961.

Those most affected by these shifts were the middle-rank combat officers, caught between an archaic and slow-moving system of promotions based exclusively on seniority on the one hand, and a cohort of less than reliable subordinates on the other. The government, in order to cope with the expansion of armed forces, had been forced to rely more and more on conscripted officers at company command levels. These *milicianos*, as they were called, dominated the lower levels of the officer corps by 1974, though in status they were clearly differentiated from the regulars.

These civilian soldiers, their careers, marriages, and professional prospects severely compromised by lengthy military service, showed even less enthusiasm for combat than the draftees they commanded. Yet, although they became unreliable in military action, the army, with 135,000 men in the field in Africa, could hardly function without them.

The burden of combat thus fell mainly on a relatively small and diminishing generation of regulars, some facing their fifth two-year tour of duty overseas. A program to allow *milicianos* to take up permanent commissions was a particular affront to these men.

The government's motivation was to entice *milicianos* "who had proved themselves in combat" to abandon their amateur status and turn professional.

Very few *milicianos*, however, relished the idea of entering the Military Academy with a group of green freshmen, so Decree-Law 353-73 created an accelerated two-semester course for conscript captains. By placating the conscripts, the government enraged the regulars. Because the archaic system of promotion within the Portuguese armed forces recognized only seniority and not merit, Military Academy graduates were listed by class rank and moved forward to higher positions in this order. What so upset the regulars was that newly converted *milicianos* were now allowed to count all their service toward seniority, thus jumping forward in a seniority line which moved much too slowly anyway in the minds of most regular officers. It was out of the protest movement organized in response to these government measures that the Armed Forces Movement emerged.

Initially, the MFA was composed exclusively of regular captains and majors. Later, some trusted senior officers were incorporated or, more often, kept informed of developments. It was a small, compact group, with strong personal interrelationships, numbering less than 200 out of a middle-rank corps of some 1,600. Members were spread throughout most units, and the MFA was especially strong in Guinea and Mozambique. After 1 December 1973, the organization was held together at the center by a fifteen-man coordinating committee, subdivided into a military committee charged with the detailed planning of the uprising and a political committee which formulated the program for the post-coup situation.

For a determined minority within the army, a protest that originated in professional concerns provided a cover for political objectives. Major Melo Antunes, an artillery officer with a long record of opposition to the regime, who had at first dismissed the captains' protest movement as being "a reactionary cooperative in defense of privilege," played a key role in drawing up the MFA program. Colonel Vasco Gonçalves, another member of the political committee, had been involved in a "putschist" attempt a decade previously, and his actions on that occasion had closely paralleled those of the Communist party. The leader of the military planning group, Mozambique-born Major Otelo Saraiva de Carvalho, was much influenced by the theories of guerrilla struggle in Guinea where he had worked on psychological warfare. The movement as a whole, however, consisted of men with divergent political views. Their coalescence was the result less of any uniform conspiratorial objective than of a convergence of resentments, loss of a sense of purpose, and emotional and intellectual estrangement from the long colonial wars. Despite conventional wisdom, the work of the young officers had to be liberalizing and liberating. The intransigence of the Portuguese regime and its commitment to the wars made that inevitable. "The Revolution had come from the Left," one officer commented in April 1974; "after fifty years of right-wing dictatorship, where else could it come from?"

It is important to emphasize this point since it serves to demonstrate an important difference between the Portuguese case and the other democratic transitions of the 1970s and 1980s in Europe and Latin America. In every other case a vital element in the process of democratization was the extraction of the military (in most cases a military regime) from power. By contrast, in Portugal it was the military that destroyed a fundamentally nonmilitary authoritarian system. Whereas elsewhere the military saw its institutional interests best served by removing themselves from the political area, in Portugal the military saw their institutional future (in fact, the avoidance of outright military defeat in Guinea-Bissau) as being served by a coup.

Yet if it was the army that pushed, it pushed a structure so fragile that it fell like a pack of cards. Professor Marcello das Neves Caetano (1906–80) was an unconvincing dictator. He embodied to an astonishing degree the limitations as well as some of the qualities that had sustained the Salazarist system in Portugal for almost half a century. Caetano was a fine scholar and historian, in addition to being a successful lawyer and administrator. In these attributes, he was not unlike many of the professors, lawyers, and right-wing intellectuals with whom the old dictator, Oliveira Salazar (1889–1970), had chosen to surround himself. Often, Salazar's protégés were men of humble origins who had risen by merit or patronage within the universities or public administration. The Portuguese dictatorship was preeminently civilian and legalistic, despite the retention of military figureheads in the presidency, and despite the fact that Salazar's authoritarian and corporatist "New State," established in the early 1930s, had its origins in a military coup in 1926.

Caetano's relationship with the military was difficult from the beginning of his prime ministership.[2] After his downfall, he would bitterly complain that the most vocal opposition to his appointment to succeed Salazar had come from those within the military hierarchy who were aware of his suggestion in the early 1960s that Portugal pursue a policy in Africa that would lead to a federation of states not unlike that proposed over a decade later by General António Spinola in his controversial book *Portugal and the Future* (Lisbon, 1974). The president, Admiral Américo Tomas, had made it clear to Caetano in 1968 that it was a condition of Caetano's appointment that the defense of the overseas territories was nonnegotiable. Without such assurance, the admiral claimed, "the armed forces will intervene." Caetano's sensitivity to the threat from the extreme Right within the military hierarchy and his lack of sensitivity to the threat from the Left among the middle-rank officers in 1974 are partly explained by this history.

The prime minister's problems were compounded by his personality and background. Caetano was a follower, not a leader. His caution, legalism, and indecision proved fatal to the regime he headed. He had stood too long in the shadow of a mentor who rewarded diligence but distrusted initiative. Caetano was also an urban-based ideologue, something Salazar, with his profound roots in rural Portugal, had never been. Although Caetano had been closely associated with Salazar for more than three decades, he had begun his career considerably to the right of the conservative Catholic wellsprings of Salazar's philosophy. Caetano had been a leading mover behind the Portuguese youth movement, the Mocidade, during the 1930s, one of the more overtly Fascist institutions of the Portuguese "New State." Much of the legislation of the Salazar regime was his handiwork, and he became—through his definitive textbook on administrative law, a work in its tenth edition in 1973—the most authoritative voice in interpreting the regime's legislation. His view of his role as prime minister was thus circumscribed by a legalistic and mechanistic view of a system that in reality had worked under Salazar not so much because of its legal niceties as because of Salazar's skillful playing-off of factions, personal control of key decisions, and draconian control of the purse strings.

Caetano thus saw his task as being that of perfecting rather than fundamentally altering the authoritarian and corporatist dictatorship he had inherited. Caetano's ideological commitment to the system was somewhat obscured during the early months of his rule when he had moved to liberalize some aspects of the dictatorship's image. Two prominent exiles, the Bishop of Oporto, Dom Antonio Ferreira Gomes, who had been prevented from reentering Portugal after a visit to Rome in 1958, and Dr. Mário Soares, a Lisbon lawyer and oppositionist who had been deported to the island of São Tomé in 1967, were both allowed back into Portugal. The regime's political movement was permitted to incorporate a handful of liberal-minded candidates, such as Francisco Sá Carneiro, Francisco Balsemão, and Miller Guerra, in its list of candidates for the National Assembly in 1969. The notorious secret police (PIDE) was renamed the DGS (Directorate General of Security). Censorship was renamed "previous examinations."

But the "Lisbon Spring" of 1968, such as it was, proved as short-lived as the spring in Prague. As time went by, Caetano rapidly retreated from his experiment with what one Portuguese Socialist called "Fascism with a human face." In retrospect, it is clear that too many misjudged Caetano's intention to carry off a successful transition to a more open and flexible system of government. He lost the opportunity to form a solid base of support for himself, which the small band of liberals in the National Assembly had been willing to provide if he had collaborated with them in a process of gradual democratization. Disillusioned, they soon resigned their seats in protest. And as a result, Caetano was constantly forced further to the Right, and further into the power of those who least trusted him.

In comparative perspective, this failure to liberalize, something the Spaniards were able to achieve in 1975–76, meant that the Portuguese missed the opportunity to negotiate a transition without *ruptura* in the immediate aftermath of Salazar's death in 1970. The modernizing elements within the old regime were unable to form alliances with the opposition and after the coup lost whatever leverage they exercised with the state apparatus. It is probable, therefore, that any chance of a *reforma pactada* (that is, reform by agreement) had been lost in Portugal as early as 1972, a situation made worse by the growing disaffection within the military institution.

Even in the final months of his rule, Caetano did not act decisively. Although he was well aware of the importance of public criticism from such figures as General Spinola, he seems to have underestimated the mortal danger his regime faced. It is true that, to many, the regime appeared to be solidly entrenched. Few inside or outside the government believed that it could be overthrown as easily as it was. The government also believed that the problem with the army's middle ranks had been resolved, and was preoccupied with the threat from the extreme Right, labor unrest, and the economic situation.

By December 1973, Caetano had reluctantly rescinded the decree that had caused so much uproar within the officer corps. Pressure from the army hierarchy first led him to exempt career officers of the rank of major and above. Then, under intensive pressure from General Costa Gomes, he agreed to reconsider the whole package, and eventually the government withdrew the decree totally. Each grudging retreat, of course, had the opposite result from that intended. The first retreat, which took place in August 1973, had stimulated the formation of the captain's movement, and by the time the decree was withdrawn, in December, the Armed Forces Movement had already committed itself to overthrowing the regime.

In December, to placate the irate officer corps, the government had also raised salaries. This pay raise was long overdue, but the timing was treated with contempt by the officers, as a bribe to buy them out of political action. Nevertheless, from the government's point of view, and in the light of past experience, Caetano cannot be blamed for believing that he had in some measure defused one potential source of danger. It was also public knowledge that an attempt in December by General Kaulza de Arriaga, a leading right-wing air force officer, to persuade the MFA to joint him in an attempt to seize power from Caetano had failed.

Again the government misread the consequences of these events which in fact had served to strengthen the links connecting the MFA, Spinola, and Costa Gomes at a critical time, and helped reinforce the democratic component of the MFA, the political complexion of which until then had been extremely hazy. Yet the government had every reason to take comfort from these developments. Given past history, the machinations of General Kaulza de Arriaga were not to be taken lightly, and the failure of the MFA to respond to his overtures was a positive sign from the government's point of view. Moreover, in March, an uprising by the Fifth Infantry Battalion at Caldas da Rainha was easily suppressed by loyalist army units, including General Spinola's old regiment, the Seventh Cavalry, and the Republican Guard. Two hundred men and officers were arrested by the DGS.

The security services were preoccupied with widespread labor unrest. This, in any case, had been their traditional area of concern, and the military had always enjoyed a certain degree of immunity from attention by the regime's secret police. Inflation by early 1974 was running at over 30 percent, the highest rate in Europe, and labor unrest was spreading not only among industrial workers but also, for the first time, among office workers and civil servants. Caetano had been warned to expect major disruptions and possibly a strike by government employees in May, a traditional month of labor militancy and antiregime demonstrations. He was also warned that the traditional methods of breaking labor unrest—the riot police, preventative detention, and censorship—might not work, and that it would be better to anticipate trouble by granting substantial salary increases before the storm broke. Caetano's response to this advice was to reshuffle his economic ministers. As to salary increases, this was a decision the government intended to take on the very day it was overthrown.

If Caetano fiddled, it was because this was his method. If he failed to act decisively, it was because the whole nature of his experience and the system he headed precluded decisive action. If he underestimated the threats, it was because few believed the regime to be in mortal danger. He was trapped both by his own personality and by the very institutions he had so diligently helped to create.

The Portuguese Revolution, therefore, occurred as much because of the collapse of the old political system as because of the strength of the forces of change. By the spring of 1974, the regime lacked viable choices and had failed to adapt internally to new circumstances. Nor had it confronted the realities of its position internationally or in Africa. It is worth remembering that, when the Portuguese army rebels took to the streets of Lisbon, Marcello Caetano could find no one but a handful of secret policemen holed up in their headquarters to defend him.

## Reform or Revolution

At first the most characteristic reaction abroad to the successful coup d'état of 25 April 1974 was uncertainty. At home it was euphoria—a springtime of exuberance which gave the revolution its popular identification as the "revolution of flowers" after the red carnations with which the victorious soldiers adorned themselves and their rifles.

Civil society was caught by surprise at the suddenness and rapidity of the young officers' success. During the weeks prior to the coup, the Armed Forces Movement (MFA) had deliberately kept away from the civilian opposition for reasons of security. The clandestine political parties were known to be thoroughly infiltrated by the secret police. Nevertheless, opposition to the dictatorship had always existed and provided almost automatically a cadre of civilian collaborators for the military in the vacuum that had emerged. The old republicans had never accepted the corporate state and its Fascist overtones, for instance, even if their countless platforms of dissent never came close to shaking the formidable apparatus of censorship, repression, and cultural uniformity that Salazar imposed. The Communist party had been the most serious thorn, and had in consequence suffered the most severe repression.

Although no one under seventy had ever voted in anything resembling a free election under the dictatorship, local political organizations called "democratic election commissions" (CDE) did exist throughout Portugal. They were used principally (most recently in 1973) as an opportunity for criticism and debate during the regime's periodic contests for seats in the National

Assembly. The electoral system itself was stacked in the regime's favor, and opposition groups regarded the whole affair as a fraud. Nevertheless, the opportunities were used to articulate a forceful critique of the dictatorship's positions. The CDE was comprised of coalitions of "anti-Fascist forces," mainly middle-class liberals, Social Democrats, Catholic radicals, independent Marxists, and the Communists (PCP).

The Portuguese Communist party had been founded in 1921.[3] Originally, the Communists had little representation among the working class, which, until the 1930s, was strongly influenced by anarcho-syndicalism. But after 1941, under the leadership of Alvaro Cunhal, the party began to develop a political base. The long decades of clandestine existence profoundly affected the psyche and behavior of the Portuguese Communists forced underground since the first days of the Salazar dictatorship. Party organization adhered to strict Leninist lines—with small cells, tight discipline, members kept unaware of one another's identities, and decisions handed down from above. Cunhal himself spent thirteen years behind bars in Portugal and another fourteen years in exile in Eastern Europe and Moscow. The party was particularly sensitive to developments in Prague, because its activities had been directed from Czechoslovakia since the 1940s.

After Fidel Castro, Cunhal was the first Communist leader to approve the 1968 Soviet intervention in Prague, strongly diverging thereafter from his Iberian counterpart Santiago Carrillo in Spain. Cunhal was a man of middle-class origins, who studied law in Lisbon. He joined the party in 1931 at the age of seventeen. In 1934, he organized the federation of young Communists in the Lisbon area and in the same year attended the Sixth Congress of Communist Youth in Moscow. He went into clandestinity on his return to Portugal and became a member of the central committee of the party in 1936.

In Portugal, the PCP possessed a strong base in the Alentejo, the grain-producing lands south of the Tagus River—a region of great landed estates. Here the party was strongly implanted among the anticlerical, landless rural laborers. In the constituent election (25 April 1975) after the coup, the PCP received its largest shares of the vote in the Alentejan districts of Beja, Evora, and Setúbal: 39.0 percent, 37.1 percent, and 37.8 percent respectively.

The PCP was also strong within the labor movement. After the incapacitation of Salazar in 1968 and during the early years of Marcello Caetano, liberalization of the rule governing election to positions within the corporative syndicate structure allowed Communists to take a leading role in union committees. In 1970 the Communist-influenced unions joined in a coordinating organization called Intersindical. Prior to the coup, the Communists were strongly entrenched in the metallurgical unions and increasingly influential among lower-middle-class white-collar workers, especially the bank workers' unions in Lisbon and Oporto.

There was a tradition of opposition, however, that coexisted uncomfortably with the Communists and gave rise in the 1960s to the Portuguese Socialist Association (ASP), and in 1973 to the Portuguese Socialist party. This current of opinion was inspired by the leading intellectual opponents of the Salazar regime, such as the Lisbon evening daily *República*, the monthly journal *Seará Nova*, and its prominent contributors, the historian Jaime Cortesão and the philosopher Antonio Sergio. In the 1960s, a younger generation took up the mantle as the old guard of dissident intellectuals passed from the scene. Three men were especially prominent: Lisbon lawyers Mário Soares and Salgado Zenha, and *República*'s editor Raul Rego. Soares and Zenha founded Portuguese Socialist Action in Geneva in 1964, and the organization was subsequently renamed the Portuguese Socialist party at a congress held in Bad Munstereiffel, West Germany, in April 1973. The Portuguese Socialists affiliated with the Socialist International and developed strong ties with Social Democrats in Western Europe, especially with Willy Brandt and the West German Social Democratic party. Soares and his colleagues were also in contact with Swedish and British Socialists.[4]

The Socialists, unlike the Communists, had very little organizational base within Portugal prior to 1974. But whereas the Communist leadership in general consisted of men of the 1930s and 1940s, mostly in their sixties at the time of the Caetano regime's overthrow, the Socialists were of a younger generation, much more closely attuned to more recent developments in Western Europe. Soares in particular had seen the unrest of the late 1960s in France at close hand. The Socialists had rarely suffered the privations that many of the Communist party leadership had endured. But men like Raul Rego, Soares, and Zenha had nonetheless taken considerable risks and suffered several periods of imprisonment for their beliefs. The strength of their dedication was something the Communists tended to disparage and, in consequence, to underestimate.

The umbrella organization from which most of the postwar opposition political groups trace their origins was the Movement of Democratic Unity (MUD), formed in the mid-1940s. Communists and others had participated in the tightly controlled electoral campaigns that the Salazar regime had periodically permitted until opposition candidate General Delgado came so close to success, in 1958, that the system was modified to protect against such near upsets in the future. After 1958, the opposition forces split, and the Socialists and Social Democrats competed in the 1969 election under their own umbrella organization, the Electoral Commission for Democratic Unity (CUED), and the Communists established an electoral front (CDE) with independents and radical Catholics led by the well-known economist Pereira de Moura. It had been for the last group that Major Melo Antunes had sought to be a candidate. In 1973, however, the Socialists and Communists came together again in the semilegal Portuguese Democratic Movement (MDP/CDE) and were consequently united at the time of the coup.

The personalities and views of the opposition were thus well known in 1974—especially to Major Melo Antunes, who had been largely responsible for drafting the MFA's program. Hence there was much less cause for clandestine or conspiratorial contacts between the military plotters and the opposition civilians than might appear at first sight. Once the coup succeeded, there was a ready-made group of clearly identified individuals to whom the military could turn if it wished to form a government composed of men whose hands were clean of any involvement with the fallen regime. Even General Spinola was aware of this—he had sent a signed copy of *Portugal and the Future* to Mário Soares in Paris.

The program of the Armed Forces Movement which was incorporated into the institutional provisions, providing a framework and timetable for the transition, called for a long period in which a new political system was to be defined. During this time, the new political parties had to find their public, and face preelectoral struggles.[5] Constituent Assembly elections were to take place within one year from 25 April 1974. In another year a parliament and president were to be elected under terms to be drawn up by the Constituent Assembly.

Apart from the Communists, no party possessed a strong organization. In the weeks immediately after the coup, the PCP took full advantage of this organizational advantage to take over key positions, especially in the trade unions and the municipalities. The Communist-dominated union coordinating organization, Intersindical, became the basis of Portugal's new trade union federation. In trade unions that had formerly been controlled by supporters of the old regime, Communist leaders were quickly elected to replace the old leaders. Also on the initiative of the Communists, new unions were organized for groups whose unionization had been prohibited by the old regime—most particularly public employees and farmworkers. In most of the country's municipalities, new councils were elected by public assemblies, the Communists often taking key positions or securing places for reliable allies.[6]

After April 1974, however, a large part of the population, intensely traditionalist and conservative, found themselves without spokesmen. Temporarily muted by the speed with which the power of the state had evaporated, the conservative rural peasantry and the Catholic community constituted a political constituency of some importance. The principal new political organizations of 1974, therefore, were not those of the Left, most of which existed before the coup and had longstanding relations with one another, but the fledgling parties of the Center and the Right. The lack of organizational capacity by conservative groups following the authoritarian regime's sudden demise and in the face of the Left's longstanding (if clandestine) organizational capacity is a phenomenon not exclusively confined to the Portuguese case. After the coup, two major parties emerged representing centrist and conservative forces, although each was constrained for many months to maintain a "Left" orientation. These were the Popular Democratic party (PPD) and the Center Democratic party (CDS). General Spinola, the provisional president, wanted to consolidate a centrist and reformist coalition that would strengthen his own authority, legitimize that authority by popular acclaim, and through the political process cirmcumvent the residual power of the MFA. He hoped to achieve this aim in collaboration with the new Popular Democratic party, which had been founded in May 1974 by the leading reformers of the early Caetano period, Francisco Sá Carneiro, Francisco Pinto Balsemão, and Magalhaes Mota.[7]

In a move that surprised even the MFA at the time, however, General Spinola invited the PCP into the provisional government. He hoped that placing a Communist in the Ministry of Labor and bringing Cunhal into the cabinet as a minister without portfolio would moderate and restrain labor militancy. As it turned out, however, Spinola badly miscalculated the consequences of his invitation to the Communists. He offered what the PCP was only too willing to concede, and he gained little from the respite in labor agitation that he hoped would follow. The PCP's strategy was to act with moderation, whatever its position in or outside the new government. The recent Chilean experience of 1973 had made the Communists wary of the military and anxious to coopt the middle class. Both factors tended to confirm the Communists' longstanding intention to direct their main attack against what they saw as the two pillars of the old regime, the great landowners and the oligarchic cartels, and to do so by forming an alliance with parts of the urban and rural middle classes. The PCP's most recent gains had been among lower-middle-class workers, especially the bank clerks, a leader of whom, Avelino Gonçalves, became labor minister in the first provisional government. During the early months following the coup, the Communists urged restraint in labor disputes, often acted to end strikes, and sought to cement an alliance with the urban middle class.

The "centrist" position of the Communists, of course, had a totally different content from that of General Spinola and the Popular Democratic party (PPD). The groups they supported and sought to encourage were diametrically opposed. Spinola hoped, as did many of the leading industrialists, that the change of regime might promote a rapid modernization of Portugal's economy and increase investments in new plants and methods, thereby raising Portugal's living standards to a level closer to the European norm. But "rationalization" of the economy along the lines proposed by Spinola's allies required the support of the very groups the Communists sought to curtail: the banks, which were the linchpin of the Melo, Champalimaud, and Espirito Santo empires, and the network of industries, insurance companies, and financial holdings the oligarchy controlled.

This contradiction would not be easily unraveled without the victory of one position over the other, for they were wholly incompatible. Moreover, it was a conflict that, rather than pitting a view of the past against one of the future, pitted two views of the future against one another. Spinola's view of a modernized country, developing the kind of large-scale corporate technology and trade that had been made other West European countries prosper, was as revolutionary for Portugal as was the objective of the Communists. But as opposition between Spinola and the PCP became more apparent, it produced one result that was to be crucial for subsequent events. It created the conditions for closer collaboration between the MFA and the PCP, because it coincided with deep divergences within the armed forces between the MFA and Spinola over decolonization.

Two major points are crucial to the Portuguese experience in the immediate aftermath of the coup. The first is the importance of the role of the Communists. Unlike in Spain, where the Communists were an important partner in both social and political pact-making during the critical transitional period, and were in any case marginal to the political forces grouped at the center of the political spectrum in whose hands the political initiative lay in this period, in Portugal, the political initiative rapidly escaped the centrist politicians and soldiers, and the PCP found itself center stage. This strategic difference was partly conjectural and partly organizational, in that the PCP alone had reliable cadres, clear ideological positions, and rapidly assessed the importance of the MFA. The second point to notice is that all other political groupings in Portugal, including the Socialists, were new and lacked organization. The old establishment, even the most modern-minded elements within it, meanwhile, found themselves outmaneuvered, discredited, and, as authority shifted into the hands of the younger officers and their leftist allies, increasingly intimidated, purged, and even jailed. Hence, Portugal stands in striking contrast to the transitional situations elsewhere in Europe and Latin America, all of which found the initiative in the hands of longstanding and organized political forces, most led by men with parliamentary and even governmental experience, many representing the conservative constituencies. In this sense at least the Portuguese experience is more like that of Nicaragua than those of Spain and Greece, or Argentina and Brazil.

## The Revolution in Crisis

When the coup occurred, the major part of the Portuguese armed forces were in Africa; the colonial warriors were war weary, and the middle-rank officers were sorely pressed. As a result de facto local cease-fires were soon arranged. General Spinola had hoped to establish a Portuguese-speaking federation of states, but the MFA overruled him and proceeded to effect decolonization. The first major crisis occurred in June 1974, when Spinola and the prime minister (a liberal law professor, Palma Carlos), attempting to reduce the MFA's influence, found themselves outmaneuvered. The crisis led to the elevation of a pro-Communist, Colonel Vasco Gonçalves, as prime minister. To foreclose the possibility of a military challenge from Spinola, the MFA consolidated its military authority by establishing a command structure (COPCON) under the control of Major Otelo Saraiva de Carvalho, the military coordinator of the April coup. In late September 1974 the conflict between the MFA and Spinola reached a climax. Spinola attempted to circumvent the MFA's influence by calling for a show of support from the "silent majority." The MFA and the Communists (under the cover of their front organization, the Portuguese Democratic Movement) mobilized their adherents and barricaded Lisbon against Spinola's supporters. As a consequence, the general resigned from the presidency on 30 September 1974. He was replaced by General Costa Gomes, whose political flexibility was reflected in his nickname, "the cork." After each of these crises major steps were taken to recognize the independence of African colonies, first Guinea-Bissau, then, in September 1974, Mozambique.[8]

The third crisis occurred on 11 March 1975. It was the result of complex subterranean maneuvering engaged in by both sides for months. General Spinola was tricked into believing that an anti-Communist putsch might succeed. When he arrived at the Tancos air base in central Portugal, he found a shambles. He barely had time to board a helicopter and flee across the border to Spain. After this comic-opera confrontation, the radical elements within the MFA removed (sometimes jailed) their more moderate colleagues and completed the purging of the old officer corps, which they had begun after the April coup. They established the Council of the Revolution as the supreme authority in the state. The Council of the Revolution decreed far-reaching measures—the nationalization of the banks, the insurance companies, and much of industry—and promised the expropriation of the great landed estates.

Despite the Left's apparently formidable assets in March 1975—control of the administration, unions, army, the media, and the political initiative—the Left's ascendancy proved short-lived. By the end of November 1975 the Left was disunited, weakened, and on the defensive.

Three aspects of those turbulent months help explain this reversal of circumstances. First, the all-important alliance with the military radicals failed. The MFA leadership split into various factions, all ostensibly "on the Left," but each with a different view of tactics and objectives. Simultaneously, discipline collapsed within the armed forces, and it did so more quickly among the "leftist" units than among the centrist or rightist units. Second, the decolonization process, which had helped cement the MFA's internal solidarity, became, after March 1975, a major irritant and divider as the situation in Angola proved increasingly intractable and as outsiders intervened there at will. Third, the economic situation in Portugal became increasingly precarious, allowing outsiders leverage which they had lacked before; during the summer of 1975 the Western governments made it clear to Lisbon that economic assistance would be dependent on political good behavior.

The behavior of the Portuguese Communist party was also an important element in the equation since by late 1974 Communist action had alienated powerful elements of the Portuguese Left which had previously collaborated with the Communists in the anti-Fascist struggle. Most especially and dramatically, the Communists were alienating the rapidly expanding Socialists led by Mário Soares.

In January 1975 the Communists took to the streets in massive demonstrations to support union legislation which would recognize a single union central organization and thereby effectively perpetuate Communist control over the organized working class. The MFA's Committee of Twenty endorsed the Communists' position. But the Catholic church, breaking a long political silence, condemned the proposal for a centralized union structure and called for pluralism. The Socialists and Popular Democrats in the cabinet succeeded in amending the details of the legislation in such a manner as to guarantee free elections for local union officials and committees.

The split pointed up fundamental differences of approach and reflected divergences on the Left long antedating the events in Portugal, raising again the classic debate between those in favor of a broad-based participatory and democratic route to Socialism on the one hand and those who espoused the role of a revolutionary vanguard on the other. The dispute forced both the Communists and the Socialists to rethink their tactics and restate their principles. The public dispute between the Communists and the Socialists that broke out in January was a conflict that reached beyond mere party factionalism because it paralleled, and to some extent intersected with, major divergences within the military. With the Right and Center effectively neutralized after March 1975, the struggle for power began in earnest within the Left and inside the MFA.

The Communists also made several major tactical blunders: they misread the balance of forces within Portugal and hence the power of their enemies; they also misunderstood the psychological impact of some of their actions, throwing potential allies into the embrace of their opponents. Finally, the election returns of April 1975 were a startling setback for the Communists and the military radicals, demonstrating graphically that although the Portuguese desired change they wished that change to be brought about by democratic means.

It was the elections that came first. Ironically, much of the foreign press, obsessed with the power of the Communists, dismissed the elections of 1975 as being of minor significance. They were wrong. In reality, the elections were of enormous significance, and their importance was well recognized once the results were in. In one of the highest turnouts ever recorded in a national election (91.7 percent), Soares's Portuguese Socialist party took 37.9 percent of the vote; the Popular Democrats, 26.4 percent; Cunhal's Communists a mere 12.5 percent nationwide, and the PCP's sister party, the Portuguese Democratic Movement (MDP/CDS), a mere 4.1 percent; the conservative CDS got 7.6 percent.[9]

The election returns revealed a marked regional polarization. Communist support was almost exclusively concentrated in the South of the country, especially in the industrial towns along the south bank of the Tagus estuary opposite Lisbon, and in the Alentejo. In the North, the Popular Democrats (PPD) and the Social Democratic Center (CDS) dominated the returns. The unintended consequence of the elections was to point up the profound differences in social and economic organization between Northern and Southern Portugal.

The Socialists (PS) emerged as a national party, with respectable percentages in both North and South. Although they tended to be the "rightist" alternative to the Communists in the South, and the "leftist" alternative to the PPD and CDS in the North, it was in the central regions of the country and the major urban centers that the Socialists did best of all. In Lisbon, they won 46.1 percent of the vote; in Oporto, 42.15 percent; overall, their support was concentrated in regions with good communications that tended to be at least partly industrialized.

There were important similarities between the regions of PPD and PCP strength. The districts of Bragança and Vila Real in the North, like those of Beja and Evora in the South, suffered the highest rates of infant mortality. All had the highest percentage of the workforce engaged in agriculture (over 70 percent). Each had a high illiteracy rate (over 40 percent). All were backward and in many respects isolated rural communities, each in its own way a traditional society. But in two critical respects they diverged: in religion and land ownership. These were the two fundamental issues in the struggle that was about to begin.

Thus, the coincidence between the seizure of power by the radical military and their Communist backers in March and the holding of the elections in April, with their victory for moderation, was of great importance. The election returns demonstrated that the base of support for the revolution was narrow indeed. The returns inadvertently provided a geography for counterrevolution, a geography that the Communists' enemies inside and outside Portugal were soon to take advantage of. Newly arrived U.S. ambassador in Portugal Frank Carlucci put the point bluntly one year later: "I think it was the election that turned the situation around."[10]

The election returns for the Constituent Assembly, and the Socialists' strong showing, therefore, also had the important effect of providing the connection that allowed Western Europe and the United States to reenter the Portuguese political scene, which they had been watching with some dismay more or less from the sidelines. The West European Social Democrats, and most especially the powerful West German party, had for some time criticized Washington's fatalistic view of the course of events in Lisbon. With the triumph of Soares and the Portuguese Socialists, their optimism was borne out. Communist leader Cunhal described the situation in his own language:

> In the Portuguese Revolution two processes have intervened, two dynamics, with completely different characteristics. On one side, the revolutionary dynamic, created by the intervention of material force—popular and military—directly transforming situations, conquering and exercising liberties, defeating and throwing out the Fascists, opposing the counterrevolutionary attempts, bringing about profound social and economic transformations, attempting to create a state in service of the Revolution, and the creation of organs of power (including military organs) which will guarantee the democratic process and correspond to the revolutionary transformation.
>
> On the other side, the electoral process, understood as the choice by universal suffrage of the organs of power, tending to subordinate any social transformation to a previous constitutional legality, and not recognizing the intervention of the military in political life, or the creative, predominant intervention of the masses in the revolutionary process.[11]

Against the background of this divided legitimacy—that of the ballot box exemplified by the political parties, and that of the revolutionary act exemplified by the MFA—the immediate reality of the situation in the spring and summer of 1975 found central authority paralyzed, with the result that a type of popular power emerged at a local level. This occurrence in turn overly accentuated regional polarization and hardened political positions. Since popular power and the rule of local vigilantes could as easily be of the Right as of the Left, the resulting volatile situation had a much more immediate impact on the development of Portugal than the protracted debates in the Constituent Assembly over the new constitution or within the armed forces over which of the many roads to Socialism to follow. The far Left and the far Right were the first to realize this situation, and their activities over the summer and fall of 1975 took on an importance out of all proportion to their numbers or their real support in the country.

As the forces of revolutionary change emerged, so did those of counterrevolution. Violence and the threat of violence were integral to both processes. The conflict remained below the threshold of large-scale armed struggle and internal war, but it was the mobilization of radicalized workers and landless laborers that, in 1974, helped propel the country to the Left, and it was the popular uprising by conservative peasants and small property owners in the northern and central provinces that blocked the momentum of revolution during the long summer of 1975.

These rural mobilizations and countermobilizations in Portugal between 1974 and 1976 gave the Portuguese crisis much of its special character.[12] It fell to Portugal in the mid-1970s, however, to reinfuse European agrarian-reform questions with the revolutionary connotations of fundamental social and political change. Closely linked to the problems of land distribution and ownership were two other factors that made Portugal's situation special. The land seizures occurred against the background of the paralysis of the state apparatus and a collapse of the state's authority. In Portugal, the old systems of deference and the old mechanisms of social control were temporarily overthrown. In the vacuum, a whole array of self-management projects emerged in the industrial sector, workers' and neighborhood commissions were set up in the urban centers, and fringe radical groups sought to articulate and harness the incoherent and spontaneous desires of a popular mass movement. Even the military was affected (the army in particular), rapidly disintegrating into a series of would-be Soviets and debating societies. Both the political parties and the more traditional military officers sensed the threat in these developments; especially concerned were the Communist party and its allies, which had based their strategy in classic Leninist style on the seizure or subversion of the existing institutional structures. These institutional structures, however, inherited from the corporate, quasi-Fascist dictatorship, had ceased to function in the fluid situation that followed the April 1974 coup. Cunhal, along with many of the political leaders returning from exile, seriously underestimated the degree to which the authority of institutions had collapsed in the immediate aftermath of the coup. The Communists were uncomfortable in the face of spontaneous action by the workers, and acted more often than not to curb such action when it occurred. As it turned out, in fact, the Communists, by associating themselves with the institutional structures and by attempting in many cases to prop them up, were badly mauled in the process. Between March and November 1975, the PCP behaved and talked very much like the dictatorial regime overthrown in 1974, and to do so was a critical error with a people emerging from fifty years of dictatorship.

As a result, since the PCP had positioned itself disadvantageously, the initiative in political terms was often taken by the radical Left, a complex and often bitterly divided collection of small groups that included several Marxist-Leninist parties, Maoists, revolutionary leftists in all but name, and advocates of popular power. These groups, marginal to the political process in most European situations, became significant in Portugal, often because they tended to reflect what was happening at local or neighborhood levels (especially in the larger urban centers) better than the more formal and traditional political parties.

### The Failure of the Communists

The failure to perceive the split that was occurring between the attitudes of the radical political and military leaders in Lisbon and the mood of the country was aggravated by the peculiar way in which the African situation and the collapse of the economy affected the chronology of the revolution. The pressures emanating from Africa were undoubtedly the most important in the short run, but economic issues dominated the revolution's second stage, which began as disengagement from Africa was complete.

The fact that the economic crisis was postponed so long resulted from Salazar's legacy of large gold and foreign-currency reserves. These reserves, which stood at $2.8 billion at the end of 1973 ($1.2 billion in gold), provided a cushion that helped the revolution postpone the consequences of its actions. At least they allowed a series of far-reaching and radical transformations to be promulgated without much apparent pain to the population at large. In the first year after the coup, in fact, workers' real purchasing power increased dramatically, stimulating a sharp rise in sales of consumer goods.[13] The reserves helped to obscure the occurrence of changes that would in time have to be paid for, and paid for not merely by the revolution's immediate victims: conservative military officers, expropriated landowners, great industrialists, and banking magnates. High degrees of sacrifice, austerity, and disciplined collective action were unavoidable if a Socialist revolution was to be made to work. Whether the Portuguese people, or a sufficiently large number of them, would be prepared for that route was a question that had been avoided. By the spring of 1975, it was apparent that the reserves could no longer provide the luxury of a revolution without tears, and that Portugal had a major economic crisis in the making. With huge and accumulating trade and balance-of-payments deficits, Portugal became vulnerable to foreign pressure and increasingly dependent on foreign aid, giving back to the western powers— West Germany and the United States in particular—the initiative that they had lost in April 1974.

The tactical problems facing the PCP leadership in the spring and summer of 1975 were certainly considerable. They did confront a new situation after March, one that to every appearance had "revolutionary potential." Their policies had until that moment been based on defeating the great landowners and the monopolists. But by mid-1975 both of these "enemies" had been put to flight. In the Alentejo, some 1.2 million hectares had been expropriated, often at the initiative of the workers themselves, sometimes by default, as workers carried on in the place of absentee owners. In any event, land seizure occurred on a massive scale and with minimal resistance. The nationalizations of industry likewise took place with ease, and again the PCP followed as much as initiated these moves. Now, with the power of the monopolists and latifundists destroyed, the editors of Cunhal's 1974 book *For a Democratic Revolution*, in revising the work in July 1975, suggested that "the present historical stage of the revolution seems to be more correctly defined as a superior stage [than that implied by the title of Cunhal's book], that of a Socialist revolution."[14]

The difficulty with this "new stage" was that it inevitably showed up the ambivalent attitude of the Communists toward their would-be allies, the small and medium-sized farmers of the Center and North of Portugal and the small shopkeepers and property owners in the town. Indeed, Cunhal had already made it clear that "the allies of the proletariat for the Socialist revolution are not the same as those for the democratic and national revolution. In the first the proletariat carried out the fundamental attack on the monopolies and latifundiarios allied with the part of the bourgeoisie (the *petit bourgeoisie* and parts of the middle class) interested in the antimonopolistic fight." "The Socialist revolution," he continued, "is directed against the bourgeoisie in its totality and for this reason, some of the allies of the proletariat in the first stage (sectors of the urban middle class, sectors of the rural peasantry, and some elements of the *petit bourgeoisie*) cease to be allies during the Socialist revolution."[15] Cunhal was nothing if not blunt.

The would-be victims, however, had a keen sense of their vulnerability. The land seizures in the South, and some highly publicized seizures elsewhere in the country, had thoroughly alarmed the peasantry and scared them into mutual collaboration. Indeed, the owners of small and medium property proved much more formidable opponents than had the great landowners and industrialists. Cunhal himself was to note a year later that there had been "without doubt deficiencies and errors" in the party's activities over these months, preeminently in "understanding the importance of these classes." He spoke then from bitter experience, for it was precisely the small land-owners who mobilized in August 1975 to burn and sack at least forty-nine of the party's offices in Central and Northern Portugal, virtually expelling the party from these regions and making it clear more than once that it was in their power to blockade and cut Lisbon off from the whole North and Center of the country if they chose to do so.

The psychological errors committed by the Communists only hastened the polarization along fundamental social and economic lines. The attack on the newspaper *República*, which the Communists may not have initiated but which they supported, became an international *cause célèbre*, and the attempt to monopolize the mass media proved to be entirely counterproductive for the Communists. The attack and takeover of the Catholic church's radio station in Lisbon also had major negative repercussions, especially among the highly religious peasantry of the North. And as if to confirm the image of Stalinist highhandedness, Cunhal gave his famous interview to Oriana Fallacci. "If you think the Socialist party with its 40 percent and the Popular Democrats with its 27 percent constitute the majority," he said, "you're the victim of a misunderstanding . . . I'm telling you the elections have nothing or very little to do with the dynamics of a revolution . . . I promise you there will be no parliament in Portugal."[16]

The PCP also overestimated the tenacity of its friends and underestimated that of its enemies. In the civilian sphere, the Socialists showed a much greater capacity to mobilize, and even to take to the streets, than the Communists had anticipated, and Mário Soares was tougher than even his friends expected. On 11 July, the Socialists withdrew from the government, followed by the PPD ministers on 17 July. On 13 July, over 10,000 Catholics had demonstrated in Aveiro against the takeover of Radio Renascença, and at Rio Maior, the same day, 200 angry farmers and Catholics destroyed the headquarters of the Communist party. It was by now apparent that a formidable popular coalition was forming against the fragmented Left.

The Communists' alliance with the military radicals was already badly strained. The Communists, as Cunhal recognized later, "badly evaluated the situation in the armed forces and were over-optimistic as to the outcome of the internal conflicts within the military." The group associated with the prime minister, Colonel Vasco Goncalves, became increasingly isolated as the summer wore on, and the initiative within the military passed to the faction with the MFA associated with Major Melo Antunes. Alarmed by the growing estrangement between the country as a whole and Lisbon, Melo Antunes's group increasingly objected to the vanguard role usurped by the Gonçalvists, and believed that a broader base of social support than that provided by the PCP was essential if the MFA was not to be placed in opposition to the majority of the population. Meanwhile, the influence of the extreme Left was growing within the command structure of COPCON and in several of the key regiments in the Lisbon area, especially the light artillery and the military police. But the power of the populists was undermined by the indiscipline that populism brought with it. COPCON was no more than a coordinating agency, and the growth of political passions at unit level tended to undermine its effectiveness, so that the troops under its nominal command disaggregated into their component parts. The most radical units tended to become the most chaotic, and a Communist attempt to subvert the more disciplined units, especially the commandos, failed miserably when the tough and popular commando colonel won over his troops in the consequent showdown. In fact it was a fourth group in the army, little noticed at the time, that was most active behind the scenes as the summer drew to a close. Known at times as the "operationals," this group was composed of officers who reflected the professional interests of the officer corps, a current of which, of course, had been a powerful element in the original captains' movement. A leading figure in this group was Colonel Ramalho Eanes, the future president of Portugal.[17]

Several factors beyond the PCP's control help explain the Communists' behavior in this critical period. From a rump clandestine organization with most of its leadership living abroad, the party had expanded by the summer of 1975 to over 100,000 members. Few of these newcomers had received the ideological indoctrination or long experience within party organizations that would have made them a reliable and disciplined force. Many of the rank and file were to the left of the party leadership, and tensions emerged between "new" and "old" Communists. The new Communists were also, according to Cunhal's own retrospective criticism, sectarian, intolerant, and indiscreet. The rapidly moving political situation in Portugal thus caught the PCP in a state of mutation, no longer the sleek clandestine organization it had been, but not yet a mass party.[18]

Second, the large and noisy factions of the far Left continued to make their presence felt during these months, and events—as with the nationalization of the banks, the land seizures, and the takeovers of *República* and the Lisbon Catholic radio station—often moved faster under grass-roots pressure than the central committee of the PCP might have wished. Cunhal was right in believing that the staying power of the far-Left factions was limited; yet the PCP was always obliged during this period to treat the criticism of the far Left seriously and to counter the far Left's impact among industrial workers and the rural laborers.

Toward the end of August and during the first week in September, the PCP suffered two serious setbacks. In the civilian sphere, a powerful coalition had formed around Mário Soares and the Socialists. Soares had led his party out of the fourth provisional government in July, and was followed by the PPD. By August, the Socialists were providing cover for large and at times violent popular demonstrations against the rump of Communists and fellow travelers appointed by Vasco Gonçalves to the fifth provisional government. In the military sphere, an equally formidable coalition had formed around Major Melo Antunes and his so-called Group of Nine. The "Nine" were officers who all had been important members of the MFA from the beginning and included the military commanders in the Center and South of Portugal. The units in the North, commanded by an officer close to Gonçalves, were refusing to obey him and had placed themselves at the disposition of the central military region.

The Communists' ally, Vasco Gonçalves, was forced out of office on 29 August. The PCP in fact had already abandoned him.[19] A sixth provisional government was established and brought back the Socialists, the Popular Democrats, and many of the original members of the MFA who, led by Melo Antunes and Captain Vasco Lourenço, had conducted the struggle with Gonçalves over the summer. But the new situation was a critical one. The crisis had split the MFA wide open. The army had withdrawn its delegates from the MFA Assembly, since the army believed the Assembly to be too heavily influenced by the Communists, and throughout the country the armed forces themselves had fragmented to such an extent that almost every unit found it necessary to define itself politically.[20]

The specter of civil strife became real. The removal of the Communist party from government power and the gradual purge of its militants and sympathizers, which began throughout the armed forces, placed the PCP squarely in opposition for the first time since the April 1974 coup. Faced with this situation, the Communists chose to ally themselves with the radical Left in a United Revolutionary Front (FUR). The Communist party's formidable organizational capacity added to the armed capability of the military units influenced by the radical Left, especially the military police and the Lisbon light artillery regiment, posing an immediate and serious threat to the new government. Within the government, the moderate Left was thus faced with the alternatives of moving against the radical Left and seeking to disarm it or running the risk of being overthrown by it. The radical Left saw the moderate Left's reaction as an immediate threat to its own position, and believed that the longer it waited, the more vulnerable it would become. The radical Left had every incentive to act sooner rather than later, especially as the government had attempted to establish an elite military intervention force (AMI) loyal to it, threatening thereby to circumvent the remnants of the COPCON security force under Otel Saraiva de Carvalho.

The demands that "internationalist" solidarity placed on the Portuguese Communists may also explain the behavior of the PCP in this period. It is impossible to speak with certainty. But there can be no doubt now that as early as August 1975 Cunhal was privately urging caution on the central committee of the PCP. Yet in October, he led the PCP into its reckless front with the previously despised far Left factionalists, an action that further alienated many Portuguese and helped consolidate a broad-based coalition of forces against the Communists. The PCP, however, has never hidden its belief that the Soviet Union is, to use Cunhal's words, the "sun" of the Communist movement. And it is at least worth noting that the behavior of the PCP between August and November 1975 provided a convenient smokescreen which did much to cover the beginning of large-scale Soviet and Cuban intervention in Angola. The Communists may also have perpetuated the struggle to secure their base in the Alentejo, since the great expansion in land seizures occurred in the fall of 1975 after the Communists had lost the power struggle at the center with the ouster of Gonçalves. The Communists, of course, abandoned their new "allies" on the far Left when the confrontation occurred in November.[21]

The West moved rapidly to shore up the sixth government. The U.S. government and the European Economic Community granted Portugal $272 million in emergency aid in early October 1975, following the ouster of Gonçalves. Both grants were openly described as political support for the moderate Socialists who had gained the initiative within the MFA and the government. The United States also pledged on 14 October to double its refugee airlift from Angola.

The Associated Press reported on 25 September that the CIA had sent between $2 million and $10 million per month to the Portuguese Socialists since June. The West German Social Democrats had also contributed several million dollars to the Soares party. Support from the Soviet Union to the PCP was placed at $45 million since the April coup, although British Prime Minister Harold Wilson claimed on 5 September 1975 that Moscow had spent $100 million on the PCP.[22]

The Center and the democratic Right acted with great skill and restraint during these months, far beyond what the Communists might have expected considering the past and continuing high jinks of the now-exiled General Spinola. As far as one can tell, the anti-Communist military in Portugal were scrupulous in keeping a distance between themselves and those nostalgic for a return to the old regime. Moreover, on several occasions when large-scale violence might have discredited and split the anti-Communist alliance now forming of Socialists, non-Communist leftists, moderates in the military, and civilian and church leaders in Central and Northern Portugal, caution and restraint prevailed. The most dangerous moment perhaps had occurred when large numbers of Alentejan workers besieged the Constituent Assembly and members of the government in the National Assembly Building in Lisbon. The commandos wanted to go in and clear out the crowd. But they were held back by General Costa Gomes, then president, who, despite his own equivocal behavior during this period, was not prepared to see Portugal plunged into civil war. The caution and the defensive strategy of the non-Communist military paid off when officerless radical soldiers in the paratroop corps led the "Left" uprising which provided the excuse for the anti-Communist alliance under the command of Colonel Eanes to crush them decisively on 25 November 1975.

Finally, it must be noted that the confused situation in the country allowed for effective action by *agents provocateurs*. Very little of a reliable nature has yet appeared covering this aspect of the Portuguese situation, but there can be little doubt that foreign intelligence operatives from the NATO countries were active in Portugal between June and November 1975. The sudden emergence (and just as sudden disappearance) of a "revolutionary" movement (SUV) within the ranks during this period, for instance, is remarkably similar in its tone and impact to the sergeants' "movement" in Brazil in 1964, which helped precipitate the coup of that year by conservative generals and politicians. In Portugal, as might have been anticipated, this development had a similar sobering effect on the Portuguese officer corps—even the leftists within it. The Communist flirtation with the rank and file during the time they were associated with the revolutionary front, and growing chaos and indiscipline among soldiers, sailors, and airmen, also helped to cement the officer corps back together again.

In any event, it was the PCP's isolation in the country, together with the isolation of the Gonçalvists within the military, that made possible the formation of a temporary alliance of anti-Communist forces after August 1975. During the 25 November 1975 showdown, when officerless paratroopers had risen in a leftist putsch attempt, this alliance delivered the decisive *coup de grâce* to the dream of "Socialist revolution" so avidly espoused a few months before by Alvaro Cunhal and his allies.

One external factor in the Portuguese experience deserves emphasis, especially in comparative perspective. Because of the role of the Communists, the social turmoil in the country, and the radicalization of the military, Portugal was, in 1975, high on the international agenda.

Unlike other transitional situations (again excepting Nicaragua), where no major geostrategical threat was perceived, Portugal not only became embroiled in East-West discussions but also provoked considerable intervention by outside forces. Surprisingly this aspect has escaped much serious attention or analysis.

This neglect is partly because the result of covert Western intervention in Portugal, unlike the result in Chile or Nicaragua, was by and large applauded by the mainstream of journalists and commentators. Intervention was also more subtle and skillful than in the Latin American cases. This approach was not fortuitous. It was caused by the peculiar constraints that would-be interveners, Henry Kissinger in particular, were obliged to work under as a direct consequence of the disruptive and demoralizing impact of Watergate and the revelation of previous operations on the U.S. government and its intelligence agencies. Kissinger was also restrained by the skillful bureaucratic rearguard action waged by the U.S. ambassador in Lisbon, Frank Carlucci, later to be appointed deputy director of the CIA. Carlucci, with strong West German backing, proposed a policy of subtle support for the Socialists. He also remained at arm's length from the old right-wing hard-liners who had previously had Washington's ear; he helped to strengthen the moderate Left within the military, and he worked mightily to provide substantial economic aid to the coalition of Socialists and moderate army officers who routed the Communists and radical soldiers in November 1975. The international context of the Portuguese crisis was, therefore, of considerable significance. In neighboring Spain, for instance, the struggle over democracy in Portugal had immediate impact. The old *caudillo*, Generalissimo Francisco Franco, was near death, and the Portuguese experience was a sobering one for both Left and Right. In Portuguese-speaking Brazil, the military regime was also seeking to manipulate a transition toward a less dictatorial system. Retroactively, therefore,

Portugal is seen as part of an evolving process of "transitions to democracy." At the time, the Portuguese experience was more one of political and social rupture than of "transition," and Portugal's impact on countries such as Spain and Brazil was to stimulate a process of managed political change intended precisely to avoid the discontinuity that Portugal suffered.

### The Problems of Consolidating Democracy

Throughout the whole period of political turmoil, social upheaval, and military factionalism, the Constitutent Assembly had been at work writing an extraordinarily long and complicated document. The assembly, reflecting in composition the electoral returns of April 1975, existed for much of its lifetime within a political climate in which history seemed to have passed it by. Under the terms of the agreement forced upon the political parties prior to the 1975 election, the outline of the constitutional settlement had been set. In particular, that agreement had demoted any future parliament to a role coequal with the Assembly of the MFA. Both assemblies were to be jointly responsible for the indirect election of the president of the Republic. The majority of the members of the Constituent Assembly—the deputies of the Socialist party, the PPD, and the CDS—therefore spent most of their energies defending what civil liberties they could within the overall conditions established by the MFA. After 25 November 1975, of course, the guidelines for the constitution changed dramatically, and the pact between the MFA and the parties was drastically revised. The most significant change, embodied in the new agreement between the MFA and the parties (February 1976), was that the election of the president was to be by universal suffrage and secret ballot, and the MFA Assembly disappeared completely from the institutional structure.

The Constitution of 1976 was nevertheless a curious hybrid. In rhetoric it was, as the Left liked to claim, a "very advanced" document. It explicitly committed Portugal to a "transition to Socialism" and a collectivization of the means of production. The nationalization and land expropriations were declared to be irreversible. The military retained an important role because the Council of the Revolution was not disbanded in 1976 but became in effect an advisory organ of the presidency. In addition, the Council acquired the significant power to judge the constitutionality of acts by the National Assembly. Constitutional revision was made difficult—any revisions being precluded before 1981, and then changes being possible only by a two-thirds vote of the Assembly. The Constitution of 1976 was thus a settlement with a built-in diffusion of power. The Council of the Revolution was intended to guarantee the progressive intent of the MFA's action in overthrowing the old regime in April 1974. The government, on the other hand, was based on the political parties in the Assembly, and the president of the Republic held extensive powers, emphasized by his election by direct popular vote in considerable autonomy from the political parties. It was, as Juan Linz has pointed out, a situation not unlike Weimar.[23]

The democratic regime inaugurated by the 1976 Constitution, moreover, had two distinct legacies which strongly affected the attitudes of those who had to work within its rules—one legacy came from the reaction against half a century of right-wing dictatorship, but no less important was the legacy that came from the reaction against a traumatic encounter with the authoritarian Left. The politicians of the new regime, especially the Democratic Socialists, Centrists, and Christian Democrats, therefore, had as clear a view of the threat to them represented by the Communists as they did of the threat from the Right.

One consequence of this dual heritage was to make the formation of parliamentary alliances an extremely complicated affair, since one possible majority—a coalition of the Left, for example, between the Communists and the Socialists—was completely out of the question. Yet a coalition between the Socialists and the Right was not easy because, although the church and the conservatives had supported the Socialists as a bulwark against Communism, the Socialists remained secular republicans who supported many social issues that the church and conservatives opposed.

The election for the Assembly of the Republic on 25 April 1976, moreover, revealed a remarkable stability of voting patterns—remarkable because the context within which the elections were held had totally changed. In April 1975, the radical military leadership closely allied to the PCP was in the ascendancy. In April 1976, the radical Left had been deposed and the colonels who had defeated them on 25 November held the reins of power. The army, which in 1975 talked of itself as "a revolutionary vanguard" and a "movement of national liberation," by 1976 praised "hierarchy" and "discipline."

Despite this dramatic reversal of circumstances, the Socialist party again gained a clear plurality in 1976 and established itself as the key element in any political equation. The election returns, however, made the formation of a viable government majority in the National Assembly extremely difficult. No general coalition could function long without the Socialists. Neither could the parties of the Center and the Right, the Popular Democrats (with 24 percent of the vote) and the Social Democratic Center (with 16 percent), form a majority of the Right. Nor could the PCP, which increased its vote (from 12 to 15 percent), join a majority coalition with the strongly anti-Communist Popular Democrats and Social Democratic Center against the Socialists, although a tactical alliance on individual issues was not impossible.

The two alternatives to a minority Socialist government—a coalition to the Left with the PCP, or a coalition to the Right with the Popular Democrats, both viable majorities in the Assembly—presented major domestic and international complications. An alliance with the PCP, quite apart from its intrinsic domestic impossibility, was strenuously opposed by Washington and the West Germans, whose economic support for the floundering economy was increasingly essential. A coalition with the Popular Democrats, who were longtime supporters of a liberal capitalist solution to Portugal's economic problems and a party opposed to the nationalizations and land reform, would risk confrontation with organized labor and the Communist-dominated rural areas of the South. Moreover, Mário Soares, the leader of the Socialists, and Sá Carneiro, leader of the PPD (now renamed the Social Democratic party [PSD]), strongly disliked and distrusted each other. In the face of these constraints, the Socialists decided to go it alone, and a first constitutional government was formed under Soares's leadership. In June 1976, Antonio Ramalho Eanes, the military mastermind of the 25 November countercoup, was elected president of the Republic by an overwhelming majority. President Eanes's first task was to reestablish military discipline and bring about an orderly retrenchment and modernization of the armed forces as a whole. The task of the Socialist minority government was to make parliamentary democracy work.

A further constraint that encompassed the new democracy lay in Portugal's geopolitical setting, something made clear by the outcome of the political and social struggles of 1975. The geographical and social balance in Portugal which had favored the anti-Communist alliance in 1975 might have mattered less had the Red Army been at Portugal's borders. As it was, Portugal was a member of NATO, and deeply embedded in the Western economic and strategic framework. Yet, whoever found the new Portugal within its sphere of influence would also find that supporting Portugal would be an expensive proposition. With the African territories gone, Portugal had lost economic advantages which, while not large in overall terms, were nevertheless highly important to those sectors of the economy that had depended on colonial markets, raw materials, and remittances. In addition, as a result of the return of Portuguese settlers from Angola and Mozambique, Portugal's population had increased by almost 10 percent, placing increasing burdens on government expenditures.

The most critical area of dispute remained the rural crisis. In the South, chaotic conditions continued in the wake of the seizures of large estates by landless workers, although the Communists rapidly asserted their control through rural unions, and collective units were established with Communist technical and organizational assistance. Practical problems abounded, however, and required government action. There was great need for irrigation, the organization of distribution, for fertilizers, technical assistance, planning for improved crop yields, and the replacement of lost breeding stock. The Socialists were understandably none too anxious to help the Communist collectives succeed. Yet the Alentejo was Portugal's breadbasket, and Portugal was a chronic importer of essential foodstuffs.

In the Center and the North of the country, meanwhile, the small landowners remained terrified that the expropriations that had taken place in the South would continue. These small and medium-sized proprietors formed the backbone of the anti-Communist riots in the summer of 1975. But some reforms are essential in the North and Center of Portugal. The average farm holding in the North is only 2 hectares, and in the Center 3.5 hectares. Many *retornados*, as the 600,000 Portuguese settlers who had fled Angola and Mozambique were called, settled in the North and Center of Portugal. Their absorption proved easier than many had expected, but the reason they could be reintegrated so effortlessly was because they tended to fill in the hollow in the demographic profile caused by mass emigration during the decades prior to the coup d'état of 1974. With economic recession continuing in the major European economies and Western Europe no longer absorbing Portuguese immigrants, most of whom came from the northern region, dangerous population pressures threatened eventually to build up.

The modern industrial sector developed in the 1960s was based on oil, petrochemicals, and motor-vehicle assembly plants (with U.S., West European, and Japanese ownership). In large part, its economic viability had been predicated on an expanding and prosperous middle-class consumer. The new enterprises were buffeted by the inflation in oil prices and the changed social conditions in Portugal. With increasing food imports and unfavorable conditions for Portuguese exports, Portugal's balance-of-payments deficits reached huge proportions in 1976, forcing recourse to the International Monetary Fund (IMF); and in consequence, because Portugal desperately needed foreign loans, Portuguese economic policy came under strict international supervision.[24]

The essence of the Portuguese dilemma in the 1980s, in fact, grows out of the ambiguous result of the struggles of 1975. In Portugal the outcome of the conflict was not clear-cut and remains in many ways unresolved. There were no martyrs such as Allende and no generals like Pinochet. Neither Left nor Right won outright. In fact, a most unlikely hybrid emerged and looked to all intents and purposes like a Western liberal and representative democracy, even if in many respects Portuguese democracy was constrained and hampered by the heritage of a long dictatorship and a tumultuous flirtation with revolution.

The break with the past after 1974 was profound to be sure. But the Portuguese Revolution was half finished. Its propagandists became isolated from the majority of the population and fell out among themselves, and as they squabbled, the tide turned. The counterrevolution was only partly successful. The compromise that resulted was thus based on two contradictory views of social and political organizations, each rooted in its own powerful but polarized social base. Both coexisted within the same system only because they possessed neither the power to overthrow it nor the desire to face the bloody consequences of the attempt to seize supremacy, although under changed circumstances the forces of the Right might be just as tempted to make the attempt as the Communists were in 1975.

The political system of Portugal that emerged after 1976, therefore, is based on a truce, a truce that muted but did not resolve the hostilities. The settlement embodied in the 1976 Constitution is thus paradoxically both remarkably stable and extremely fragile. The contradictions beneath the compromise, however, are part of the explanation for the inability of the constitutional governments to act effectively or to resolve the structural problems that Portugal must solve.

Despite the formidable transformations set in motion by the events of 25 April 1974, much in Portugal did not change. The social composition of the new political class differs little from that of the old regime. The bureaucracy remains in place, merely expanding to accommodate a new political clientele superimposed upon it, rather than being modernized by the infusion of new people and ideas. Workers whose purchasing power was temporarily increased after 1974 might have marched in demonstrations and chanted slogans of Socialist revolution, but they spent their money on the clothes, appliances, and artifacts of West European consumer societies to whose standard of living they aspired. The white-collar workers in particular, who had been among the most vociferous "leftists" in 1975, moved quickly to the Right as economic conditions worsened. In behavioral and psychological terms, it is not yet clear how much really changed in Portugal, beyond the traumatic recognition, as revolutionary optimism evaporated, of the resilient power and divisiveness of class, regional, and personal antagonisms and jealousy.

The economic dilemma is much like that which affects the political system established in 1976—it is that Portugal is in many ways straddling the divide between the consequences of a capitalist transformation that was only partly completed and a Socialist revolution that had no more than begun, suffering the disadvantages of both and the benefits of neither. Land and enterprises remain expropriated and nationalized under the constitutional regime established in 1976. Many of those who lost much of their patrimony, therefore, remain bitter and unsatisfied. The two principal areas from which the oligarchy was expelled—the modern industrialized enterprises and the grain-producing plateau of the South—are the two sectors on which Portugal most depends for the increased productivity in both industry and agriculture needed to bring Portugal's payments deficits into balance and to prepare Portugal for the harsh competition that entrance into the European Economic Community will cause.

The revolution has had other paradoxical consequences. The nationalizations, for instance, have important implications for Portugal's ability to bargain effectively in the international arena. The result of taking so vast a sector of Portuguese industrial enterprise into the hands of the state, and of simultaneously allowing foreign enterprise to remain inviolate, has been that the nationalization of nationally owned enterprises has tended inadvertently to promote a denationalization of the economy as a whole. Given the political and economic trajectory of Portugal since the end of 1975, it is perhaps inevitable that this outcome should occur. The state, because of the paralysis and the failure to rectify the problem of chronic deficits in the balance of payments, has been in no position to argue against the predispositions of the international financial community, which is innately distrustful of nationalizations in any case. The preference of outsiders to place their investments in private and foreign-affiliated business, combined with the state's lack of capacity effectively to manage nationalized enterprises, and compounded by the virtual abandonment of control over economic policy-making to IMF dictation, all served to confirm this pattern.

The historical record, in any case, does not offer much support for the hope of many well-meaning economists and foreign bankers that denationalization of enterprises and the working of the free market will dynamize Portuguese business.

This interplay of dependency and nationalism is a recurrent problem of small nations forced to live with overpowering neighbors, and Portugal has always faced the difficulty of balancing the need for external support against the desire for national independence. Yet, when this economic constraint is paralleled by political paralysis, there is potential danger. Too great a reliance on outside support, within a fragile political system, risks abandoning the potent claims of nationalist sentiment to the enemies of democracy.

The Portuguese case is thus an unfinished one. Many Portuguese are more concerned than ever about the future of their system, dissatisfied with its functioning but uncertain how it should be improved without reopening old wounds, hoping that the panacea of engagement with Europe will solve their problems but fearful that engagement with Europe may make their problems worse.

# 6 ·

# Regime Change and the Prospects for Democracy in Greece: 1974–1983

## P. Nikiforos Diamandouros

The transition from authoritarian to democratic rule in Portugal, Spain, and Greece in 1974 and 1975 coincided with, and added momentum to, the growing scholarly interest in the nature and internal structure of authoritarian regimes and, especially, in the dynamics of regime change. The obvious and significant differences in the transition patterns followed by each regime-in-crisis offer a rich ground for theoretical and empirical analyses. What, for example, accounts for the striking differences under which Portugal and Spain, the two longest-lived authoritarian regimes, both originating in the era of Fascism, acquired a democratic regime? Is the obvious significance of the external factor (i.e., colonial crisis) in Portugal of such crucial importance as to explain the different crisis outcomes in and of itself? Or, as Philippe Schmitter has suggested, do the dynamics of the regime's internal contradictions have to be assigned a preeminent role in any analysis seeking to account for the causes of regime crisis and transition? What were the confining conditions under which change occurred in each regime, and what were the perceptible differences in the consolidation strategies followed by the successor leadership in each case? Finally, the even more general theoretical question raised by Schmitter concerns the whole issue of the dynamics of change within authoritarian regimes. Indeed his analysis constitutes an attempt to inject the dimension of change into what he seems implicitly to regard as too static a conception of the authoritarian regime analyzed by Linz in his classic statement on the subject.[1]

The use of Spain and Portugal as archetypal examples from which to generalize about authoritarian regimes is not a novelty. On the contrary, such use would, for a number of reasons, appear to be eminently sensible. The very longevity of these regimes allows analysis to stretch far enough back in time to afford a better understanding of the constellation of forces that not only brought about but also sustained them over time, in the process transforming them and giving them their distinctive flavor. Their consolidation and subsequent institutionalization permit, in turn, the study of the internal balance of those forces which, according to Linz, allow us to speak of "limited pluralism" as a distinctive characteristic of authoritarian regimes.

Still, it is this very distinctness which, in my mind, raises the questions regarding the extent to which we can extrapolate general propositions from the Portuguese and Spanish experiences. More specifically, time, in the concrete form of the longevity of a regime, inevitably becomes a variable that cannot easily be ignored in any attempt to study authoritarian regimes systematically. Taken as a variable, time is important to the extent that it relates to the success or failure of any given regime to institutionalize itself. In that sense, the use of Spain and Portugal as typical examples of authoritarian regimes may pose some problems in that their very longevity and long-achieved institutionalization could obscure certain characteristics of shorter-lived authoritarian regimes which may have a bearing on the comparative analysis, and on improved understanding of regime crises and transitions.

It is in this light, then, that I should like to focus on the recent Greek authoritarian regime and on the conditions leading up to the 1974 transition to democratic rule in that country. The much shorter life of the colonels' regime and also its establishment, unlike that of its Portuguese and Spanish counterparts, in an international, or at least European, climate that was hardly receptive to its ideas, make the Greek regime a useful tool for comparison and for juxtaposition with which to attempt to confirm, deny, or modify some of the tentative theoretical generalizations regarding authoritarian regimes that have been formulated in the literature in recent years.[2]

The nature, meaning, and long-term significance of the 1974 transition from authoritarian to democratic rule in Greece have been the subject of various and conflicting interpretations. Some have hailed it as a "return to normalcy"; others have questioned the significance of the change brought about by the return of the military to the barracks by pointing out the various undeniable continuities linking the post-1974 democratic regime with its immediate or recent, but discredited, predecessors. Among the proponents of the continuity theory, two versions seem to have gained wide acceptance. According to the first, the transition was more apparent than real since it resulted in the return to power of the same political leader and of the same political forces that had dominated Greek political life in the post-World War II period. A more radical version of the continuity theory considers the post-1974 regime as only marginally different from its immediate predecessor since, like the latter, it owes its existence to decisions taken outside Greece, decisions that, ostensibly, constitute just a more recent example of a long series of foreign interventions, overt or covert, in modern Greek politics.[3]

Of the two interpretations, the latter—which tends to be more popular among a certain segment of the Greek Left—is clearly the more treacherous, because of its simplistic and disorienting methodological implications. Both, however, suffer from a common weakness: their failure to appreciate that, alongside the return of Karamanlis and of the Greek Right to power in 1974, the internal balance of power of the Greek political system has been deeply affected by the significant structural changes that have taken place in Greek society over the past thirty years. The most obvious political manifestations of these are: the emergence of the Panhellenic Socialist Movement (PASOK) as the second largest party in the land and as the major opposition party in Parliament; the crushing defeat of the traditional Center political forces; the elimination of the monarchy as the pivotal issue in Greek politics; and the establishment of what, by all accounts, is the most openly democratic regime in modern Greek history.[4]

Far from reflecting the ephemeral verdict of a volatile electorate, these developments constitute, on the contrary, evidence of long-term societal changes in Greece, changes that have already resulted in the first significant opening up of the Greek political system in more than half a century, and that are certain to influence its future evolution. To the extent that they bear directly on the nature and particular dynamics of the 1974 transition to demo-cratic rule in Greece, but also because they help throw light on the long-term social and political mobilization affecting the development of the Greek polit-ical system, these changes have to be analyzed in greater depth, and to be placed within the context of the evolution of the Greek political system in the last fifty years, and especially since World War II.

At the risk of overschematization, I would argue that there are three major aspects of the Greek political system of the interwar period: first, what came to be called the "schism" or *dichasmos* of the Greek nation into two mili-tantly opposed camps, one revolving around the Greek monarch, the other around Eleftherios Venizelos, the great Greek statesman of the early twentieth century. The clash of the latter with King Constantine over what ostensibly was merely a constitutional issue in 1915 gave rise to a passionate division of the Greek middle class into Venizelists and anti-Venizelists, a division that soon spilled over into the entire society, and consumed all its attention and energies for the remainder of the interwar period. The social bases of the "national schism" are extremely complex and, to this day, remain largely unexplored. Still, there is little doubt that, to a certain extent at least, the intensity of this intrabourgeois conflict was intimately related to the passage of Greek society from its precapitalist to a more fully capitalist phase. Though this process had its origins in the latter part of the nineteenth century, it was not until the years after 1912 that it acquired a significant and sustained momentum that was to lead to major structural changes in the decade of the 1920s. The acute, indeed passionate, conflict between Venizelism and anti-Venizelism reflects diverging strategies on how that transformation was to be effected, pitting the more traditional and conservative elements of the Greek bourgeoisie d'état against the more liberal commercial and incipient indus-trial sections of the middle class. More than anything else, this division was to dominate interwar politics and society, and to subsume all other conflicts within its bounds.[5]

The second major feature of the interwar Greek political system springs from the devastating military defeat suffered by the Greek armed forces during the Greek-Turkish War of 1919–22, in the course of a vain attempt to realize the century-old Greek irredentist aspiration of uniting under the Greek flag all the Greek-speaking populations in the Ottoman Empire. The defeat of the

Greek armies, indicatively known in Greek as "*the* Catastrophe," had two far-ranging consequences: first, it resulted in the uprooting of over one and a half million Greek-speaking inhabitants of the Ottoman Empire who, mostly as destitute refugees, arrived in Greece in the space of a few months. Their presence in Greece during the period when Greek society was experiencing rapid change had an undoubted impact on interwar social and political developments. Politically, the support that the refugees extended to the Venizelist camp seriously affected the internal balance of power by enhancing the strength of the liberal, antimonarchist forces. Economically and socially, the ready availability of a huge number of potentially employable, uprooted, and impoverished individuals benefited not only the Greek economy during the critical phase of its industrial "takeoff," but also, and inevitably, strengthened the social and political power of the small but growing Greek working class.

On the ideological level, the Greek defeat of 1922 signaled the end of Greek irredentism, and the irreversible loss of the "Great Idea," that potent expression of modern Greek nationalism which, for a century following Greek independence, had fired nationalist aspirations and acted as a powerful ideological instrument of social demobilization and social control, managing to contain social conflict, and to impart some semblance of unity to a deeply fragmented society. Its death left Greece with a huge ideological vacuum precisely at the time when it was badly shaken by defeat and the new social forces and increased tensions produced by the rapid transformation of Greek society rendered all the greater the need for an ideological principle of legitimation.

Indeed, the third salient characteristic of the Greek political system in the interwar period was the slow but unmistakable rise in social and political pressures which, because of the weakness of Greek capitalist development, and because of the powerful hold of the Great Idea, had, until then, remained relatively undeveloped and politically quiescent. Augmented in numbers by the rapid socioeconomic change, and through the influx of refugees (who, free from the ideologically inhibiting influences of the Great Idea, were more inclined to engage in political struggles), these new social strata were to play a significant role in the politics of interwar Greece.[6]

The years following the 1922 Greek defeat were critical for the development of the Greek political system not merely because of the simultaneous existence of these three factors but also because of their intimate interrelationship and their cumulative impact upon a weak liberal regime which was patently ill equipped to face severe social and political strains and turmoil. The years between 1922 and the imposition of the Metaxas dictatorship in 1936 are, from the perspective of this analysis, increasingly marked by two developments: the rising demands of the working classes for a greater share of the social goods and services; and the determination of the fragile and divided Greek middle class to safeguard the Greek liberal state from what it perceived to be a mortal threat. To be clearly understood, the reaction of the Greek middle class has to be placed within its proper domestic and international contexts. Shaken by the after-effects of defeat and humiliation in Asia Minor, bitterly divided over the issue of monarchy versus republic, deprived of the powerful ideological instrument of legitimation which the Great Idea had long represented, mired in a psychological climate of despair and broken morale, surrounded by an international situation marked by the social and political convulsions of the world war, gripped by the fear the Bolshevik victory in Russia had created throughout the liberal regimes in the West, faced with a serious financial crisis and with massive domestic problems, the Greek middle class reacted defensively to the increasing wave of social agitation, and to the mounting disaffection of the working class, by taking a series of repressive measures designed to safeguard what came to be described in Greek legal texts as the "established social order." The newly founded Communist party of Greece, which claimed the allegiance of the most militant segment of the small Greek working class, became the major target of these measures, despite its objective inability to challenge directly the Greek middle class's control of political power. The Metaxas dictatorship represents the final act in a process of gradual reconciliation between the two separate segments of the Greek middle class, a strategic closing of ranks in the face of the ostensible common enemy, the ultimate purpose of which was to deny the rural and urban working classes fuller participation in the political system. The closed nature of that system was further reinforced by the restoration of the monarchy, which had been abolished in 1923, in the wake of the Asia Minor defeat, and was ultimately guaranteed by the armed forces which, following an unsuccessful Venizelist coup in 1935, had been thoroughly purged of liberal (republican, Venizelist) elements, and had emerged as the ultimate bulwark of the regime.

Under these circumstances, and within an international environment marked by the crisis of democratic regimes and the rise of Fascism, the anti-Communist state slowly emerged in Greece. Indeed, anti-Communism and the defensive mentality that it exemplifies can be regarded as the mechanism employed by the Greek middle class to fill the ideological vacuum created by the collapse of the Great Idea. Put somewhat differently, anti-Communism was the ideological instrument of legitimation adopted by a fragile and insecure liberal regime faced with territorial loss, psychological withdrawal, a profound sense of malaise, moral crisis and despair, and by the need to consolidate itself against real or perceived enemies, external or internal.[7]

It was not, however, until the dramatic events of the 1940s, and especially of the Civil War (1946–49), that anti-Communism was transformed from a mere instrument of state legitimation to the governing principle of an aggressive strategy of social demobilization and of social control designed to safeguard the closed nature of the Greek political system, to reinforce it and, above all, to ensure its perpetuation. If the rise of the anti-Communist state in Greece has to be understood in the context of the deep crisis created by the national schism and by the Asia Minor defeat, the key to its postwar expansion, consolidation, and institutionalization lies in the mortal threat posed by the rise, during the Axis occupation, of a massive resistance movement which, irrespective of the specific political orientation of individual organizations, represented an unmistakable rejection of the discredited institutions of the interwar political system—further tainted by its association with the Metaxas authoritarian interlude—and a clear preference for a more open system which would allow new entrants to organize autonomously, and to participate fully.

It was in the course of the Civil War that the legal-institutional nexus, which was to dominate state-society relations in Greece until 1974–75, was slowly erected. This crucial fact is clearly borne out by an important recent study on the subject which points out that the "significance of these measures lies not so much in their application during the course of the civil war, but in the fact that, by means of an astute juridical construction, they survived the tensions of the 1940s practically intact, and did not cease from being vigorously applied until recently." The distinctive characteristic of this "paraconstitution," which operated alongside, and in flagrant violation of, crucial provisions of the liberal Greek 1952 Constitution, was the division of Greek citizens into two mutually exclusive categories: the "nationally minded" who included supporters of the militantly anti-Communist political system; and those whose commitment to the "political regime" and to the "established social order" could be questioned and who, therefore, were to be denied equal rights of participation in the system through a variety of repressive and arbitrary laws and executive decrees.[8]

Indeed, the postwar Greek political system is indelibly marked by the effort of a politically triumphant but deeply traumatized Greek Right to institutionalize the anti-Communist state in Greece, and thereby to safeguard the exclusivist nature of the system and its own political ascendancy. The success of the strategy employed in pursuit of this goal depended ultimately on the close cooperation of three major institutions: the armed forces, the crown, and the political leadership of the Greek Right in Parliament.

Already purged of liberal, Venizelist elements in 1933 and 1935, the Greek officer corps underwent further massive "purification" in 1943–44 and, finally, during the Civil War. Thus, by the early 1950s, the main characteristics of the Greek military were militant anti-Communism, anti-Venizelism, monarchism, and antiparliamentarism. In addition, the armed forces acquired, in the course of the Civil War, an institutional autonomy vis-à-vis the civil authorities which further accentuated their role as ultimate prop and arbiter of the regime, and as a major actor in the operation of the political system. Though this autonomy was legally terminated in 1951, an enlarged and extremely elastic definition of "national security" kept a wide array of normally civil responsibilities within the realm of the armed forces' competence.[9]

Having returned to Greece through the sheer determination of Britain (and especially of Churchill), the Greek crown owed its power within the postwar Greek political system to two major factors: first, that it was able to emerge as the champion of the anti-Communist cause, and to receive the support of the Greek Right; second, because of its pivotal position as the rallying point for

Greek anti-Communists it received massive political support from the British, and, after 1947, the U.S. governments.

Having survived the challenge posed to their continued political preeminence by the almost universal demand of the major resistance organizations for structural changes in the Greek political system, the traditional political parties emerged practically intact from the crisis of the Civil War. In fact, the undoubted beneficiary of the defeat of the Left, the outlawing of the Communist party of Greece, the polarization of the electorate, and, above all, the emergency legislation which lay the foundations for the paraconstitution and for the institutionalization of the anti-Communist state in Greece was the traditional Greek Right. Enriched by the adhesion of a number of erstwhile liberals and Venizelists who had made their peace with the crown, the Right dominated the Greek political scene throughout the 1950s, first under the leadership of Marshal Alexander Papagos, and, after his death in 1955, under Constantine Karamanlis.

The Right's eleven years of uninterrupted rule (1952–63) should be analyzed on two levels. On the first—the political-institutional level—the efficient use and systematic application of the legal and quasi-legal apparatus inherited from the Civil War; the undeniable momentum which victory in the war had generated; the inevitable quiescence of the opposition; and the strongly anti-Communist atmosphere in the West and in the NATO alliance, which Greece had joined in 1952, allowed the Greek Right to consolidate its political power, and to institutionalize the anti-Communist state in Greece. Despite small and ephemeral victories here and there, the Center and Left parties remained effectively isolated, fragmented, and politically marginal for most of the decade.[10]

On the second or socioeconomic level, however, the decade of the 1950s was a period of far-reaching structural changes. Unlike Portugal and Spain which, during the same period, were still pursuing policies of relative isolation and of low growth, Greece, in urgent need of internal reconstruction and of economic development following a decade of destructive foreign occupation and Civil War, opted for a policy of full integration into the international market, and for rapid growth. Aided by monetary and political stability, by low wages, and by significant emigration of unskilled workers, Greek capitalism made impressive strides, achieving an average rate of growth of 6 percent throughout the decade. However, this development was sharply uneven. The social dislocation and disintegration that rapid change brings about were exacerbated by the growing inequalities within the industrial labor force and the lower middle classes. The resulting social and political discontent became apparent in the late 1950s, and took a much more crystallized form in the early 1960s. The election victory of the Center Union party in 1963, and again in 1964, was evidence that the politically repressive, exclusivist parliamentary system in Greece could not survive without changes. Such changes, however, were bound to affect some of the main institutional pillars of the political system, and to alter fundamentally the distribution of power among them.

The great dilemma faced by the Greek political system at that specific juncture was succinctly summarized by Nicos Mouzelis: "Either parliament, through its opening up to the masses, had to become the dominant force in this [throne, armed forces, Parliament] triarchy, in which case the army would lose its leading position with inevitable internal consequences for those holding posts within it; or else, the army had to prevent this by the overall abolition of parliamentary rule."[11]

In the light of the preceding analysis, then, the 1967 coup should be regarded as an attempt by the Greek Right to safeguard its political ascendancy by forestalling a democratization of the political system which would have allowed recently mobilized sectors of Greek society to play an autonomous role in the political process. On another level, however, the coup constituted evidence of a radical redistribution of power within the triarchy on which the Right's postwar dominance had rested. As such, the coup signified the attempt by the armed forces to assert their full autonomy vis-à-vis their erstwhile partners, now seen as corrupt and incapable of defending the integrity of the formula upon which the postwar political system had been based, in order to ensure the perpetuation of the anti-Communist state in Greece. Their action was thus the last step in a long process of progressive autonomization through which, ever since 1935, and especially since the Civil War, they had been allowed to emerge as the ultimate guarantor of the exclusivist state in Greece. The passage to authoritarian rule, finally, meant that the "paraconstitution"—the unofficial reality on which the operation of the anti-Communist state had depended throughout the period of parliamentary government—had finally become the official constitution, and the governing principle of the new regime. In the final analysis, the Greek attempt at "guided democracy" had failed, as the authoritarian element in the formula of governance, devised during and after the Civil War, had slowly superseded and eventually engulfed the pluralist.

The fundamental weakness of the colonels' regime was its failure to consolidate, to institutionalize, and to legitimate itself. A study of the circumstances under which their efforts fell far short of their goal suggests, in broad outline, the qualitative differences distinguishing the Greek from the Portuguese and Spanish experience with authoritarian rule. Instituted at a time when the legitimacy of democratic rule was clearly on the defensive, the Iberian regimes could, during their critical initial phases of consolidation and institutionalization, count on the general climate of psychological insecurity and fear, brought about by the international economic crisis, the apparent collapse of the liberal democratic order, and widespread unemployment, to promote social order and discipline. Similarly, the strong wave of protectionism and isolationism fostered by these international conditions further facilitated the consolidation of the authoritarian regimes in Spain and Portugal by providing the protective vacuum within which they could grow relatively free of international pressures, whether economic or political. Finally, distance from the main theaters of war during 1940–45 made it much easier for Franco and Salazar to pursue, more or less unhindered throughout the 1940s and most of the 1950s, policies of political and economic isolation, and of low economic growth designed to avoid the social dislocations and political turbulence caused by the social and political mobilization of sectors excluded from full participation in the political system. Thus, under fairly unusual, if not unique, circumstances, an initially receptive international political climate, an international economic situation conducive to isolationism and protectionism, and a subsequent period of international indifference and neglect combined to provide both regimes with time to consolidate their hold over their respective societies, to institutionalize themselves, and to gain and maintain a considerable degree of legitimacy among strategic segments of the society.[12]

By contrast, the international climate facing the Greek regime in 1967 could hardly have been more different. In Europe, which was the region with the greatest political, economic, and cultural influence upon Greece, except for the United States, the disrepute into which authoritarian rule had fallen since the days of Fascist experiments; the widespread acceptance of the legitimacy of democratic rule and of pluralist politics; the multiplicity of international organizations committed, with varying degrees of intensity, to the preservation and defense of democratic politics; and the high degree of integration of the international (especially the European) system—certainly by comparison with the situation that prevailed in the 1930s—combined to create a situation marked, above all, by the absence of compartmentalization. There were no interstices where a newly established authoritarian regime could, with minimum external interference and pressure, slowly attempt to cope with the critical problems of regime consolidation, institutionalization, and legitimation.[13]

At the risk of overschematization, I would argue that, in their attempt at regime consolidation and regime building, the Greek colonels were caught in four major dilemmas which were to plague them throughout their seven-year rule, and which were to contribute decisively to their downfall. These dilemmas were: the political cohesion of the anti-Communist bloc; the ideological legitimation of the regime; economic development; and, finally, liberalization which overarched the others, and emerged as a necessary, though by no means a desired, alternative whenever the contradictory forces inherent in the other dilemmas tended to lead to policy impasses.

The breakup of the internal cohesion of the conservative coalition was one of the major problems created by the military's attempt unilaterally to gain full autonomy within the Greek political system. Suddenly cut off from the exercise of power, the throne and the parliamentary Right reacted by withdrawing their support from the new regime. The opposition of the crown, latent from the start, open during the ill-planned and ill-executed countercoup of 13 December 1967, and muted but continuous after that, meant that a significant and politically powerful segment of the Greek political establishment refused to act as an instrument of legitimation for the new regime. Even more significant, from the perspective of the internal cohesion of the armed forces, the clash between crown and colonels resulted in a sharp split within the Greek officer corps, pitting the vast majority of the navy officers and large numbers of their air force counterparts against their army colleagues. Though the problem of the crown's opposition became less acute following the king's flight to Italy, and the purging of royalist officers who became implicated in the failed coup, it was by no means overcome. Indeed, the 1973 attempt by Papadopoulos to establish a republic in Greece was, in one real sense, clear evidence of the intractable problem of legitimacy *within* the Greek Right which the royalist camp's enduring alienation continued to pose for the Greek authoritarian regime.[14]

Much as the opposition of the crown and its allies represented a serious obstacle to the regime's attempts at consolidation and institutionalization, what rendered the split within the Right lasting was the quasi-unanimous refusal of the parliamentary Right to cooperate with the military, and to lend their regime a badly needed mantle of legitimacy.[15] Three factors, above all, seem to have contributed decisively to this, the major *political* contradiction of the regime, and the greatest impediment to the colonels' legitimation strategy: first, the attempt, by means of the crudest form of virulent anti-Communist rhetoric, to resuscitate the most extreme aspects of the anti-Communist state which fading memories, generational change, and the rapid structural transformation of Greek society had rendered obnoxious to the vast majority of the Greek population; second, the unqualified rejection of Greek parliamentary institutions, which were uniformly characterized as "corrupt," "permissive," and easily susceptible to Communist penetration and subversion; and third, the vicious attacks on the Greek parliamentary elite, which was denounced for its alleged ineptitude and corruption, and held responsible for the "degeneration of the moral rectitude" of the Greek people.

To a political class that had, for more than twenty years, successfully managed a political system that ingeniously combined parliamentary rule with an anti-Communist state in Greece, the attempt to force a choice between the authoritarian and the liberal elements of the political system, between the constitution and the paraconstitution, was all the more unacceptable, because it threatened them with permanent eclipse, and affronted their ideological commitment to "circumscribed parliamentarism."[16]

Thus, in an ironic turn of events, the colonels' attempt to resurrect militant anti-Communism as the rallying point around which to reunite the social and political forces opposed to the opening up of the political system backfired. Instead of the hoped-for polarization of the society along "Communist" versus "non-Communist" lines, it served rather as the catalyst which rendered overt a long-standing, latent conflict within the Greek Right between supporters of extraparliamentary, authoritarian rule, and proponents of a constitutional form of government, however severely circumscribed by paraconstitutional arrangements. The chief victim of this conflict was undoubtedly the unity of the anti-Communist Right in Greece, a development that resulted in the isolation of the military, and of their extreme right-wing adherents, and that posed an insuperable obstacle to their attempts at regime legitimation.[17] The absence of solid support among their natural constituency translated, in turn, into a crisis of legitimacy, and brought to the fore, much earlier than would have otherwise been the case, the need to consider liberalization of the regime as an alternative mechanism for ensuring the support of strategic elements of the Greek Right, and thus of obtaining legitimacy.

The very fact that liberalization had to be posed as a major issue at such an early stage points, once more, to the significant differences distinguishing the Greek from the Iberian experience with authoritarian rule. Neither Franco nor, for that matter, Gomes da Costa, Sinel Cordes, or Carmona had to face a deeply divided Right in their respective countries at the time of coming to power. On the contrary, whether because of the Civil War polarization in Spain, or because of the bankruptcy of the Republic in Portugal, both regimes assumed power with significant support from within their natural constituencies—support galvanized, in the case of Spain, by war and anti-Communism, and in Portugal by the revulsion felt by most of the military, the church, businessmen and bankers, as well as landed aristocrats, for the Republic. Neither Iberian regime found it necessary to consider alternative mechanisms of legitimation. Hence, liberalization was not a necessary option. Indeed, the intervening war and cold war atmosphere would postpone consideration of such an alternative until the late 1950s for Spain, and the 1960s for Portugal.[18]

From the very start, the Greek regime's arsenal of ideological weapons included an appeal to the mystical values of the Hellenic nation, a call for the return to the authentic Greco-Christian tradition (expressive of the deep-seated xenophobia of Eastern Orthodoxy vis-à-vis the West), and an extensive use of anti-Communist slogans. Yet, without a doubt, the regime's ideological legitimation strategy assigned a preeminent role to the eventual return to democratic institutions and competitive politics. Even the utterances of the most militant among the colonels spoke not of a total abandonment of democratic practices, and an alternative model of political organization for Greek society, but of a *restoration* of democracy, and of the creation of a "healthy" and "regenerated" political system.

This paramount concern with the reestablishment of political institutions that would bear testimony to principles of democratic and competitive politics is sufficient evidence of the radically different context, both domestic and international, within which the Greek authoritarian regime, by contrast to its Iberian counterparts, had to seek its legitimacy. The profound crisis of confidence in liberal institutions during the 1930s, as well as the simultaneous existence of an alternative model of government, made Franco's and Salazar's choices much easier, and their legitimation strategies much simpler. Both the *Estado Novo* and the Franco state could speak of their efforts to rebuild Portugal and Spain in positive terms, utilizing a conception of the political organization of their respective societies that looked and *was* different from what had been tried and discarded, and which promised to usher into a new era free of class conflict, civil strife, endless political instability, and malaise.[19]

In Greece, on the other hand, the crisis of parliamentary institutions which preceded and, to a certain extent, contributed to the creation of a climate conducive to the installation of the colonels' regime was qualitatively different in at least two cardinal ways. First, it represented a bankruptcy of the institutions of the anti-Communist state, and not a loss of faith in the democratic process.[20] On the contrary, increasing pressure placed upon the exclusivist political system by social forces barred from participation in it, and clamoring for democratization and for an autonomous role within a more liberalized system, led to the crisis of confidence in these institutions. Second, the reigning international climate in the 1960s was one of unquestionable legitimacy of pluralist democracy, and of equally undoubted rejection of authoritarian rule. Greece was a member of a large number of international organizations that professed their commitment to democratic principles; and some of these reacted strongly to the imposition of authoritarian rule in the country. In short, the near impossibility of disengaging from what in the 1960s was a mostly hostile international community meant that, unlike its Spanish and Portuguese counterparts, the Greek authoritarian regime could not benefit from a protective vacuum created by a climate of international isolation and indifference in its initial efforts to gain legitimacy at home. Hence the need to consider liberalization as an alternative strategy of legitimation despite all the pitfalls that such a course of action entailed for a regime that had not yet succeeded in consolidating itself, and which lacked the solid support of its natural constituency. Indeed, one of the significant advantages of liberalization was precisely that it could be geared at two targets at the same time: the public at large and the parliamentary Right. And cooperation of some sort with part of the political world of the Right would be a major boon in the regime's search for legitimacy.

Economic development constituted more of an intractable set of problems than a dilemma for the new regime. As has been pointed out in a number of studies, and most recently by Mouzelis, economic growth in Greece from the mid-1950s on had resulted in uneven economic development, making for sharp inter- as well as intrasectoral differences, and resulting in increased inequalities within the industrial labor force and within the lower middle classes which colonized the tertiary sector. There can be little doubt that the social unrest and political mobilization of the early and middle 1960s were directly connected to the increased awareness, politicization, frustration, and resentment brought about by rapid but unequal change among these segments of the Greek population. Indeed, it was pressure from these very classes that began to place an intolerable strain on the institutions of the exclusivist political system of the post–Civil War years and which finally posed the dilemma of "repression or liberalization," and led to the 1967 coup.[21]

For as long as it was not realistically possible for the colonels to reverse the tide, however, and to arrest economic development in order to put a brake on long-term social mobilization, the basic dilemma remained, and was compounded by the regime's decision to opt for liberalization as a mechanism of legitimation. There can be little doubt that the regime's commitment to continued economic growth made the prospects for successful liberalization even more difficult, if only to the extent that, for as long as the doctrine of rapid economic growth remained unquestioned, popular expectations continued to rise, bringing with them the danger of more frustration, resentment, discontent, and potential unrest.

I would not argue, of course, that doing away with rapid economic growth as a goal was a realistic option for the colonels. Given the degree of Greece's integration in the international market, the extent to which the values associated with rapid economic growth had been internalized by the Greek population, and the benefits derived from such growth had become a part of life, a reversal of that policy was politically impossible. If an alternative existed for the colonels, it was more the bureaucratic-authoritarian model described by Guillermo O'Donnell. The decision, however, to use liberalization as a legitimation strategy effectively precluded that option. Rather, the purpose of this argument is to point to the problems that economic development and its concomitant, social and political mobilization, posed for the successful consolidation and legitimation of the Greek authoritarian regime, and, once again, to contrast the Greek with the Iberian experience. In the latter case, the prevailing economic crisis and rampant protectionism of the 1930s, combined with the isolation provided by neutrality during World War II, rendered feasible in the 1950s the pursuit, in both Spain and Portugal, of economic policies of low growth which avoided the hazards of rapid social and political mobilization. In Spain and Portugal, unlike Greece, regime institutionalization and legitimation were effected without the dangers posed by simultaneous rapid economic growth.[22]

Liberalization posed a double problem for the colonels: how to proceed with it so as to ensure the adherence of those segments of the population which would contribute to the regime's legitimation; and, at the same time, contain it in such a way that regime consolidation would not be endangered, and its long-term prospects not undermined. This problem and the dilemma that it encompassed are, I believe, graphically reflected in the regime's two constitutions, and in the different rationale by which each was presented to the population.

Prepared by a committee of jurists, and not by a constituent assembly; presented to the voters in a frenetic propaganda campaign designed to ensure its approval, and benefiting from the official prohibition of an opposition campaign; voted upon in a plebiscitary fashion under a state of siege, and of continuing martial law, the Constitution of 1968 had three major targets: the public at large, the parliamentary Right, and the crown. To the first, the new charter offered the familiar trappings of constitutional government, parliamentary rule, and provisions regarding civil liberties and rights. The substance of the bid to gain the support of the second group lay in the reinstitution of parliamentary practices of a kind that was thoroughly familiar to the Greek Right. It was, in effect, an attempt to placate those who would wish to be placated, and to offer them a chance to continue to do what they had been doing since Civil War days, albeit under stricter supervision by the armed forces. By maintaining the so-called fundamental clauses of the 1952 Constitution intact, the colonels hoped to gain the adherence of the crown and of its loyal allies inside and outside Parliament. It was in this hope, in fact, that they allowed the monarchical aspects of that constitution to be retained in the first draft of the committee of jurists which was submitted on 23 December 1967, just ten days after King Constantine's failed countercoup.[23]

To be sure, the liberal trappings of the new document were counterbalanced by more authoritarian elements designed to ensure the army's control of political power and, thus, to advance the regime's consolidation. Two devices were employed in order to render such control effective: the complete, though covert, autonomization of the armed forces vis-à-vis the civilian government, which was rendered incapable of intervening in the internal affairs of the armed forces, including the promotion of officers at the highest levels; and, second, a vastly expanded definition of "national security" which made it easy for the military to invoke whenever it judged that "the existing political regime, and the established social order" were being threatened by internal or external dangers.[24]

In this two-pronged formula, the functional and administrative autonomy of the armed forces vis-à-vis the civil authorities represented the structural mechanism through which the affairs of state could conveniently, if unrealistically, be divided into two domains: one encompassing the "vital" interests of the nation and assigned, therefore, exclusively to the armed forces; and a second, involving the "day-to-day" affairs which could safely be entrusted to the civilian government. The vastly enlarged definition of national security, on the other hand, provided the dynamic through which the whole system could be put into operation by allowing the armed forces, as guardians of the nation, to invade the areas officially outside their reserved domain in case they perceived a threat to the "existing political regime and established social order." The net result of such an arrangement would be to grant the military a preponderant role in the political organization of civil society, and to ensure the institutionalization of the Greek authoritarian regime.[25]

As a final insurance against the dangers inherent in too early a return to "normalcy," even one that was so severely, though covertly, "controlled" from within, the colonels put the new constitution "into force" on 15 November 1968, but postponed its "application" until some unspecified time in the future. Placing the constitution in suspended animation was an astute act designed to buy time during which to build bridges toward the royalist and parliamentary camps, and to search for allies whose adherence would make it possible to place the system in operation, an act that would contribute decisively to the regime's chances of institutionalization and legitimation.

Over the next five years the colonels repeatedly sought to overcome the problems stemming from the continuing refusal of the crown and of the major, as well as most of the secondary, figures of the parliamentary Right to make their peace with the regime. Frustrated with the fruitlessness of his long discussions with a number of political figures who flirted with the idea of joining forces with the regime, but never crossed the critical threshold; faced with mounting evidence of division within the armed forces, and of increasing opposition within the society, especially the students; confronted, finally, with an unsuccessful coup organized within the traditionally proroyalist navy in May 1973, George Papadopoulos, already the regime's strongman, made a new bid for legitimacy, this time in the form of a more authoritarian constitution prescribing a "presidential parliamentary republic." The chief characteristics of the new constitution were two. First, it attempted to derive legitimacy out of the repudiation of the monarchy, long a source of intense and divisive controversy in Greek politics, and, more to the point, no longer, after its suspected implication in the navy's coup, a potential political asset for the regime. And second, it concentrated in the hands of the president of the new Republic, a post that Papadopoulos filled himself in a plebiscite barring an opposition candidate, of such extensive powers as to render the presidency the pivotal force of the new system.

Bidding for a new legitimacy, and no longer constrained by the need to make concessions to the monarchy, the Constitution of 1973 rendered overt the division of state affairs into "national" and "ordinary" which, however covertly, was already present in its predecessor. The president of the Republic, elected by universal suffrage for seven years, was invested with both legislative and executive competence in the areas of national defense and national security, public order, and foreign affairs in which he named ministers responsible only to himself, and not to Parliament. As supreme head of the armed forces, which he governed through the newly created post of "chief of the armed forces," he commanded, in addition, such a vast array of weapons as to be a veritable "superpresident" before whom the elected representatives of the country and their government were practically powerless, their role, in essence, being limited to that of executive organs carrying out decisions taken elsewhere.[26]

As the November 1973 events were to demonstrate so dramatically, however, the ultimate weakness of this construction was that it rested, after all, on too delicate a balance between an immensely expanded presidency—an institution that, in this new form, was entirely untried in Greece—and the armed forces, and depended for its continued smooth operation on the complete cooperation between these two institutions. The withdrawal of support by the armed forces could easily bring the whole edifice down.

As concrete evidence that the rationale of "suspended animation" was being abandoned, and that the country was being steadily led back to "normalization," the state of siege was lifted throughout Greece, a broad amnesty freed most political prisoners, constitutional guarantees of civil liberties were officially put into effect, and parliamentary elections were promised for no later than the end of 1974. This time, the search for legitimacy received a major boost by the decision of Spyros Markezinis—the head of the tiny Progressive party, but a figure of prominence and controversy within the Greek Right, and certainly an established member of the Greek political elite with strong, though turbulent, ties to the Greek monarchy—to assume the responsibility of forming a government, and to lead the country to elections, within the timetable prescribed by Papadopoulos. The Markezinis experiment, which began on 8 October 1973, when his government—free of military and with less than one-third carry-overs from the previous cabinet—was sworn into office, represented the most serious attempt yet by the Greek authoritarian regime to attain legitimacy through liberalization, and to institutionalize itself. Had Markezinis succeeded in his goal of turning power over to the civilian political elite, albeit under the constraints imposed by Papadopoulos's streamlined "democracy," it is a fair guess that the regime would have cleared a critical hurdle in its search for a broader base of support, and would have gained a minimum degree of wider acceptance that was the sine qua non of its viability in a form other than that of sheer repression.[27]

In the end, the student uprising of the National Polytechnic, coming as it did during this most delicate moment, shook the regime to its foundations, obliged to resort to even greater force, and led to an internal coup which imposed the rule of the hard-liners and the military police over the moderates within the Greek junta. Broken, disoriented, and relying increasingly on repression, the new and harsher version of the colonels' regime drifted on for seven more months before the external crisis created by its folly in Cyprus brought it down for good, ensuring the return of the old Greek political elite under highly traumatic circumstances.[28]

There can be no doubt that the Cyprus debacle was the immediate cause for the regime's collapse, yet it is equally true that the regime had suffered irreparable damage as a result of the November 1973 Polytechnic events. Coming at the end of a growing number of acts of defiance against the regime throughout 1973, acts that included mounting student unrest in the universities during the first months of the year; a sharply worded statement by Karamanlis from Paris in April warning of "grave dangers" for Greece if the military regime continued in power; and, above all, the foiled navy countercoup in late May, which prompted the abolition of the monarchy and the proclamation of the republican constitution; the November confrontation did not represent an isolated challenge to the regime. On the contrary, it was the last in a series of actions that tended to place the regime on the defensive at the same time that it emboldened its opposition.

In fact, the Polytechnic events represented the moment when the belated attempt to make up for lost time, and to move decisively away from "suspended animation" to a new reality came face to face with powerful political forces generated by long-term social mobilization, forces that had been contained since 1967, but which had continued to grow, to remain restless, and to represent a potential source of destabilization against which the regime sought to guard itself. Unable to bear the combined strain of liberalization and simultaneous political mobilization, the regime cracked, attempted to retreat in the illusory safety of repression, and eventually collapsed a few months later. Indeed, it is a major contention of this chapter that the collapse of the Greek authoritarian regime involves, at its very center, an inability to overcome the major difficulties created by the need to accommodate liberalization with social and political mobilization before institutionalization and legitimation had been secured. Given an international climate decidedly hostile to authoritarian rule, and the existence of significant social and political mobilization in the country, the Greek regime, unlike its Iberian counterparts, was unable to benefit from circumstances favorable to its legitimation and institutionalization without liberalization; instead, it was forced to pursue the latter in search of the former, and was unable to avoid conflict between regime and civil society which eventually brought about its demise.

Time, in the form of the longevity of a regime, is also of importance in understanding the different trajectories followed by the three authoritarian regimes as they approached "dissolution." In the Greek case, the existence of a significant degree of social and political mobilization, which had been achieved prior to the regime's coming to power, made institutionalization and legitimation all the more difficult, and forced the colonels to opt for liberalization before sufficient time had elapsed. In the case of Spain, which embarked upon a policy of rapid economic growth only in the late 1950s, social and political mobilization did not occur until almost thirty years after the installation of the regime; the regime had become institutionalized before it had to face the strains resulting from social and political mobilization. In Portugal, where social and political mobilization had, for all practical purposes, been contained almost to the end, the regime did not have to face a challenge to its strength arising from civil society.

When it comes to considering the causes for the eventual demise of authoritarian regimes, then, the different transition experiences of the three regimes might suggest a partial reformulation of the generalization proposed by Philippe Schmitter in his "Liberation by *Golpe.*" Rather than seeking "the sources of contradiction, necessary if not sufficient for the overthrow of authoritarian rule, . . . within the regime itself, within the apparatus of the state, not outside it in its relations with civil society," such a reformulation might introduce "social and political mobilization" as a variable in the process, and suggest that Schmitter's statement stands in cases such as Portugal, where social and political mobilization had been minimal; but that where such mobilization has occurred, the overthrow of an authoritarian regime is very much a function of its relations with civil society (Spain and Greece). To refine the point further, in countries where social and political mobilization chronologically precedes the installation of the regime, and acts as an impediment to its institutionalization, the regime overthrow tends to be the result of a breakdown arising out of its relations with civil society (Greece). Conversely, where such mobilization occurs after regime institutionalization, then the regime's overthrow, which again arises out of the inability to contain forces within civil society, can more easily take the form not of breakdown, but of self-dissolution and self-transformation (Spain).[29]

Time also affects the picture, by reinforcing the potential impact of global and political mobilization upon regime institutionalization. Where such mobilization precedes institutionalization, the need to obtain the latter acquires a great urgency, and may impose alternative and more precarious strategies designed to achieve it, but also capable of undermining it. Where the reverse situation obtains, the passage of time seems to act as a force that strengthens institutionalization, and renders the regime better equipped to face the strains that mobilization will eventually bring about.

The central role assigned to regime institutionalization in this chapter raises a relevant question. If a chief characteristic distinguishing an authoritarian regime from a mere dictatorship, as suggested by Linz and most observers, is precisely the presence or absence of institutionalization in the exercise of power, does the failure of the colonels to institutionalize deny the authoritarian nature of their regime? My answer would be that, by its very concern with constitutional formulations that sought to divide state affairs into "national" and "ordinary" so as to ensure the armed forces control over politics in Greece, the colonels' regime had all the characteristics of an incipient authoritarian regime seeking to render itself permanent. According to this analysis, opposition from within civil society and insufficient time prevented it from realizing its aims.

The remainder of this chapter will concentrate on the Greek transition *stricto sensu*. As such, it will focus on the relatively brief four-month period extending from the 20 July 1974 Cyprus crisis, which constitutes the formal *terminus ad quem* of the Greek authoritarian regime, to the 17 November 1974 parliamentary elections which mark the onset of the new democratic regime's consolidation phase. This shift in emphasis implies a corresponding shift in perspective away from the macrolevel factors which have concerned us thus far to the more conjunctional forces which tend to surge to the fore during such periods and which place a premium on human ability and ingenuity to cope with often fluid, uncertain, and unpredictable outcomes.

The transition phase of regime change involves a series of critical decisions and delicate political choices designed to cope with the problems relating to regime legitimation and enhancing the chances of its eventual consolidation. More specifically, these measures seek to: (1) ensure the active cooperation of social and political actors crucial to the maintenance of the momentum sustaining the regime-in-genesis; (2) secure the acquiescence of wavering but potentially hostile forces; (3) minimize the probability of regression, breakdown, and relapse to noncompetitive politics posed by calls for a return to the *status quo ante* or for immediate social and economic transformation; and (4) bring about the delegitimation of the predecessor regime among as many of the public as possible.[30]

How open-ended a transition is varies from case to case, because a variety of factors both domestic and international limit the degree of choice available to decision-makers. Thus, in Spain, the strength of the "bunker" and the issue of peripheral nationalisms posed definite and very real limits to the options entertained by the transition managers in that country. Conversely, the weakness of the extreme Right and the ease with which the disintegration of the authoritarian regime was brought about in Greece tended, in the short run, to create the impression of the absence of such limits, thereby facilitating the potential for a rapid radicalization of the situation.

In this context, the Greek case acquires particular interest because of an apparent paradox relating to the impact of the Cyprus crisis on the transition as a whole, but especially on its initial moments. On the one hand, the circumstances under which the crisis was brought about (a Greek-led coup against the government of Archbishop Makarios); its dismal handling; and the subsequent popular reaction to it, which revealed the enormity of the authoritarian regime's ineptitude and led to its immediate collapse and profound delegitimation, all created the possibility for radicalization and for a powerful "popular emergence," to use O'Donnell's and Schmitter's terminology. Indeed, the crowds that filled the streets of Athens and other major cities on 23 July, when the surrender of power to the civilians was being negotiated, pointed in that direction. What rendered radicalization even more likely was the additional fact that the badly managed general mobilization, spasmodically announced and carried out by the regime, had brought reserve officers and many civilians from the more radicalized urban centers to the countryside and gave the "popular emergence" a national dimension.[31]

At the same time, however, the very real threat of war which the crisis produced acted as a powerful counterweight, containing radicalizing forces, imposing self-restraint on mass actors, and producing a wave of national solidarity which greatly expanded the new civilian leadership's freedom of movement and effectively neutralized substantive opposition to its handling of the transition. To understand the dynamics of this process and to appreciate the extent of the change that it brought about, it is necessary to look at three contrasting transition strategies: (1) the outgoing regime's preference for a transfer of power; (2) the formulas for surrender of power envisaged by the civilian leadership in the "national council" convened by the moderate elements in the collapsing regime for that purpose; and (3) Karamanlis's own strategy for the democratization of the Greek political system.[32]

The outgoing regime's search for a formula that would make possible a transfer of power to a segment of its supporters has to be understood in the context of the internal divisions brought about by the suppression of the Polytechnic uprising in November 1973, the end of Papadopoulos's liberalization experiment, the rise of the *hard-liners* to power under Ioannides and his supporters within the military police and the lower ranks of the army, and the latters' deep involvement in the events that led to the Cyprus crisis and to the brink of war with Turkey. These events, starting on 21 July, the day following the mobilization order, produced a major split within the regime and led to the decision of the Joint Chiefs of Staff to seek a "political solution" out of what was fast threatening to become a major domestic crisis as well. Having gained the support of the regime-appointed president of the Republic, Lieutenant-General Phaedon Ghizikis, the Joint Chiefs, invoking the threat of war, reasserted the hierarchical lines of command within the armed forces and effectively neutralized the power base sustaining Ioannides and the *hard-liners*. This move signaled the distancing of the armed forces from the disintegrating regime and made easier the search for a transfer-of-power formula under their initial aegis.[33]

The Joint Chiefs' next move was to convene a meeting with selected civilian leaders to explore the specific format under which the transfer of power could be effected. Documentary evidence concerning the nature of the transfer of power envisaged by the military is scant. What has come to light, however, suggests that the Joint Chiefs' distinct preference lay in a transfer of power that would ensure the liberalization of the existing political system, leaving, at least initially, significant power in their and their moderate civilian supporters' hands, and containing the forces clamoring for more structural change. The very composition of the group brought together to act as a mechanism for the transfer of power points in that direction. Of the thirteen individuals sitting on it, five were military (the president of the Republic, and the chiefs of the armed forces, the army, the navy, and the air force); three (George Athanassiades-Novas, Petros Garoufalias, and Stefanos Stefanopoulos) were protagonists in the July 1965 royal intervention in Greek politics which destroyed the parliamentary majority of the ruling Center Union party and precipitated the grave political and constitutional crisis that ended with the imposition of military rule in April 1967; one, Markezinis, was the regime's handpicked candidate to head the liberalization experiment that ended dismally in November 1973; two (Panayotes Kanellopoulos and Evangelos Averoff-Tossizza) were prominent members of the parliamentary Right; one (Xenophon Zolotas) was a respected conservative banker; and just one, George Mavros, represented the moderate wing of the pre-1967 Center Union. Of these, only three, Kanellopoulos, Mavros, and, to a certain extent, Averoff-Tossizza, had become involved in overt resistance activities against the regime. Conspicuously absent were representatives of the country's Left and Left-of-Center forces, whether identified with the pre-1967 political formations or with the resistance to the regime.

Subsequent reconstructions of the group's deliberations provided by some of the participants throw further light on the outgoing regime transfer-of-power strategy. President Ghizikis initially expressed the wish that the military retain control of the "sensitive" ministries of National Defense, Public Order, and the Interior, but hastily withdrew it when confronted with strong objections by Mavros and Kanellopoulos. The chief of the Armed Forces, General Gregorios Bonanos, apparently hoped to promote Garoufalias, the king's intimate and the man who was to lead the proregime forces in the 1974 elections, to head the transitional government. Markezinis recommended a caretaker government under the conservative diplomat Christianos Xanthopoulos-Palamas, the minister of foreign affairs in his short-lived 1973 government. Ghizikis seems to have favored a "national government" format consisting of those present at the meeting.[34]

The transfer-of-power scenario favored by the military, and the preference for a liberalization that it so clearly implied, suffered from a fatal weakness: it was based on an essentially defensive strategy designed to end the external crisis and to contain its potential domestic repercussions. As such, it was unable to appreciate the need for a long-term solution that would respond to, and accommodate, the great popular expectations for a more open and inclusive political system which a generation of socioeconomic change and considerable radicalization during the seven years of authoritarian rule had produced. Not surprisingly, it was Kanellopoulos and Mavros, acknowledged leaders of the two political formations (National Radical Union and Center Union) that in the last elections before the 1967 coup had together received close to 90 percent of the popular vote, who proved most sensitive to this dimension of the crisis and who successfully opposed the liberalization scenario as a woefully inadequate response to the problem. Armed with the great authority they derived from their outspoken opposition to the regime, and capitalizing on their role as the recognized spokesmen for the two largest political parties in the country, the two sought, and initially obtained, authorization to form a transitional coalition government based on the two parties, with Kanellopoulos as its head and Mavros as deputy prime minister and minister of foreign affairs.

In opting for this solution, the informal emergency council managing the first moments of the transition signaled that it was prepared to acquiesce to a surrender-of-power scenario that would give ascendancy to the regime's moderate opponents, and would presumably bring about a partial restoration of the postwar political system, shorn of the most obnoxious and politically discriminatory elements that had led to its demise in 1965–67. It is within this context and the limited political democratization logic that underpins it that one has to understand the final decision to forgo the Kanellopoulos-Mavros solution and to opt instead for Constantine Karamanlis, the charismatic founder and former leader of the National Radical Union (ERE), as the best person to undertake such a difficult task.[35]

Leader of the anti-Communist Right during most of the 1950s, a powerful personality who had dominated Greek politics into the early 1960s and had gone into self-imposed exile in Paris following a clash with the monarchy and defeat in the 1963 elections which first brought the Center Union to power, Karamanlis had remained untarnished by direct involvement in the events that led to the demise of parliamentary politics in 1967. Acceptable to the military on account of his past anti-Communist record, he could also command the support and confidence of the nonroyalist Right and of large segments of the traditional Center, and he was tolerated as the lesser of two evils by monarchists opposed to the military regime. Therefore, he appeared to possess the ideal credentials for the delicate mission of not merely managing the transition crisis but also of presiding over an effort to construct an improved version of the postwar political system capable of coping with the uncertainties generated by political mobilization and radicalization among major segments of the electorate in the previous decade. Simply put, once the dynamic of the situation had made it clear that a mere transfer of power was no longer a viable option, Karamanlis emerged as a better candidate than Kanellopoulos and Mavros for carrying out a strategy of surrender of power that envisaged more a restoration of the previous system than an instauration of political democracy in Greece. The Karamanlis solution implied an unspoken decision to deemphasize the role of existing political parties in the transition process and suggested instead a preference for leadership that stood "above parties" and appealed to the "nation" as a whole. This perspective, which Karamanlis shared with those who recalled him and which was in conformity with his charismatic image, was best reflected in the fact that he was initially invested with sole political power and only subsequently appointed the first members of his government.[36]

What, above all, characterized Karamanlis's strategy during the 116 days between 24 July, when he was sworn into office, and 17 November, when his electoral triumph provided him with popularly derived legitimacy and independence vis-à-vis earlier partners and supporters at the elite level, was his studied attempt to minimize commitments to collective and individual actors, to personalize crisis management, to maximize his freedom of movement, and to create the preconditions for a genuine political democracy in Greece. The last goal, which went far beyond the assumptions and expectations of those who had recalled him, and which envisaged more a new democratic regime than a restoration of some improved version of the postwar political system, constituted Karamanlis's central long-term aim which, though unspoken at the outset, permeated his entire transition strategy and surfaced slowly over time.

In pursuit of these goals, Karamanlis adopted a deliberately gradualist course of action in which elements of continuity and change as well as substantive and symbolic acts were judiciously balanced in an effort to attain three distinct short-term objectives: (1) the maintenance, for as long as possible, of the unity of the founding coalition and of the momentum for national solidarity generated by humiliation over Cyprus and exhilaration at the fall of the military; (2) gradual distancing from, and eventual isolation of, the more recalcitrant and unreconstructed elements of the Right; and (3) the need to reassure, and even to placate, that significant part of public opinion and those emerging political forces which clearly favored a radical democratization of the postwar political system and a major change in the rules of the game.[37]

A deliberate mixture of continuity and change in Karamanlis's strategy was striking from the start. In addition to Karamanlis himself, the civilian cabinet sworn in on 25 and 26 July consisted of well-established political figures associated with the Right and Center-Right in postwar years. The new cabinet (much like the initial body that had engineered Karamanlis's recall) totally excluded the Center-Left forces identified with the Andreas Papandreou faction of the old Center Union, as well as the traditional Left, yet its inclusion of such figures as George Alexander Mangakis (hallowed by resistance activities against the colonels) and, in general, men with impeccable antijunta credentials was important on both symbolic and substantive grounds. It was the first oblique—and, at the time, unrecognized—indication of Karamanlis's intention to break with the recalcitrant anti-Communist Right, and to strive for a different balance in the new political system, in which the center of gravity would be located more toward the Center than the Right.

The same principle seems to have lain behind his decision to announce, on 1 August, the return to the 1952 Constitution as the interim law of the land, while suspending the articles pertaining to the monarchy; to maintain General Ghizikis as interim head of state, while stating that the nature of the permanent head of state would be settled in the near future, either by popular referendum or by a constituent assembly; to opt finally for a constituent assembly as the appropriate organ for the preparation of a new constitution, while restricting its role to that of a *revisionary* body. Similarly, he decided to return to prejunta legality by means of a series of constituent acts relating to the judiciary, the universities, the civil service, and local government, while, at the same time, freeing political prisoners, proclaiming a general amnesty for political crimes, and declaring Civil War and related postwar restrictive legislation to be no longer in force. He also legalized all political parties, thereby making it possible for the Communist party of Greece to operate in the open for the first time since the Civil War, and, more generally, for forces of the Left to participate legally and formally in the political system.[38]

Karamanlis's gradualism was equally evident in the careful timing of these measures, in the incremental approach adopted in the announcement of changes, and, especially, in the deliberately slow pace at which the government proceeded in dealing with the most sensitive and explosive popular demands: purges of the military, the state bureaucracy, the universities, the security forces, and, above all, the prosecution of the protagonists in the 1967 coup, in the suppression of the Polytechnic uprising, and in the torturing of prisoners during the seven-year authoritarian regime. Here, Karamanlis's attitude seems to have been largely determined by his justified fear of a military reaction in the event of a thorough purge, or even of one that was perceived as "excessive" among military and civilian quarters close to the fallen regime.[39]

The gradualist component of Karamanlis's transition strategy included three additional implicit assumptions: first, that these issues should not be directly addressed until after the election, when the legitimacy of the new civilian government would place it in a much better position to face such a delicate enterprise; second, that, before dealing with these intractable issues, measures had to be taken to ensure civilian control of a number of agencies and institutions (police, security services, intelligence agencies, chiefs of staff) whose loyalty would be a crucial precondition for the uneventful handling of these emotion-laden issues; and third, that, in the application phase of the strategy, a line had to be drawn between retiring, and therefore isolating, those officers implicated with the former regime, and prosecuting them for various offenses. This line he carefully observed until after the elections of 17 November.

It is characteristic that the only criminal prosecution proceedings initiated against protagonists of the colonels' regime prior to the elections were the result of a private suit, and did not involve government initiative. Equally significant, the case was not tried until almost nine months later, long after an overwhelming electoral victory had provided Karamanlis with unquestioned legitimacy, with independence vis-à-vis other actors in the transition, and with a crushing parliamentary majority—in excess of two-thirds of all seats. It was only after a foiled coup, in February 1975, that he was given the long-awaited opportunity to move decisively against adherents and sympathizers of the previous regime, and to eliminate a source of major potential resistance to further change without risking serious erosion of his political support.[40]

At this point in the transition, gradualism gave way to a policy of swift, decisive, credible but contained retribution. It was designed to enhance the legitimacy of the new regime, further to delegitimate its discredited predecessor, and, at the same time, to appear equitable, to avoid the potentially negative repercussions from too protracted a public focus on past traumas, and to prevent excesses that might undermine the climate of national solidarity so crucial to the regime's long-term consolidation chances. Thus, in less than six months, the protagonists of the 1967 coup, the leaders of the foiled February 1975 coup, together with the major figures in the suppression of the Polytechnic uprising, and in the torturing of prisoners during the seven-year regime were brought to trial, and received sentences ranging from life imprisonment for the major figures to lesser sentences for others. In line with the government's determination to avoid action of a potentially destabilizing and divisive nature, the death sentence handed down by the courts against the three leaders of the previous regime, George Papadopoulos, Stylianos Pattakos, and Nikolaos Makarezos, was immediately commuted to life imprisonment. The government's announcement of clemency significantly stated that "in the fair state, the work of justice is completed by the final procedure . . . which permits the reduction of sentences. In this final phase, a high sense of political responsibility must prevail."[41]

By the end of 1975, therefore, and despite opposition accusations that it had exercised excessive restraint, and that the commutation of the death sentences "smacked of a deal," the new Greek democratic regime had effectively dealt with what John Herz has recently referred to as the "legacy problem" crucial to the definition of a successor democratic regime's self-image, and for the demystification of its predecessor.[42]

If the conclusion of the various trials marks the natural end of the new government's policy for dealing with the "legacy problem," a series of actions taken early in the transition attests to the significance attached to this issue:

the immediate banning of the authoritarian regime's symbols, including the universally loathed "phoenix"; the prohibition of all references to the "revolution" as a term to describe the 1967 coup in school textbooks; the appointment of men with known antijunta and even leftist sentiments in key positions in the sensitive Ministry of Education; the early dismissal of junta appointees from the university system; and numerous official and unofficial utterances concerning the freedom of the press. All these constituted symbolic acts designed to serve the dual goal of demonstrating the new regime's unequivocal condemnation of its predecessor, and, equally important, to signal its determination to proceed with the democratization of the political system, and to work for the consolidation of democratic politics in Greece.

If a judicious mixture of continuity and change and deliberate gradualism in dealing with potentially divisive issues were conspicuous elements in Karamanlis's transition strategy, a less obvious but equally important component focused on the need to maximize the benefits that the circumstances of the surrender of power gave to the Center and Center-Right forces, and consequently to contain the opposition and neutralize the Left. In pursuit of these objectives, Karamanlis exploited the *carte blanche* context of his accession to power, ran an issueless campaign, took advantage of the colorless opposition provided by George Mavros's Center Union, and, above all, opted for elections sooner rather than later. He knew that an early election would allow his potentially more dangerous opposition, the recently surfaced Communist party and the newly formed PASOK, minimal time to mobilize or to articulate an effective electoral platform. It would also make it easier to give the whole event a plebiscitary flavor in which the slogan "Karamanlis or the tanks" would become the dominant theme, ensuring his success, and enabling him to proceed with the implementation of his consolidation strategy.

As noted earlier, this strategy, which went beyond the expectations of the predominantly conservative forces that had engineered his recall, sought to ensure consolidation through a genuine democratization of the political system designed to make it responsive to, and congruent with, the deep structural changes that had occurred in Greece over the previous quarter century. In the course of the transition, Karamanlis carefully sought to pave the way for such an eventuality by pursuing a policy of national reconciliation which put an end to the Civil War divisions perpetuated by the postwar exclusivist state, and by bringing about a radical redistribution of power. The first goal he achieved through the thorough dismantling of the postwar legal and institutional nexus which effectively reserved the benefits of the political system exclusively for the victors in the Civil War, and through a series of actions designed to underscore that a new system open to all Greeks was in the process of being constructed. The second, more troublesome, task entailed the subordination of the military to civilian authority, and the settlement of the nature of the head of state. The latter was decisively settled on 8 December 1974 with an impressive 69.2 percent of the electorate favoring a republic in what by all accounts was the fairest and freest plebiscite in modern Greek history.[43]

The elimination of the monarchy fullfilled a central precondition for genuine democratization. Another central precondition, the subordination of the military to civilian authority, required putting an end to the institutional autonomy that the military had acquired over the previous forty-five years and especially since the Civil War. Though this was more of a long-term proposition, there can be little doubt that the dismal failure of the military's seven-year experiment with direct government, and the humiliation it suffered in the context of the Cyprus crisis, had had an immensely sobering effect and had served greatly to redress the balance between the military and civilian elements in the political system in favor of the latter. Karamanlis's post-1974 policies certainly reinforced that trend and, especially after the elimination of recalcitrant elements in the course of 1975, strengthened the likelihood that the Greek military would henceforth confine its activities to the barracks.[44]

Thus, less than half a year after the dramatic events that led to the collapse of the authoritarian regime and to the recall of Karamanlis, the basic political and institutional arrangements establishing the first genuine political democracy in Greece had been completed. In the ensuing years, the new political system would evolve smoothly, coping successfully with the reentry of the Left in the political arena; the meteoric rise in the strength of new Left-of-Center forces (PASOK) under Andreas Papandreou; Karamanlis's rise to the presidency of the Republic in 1980 and the orderly election of his successor by the New Democracy party he had founded in 1974; and, as of 1981, with its first and impeccably conducted alternation in governmental incumbency which brought PASOK to power and signaled the end of forty-five years of almost uninterrupted rule by the Greek Right. The smooth operation of the system over the past three years bears testimony to its legitimacy and institutionalization and serves as a reminder that, whatever its weaknesses, it is by far the most open, inclusive, and democratic regime in modern Greek history.

Looked at in comparative perspective, the Greek case amply bears out O'Donnell's and Schmitter's generalizations regarding successful transitions to political democracy: the dominance of Right-of-Center forces in the transition; the judicious handling of the military, despite the fact that its own mismanagement of the Cyprus crisis had drastically reduced its ability to react effectively; the preference for an inclusive system in which all political forces could legally participate; all tend to confirm the general observations that emerge from the study of transitions in these volumes. What is striking about the Greek transition, however, is that it occurred under initial conditions of a grave external crisis and was accomplished smoothly in a short period of time. As I have argued above, the conditions of external crisis paradoxically facilitated the transition to the extent that they tended to act as a powerful restraint against popular mobilization and radicalization, while, at the same time, they enormously enhanced Karamanlis's freedom of movement, providing him with a golden opportunity to determine the pace, timing, and scope of various measures deemed necessary to lay the foundations for a new political system which vastly transcended the expectations of those who recalled him and radically democratized political life in Greece. There can be little doubt that, in the absence of these conditions, Karamanlis's ability to impose his own agenda on the transition would have been quickly and strenuously opposed from a number of quarters: at the very least, the whole process would have been more protracted and the end-result quite different. In the absence of comparable cases (the Argentina/Malvinas crisis comes closest, but lacks the direct temporal overlap linking the crisis with the transition), the judgment as to whether this can be considered a useful addition to the growing body of tentative generalizations regarding transitions, or merely a Greek paradox, will have to await further evidence.

# 7 •

# Democracy in Turkey: Problems and Prospects

## Ilkay Sunar and Sabri Sayari

When Turkey's parliamentary democracy was terminated by a military coup in September 1980, neither the military intervention nor the political crisis that preceded it were new. Since the transition, after World War II, from an authoritarian monoparty system to a competitive parliamentary democracy, Turkish politics has been marked by periods of instability and on three occasions interrupted by military interventions. On every occasion, however, when the military was either directly (1960–61 and 1980–83) or indirectly (1971–73) in power, the relatively short periods of military rule have all been followed by the resumption of electoral politics. Nevertheless, the reconstruction of the Turkish political system at roughly ten-year intervals since 1950 and the vacillation between periods of competitive politics and military rule are clearly signs of a political system with serious problems. Our purpose in this chapter is to examine these problems and to offer an explanation for their persistence.

The breakdown of democratic regimes and the establishment of authoritarian ones in South America, and the transition from authoritarian rule to democracy in Spain, Portugal, Greece, Brazil, and Argentina have recently generated a substantial body of research and speculation on the causes, dynamics, and probable outcomes of such regime transitions.[1] Although a bewildering number of suggestions, hypotheses, and variables have been proposed to analyze these regime changes, in practice two main types of research have been predominant. One type is concerned with the objective determinants of regime transition, transformation, or breakdown, whereas the other concentrates on political actors, their strategies, possibilities, and choice. The former school emphasizes objective conditions and seeks to understand the structural determinants of political change. It views regime changes as products of specifiable economic, social, political, or cultural conditions, whether these consist of phases of industrialization, types of economic development, levels of political institutionalization, or patterns of culture. The latter inquires into possibilities, tends to stress the behavior of strategic political actors, sees choice as central to politics, and speaks in the language of possibilities rather than determinants.

These two types of research are deeply rooted in theoretical and epistemological assumptions over which there has been much debate but little or no resolution. It will suffice here to say that any historical circumstance is the outcome partly of objective conditions and partly of politics in which calculation, choice, learning, even *fortuna* have varying and uncertain roles to play. In the exploration of the Turkish case, our emphasis is upon objective conditions as constraints involved in the exercise of a choice for democratic politics. In this respect, all democratic governments carry to some extent the weight of their old regime legacies; or, to put it differently, the extent to which a democratic regime is able to overcome the "confining conditions" antecedent upon its emergence shapes to an important degree its ensuing course and character.[2] In Turkey, a strong centralist state and an elite tradition, inherited from the Ottoman Empire and dominated heavily by a bureaucratic structure and culture, have exercised strong effects on the development and consolidation of democratic politics.[3] In the following pages, we attempt to show that the advent of democracy in Turkey and its difficulties have been closely bound up with an overbearing statism and the deep marks that it has left on Turkish political institutions and culture.

**The Ottoman Legacy**

Ottoman rule was based upon a mixture of imperial and patrimonial modes of governance. The imperial features were most pronounced in the high level of symbolic and organizational distinctiveness of the ruling center, and its high degree of differentiation from the ruled periphery. At the apex was the sultan, under him the two fundamental pillars of his rule: the military and the civil administrative staffs.[4] In its earlier efforts to consolidate the empire, the center had eliminated local princes and magnates and never allowed the subsequent rise of local powers tied to land, which might have had any resemblance to an aristocracy. While the standing army at the center existed in complete isolation and was subordinated to the sultan through the *devsirme* (conversion) system, the provincial armies were raised by the appointees (*Sipahi*) of the state and integrated into the central military-administrative machinery. With the lack of an independently organized church in Islam, and more than any other Islamic state, in the Ottoman Empire the religious elites (*ulema*) were incorporated into the patrimonial-bureaucratic organization of the center.

The patrimonial characteristics were prominent in the limited institutional permeation of the periphery by the center, and the restricted access of the local elites to the state. This low level of interpenetration between the state and local groups was hedged, however, by a number of qualifications: it was most conspicuous in the cultural realm, and least relevant in the fiscal-economic sphere. The regulative structures of special importance were those that aimed at the accumulation of resources in the center and the monopolization of economic surplus.[5] Otherwise, there were no attempts to disrupt the plurality of local arrangements; neither was there any encouragement for the formation of civic, associative organizations with access to each other and to the center. The social and cultural groups of the periphery were largely left to their own devices, embedded in their primordial loyalties, and segregated from the center and other ascriptive collectivities. Stratification, therefore, was discontinuous, with a sharp break in the structuring elements of status in the center and the periphery.[6] In fact, the state enforced social and status segregation in order to prevent a countrywide status consciousness, and to forestall attempts by local groups to convert their resources into means of participation in the center, and autonomy in the periphery.[7]

The attitude of the center toward the periphery was suspicious. From the point of view of the periphery, the center was seen as alien and burdensome. The state machinery was more superimposed upon the periphery than it was integrated with it; and in the lack of autonomous intermediate associative organizations with access to the center, the relationship of the state to local communities was marked more by control, cooptation, and regulation, than by consultation, coordination, and consociation. There were no estates (*Stände*), assemblies, corporations, or autonomous towns, nobility, clergy, or guilds with resources and prestige that could be converted into means of independent association with the political center. Land was largely a monopoly of the state; peasant labor was mainly regulated by the appointees of the sultan; guilds were largely means of administrative control over artisans; towns lacked autonomy and corporative standing; and the influential cultural elites of local communities, and religious enclaves, were coopted into acquiescence.[8]

Consequently changes in the empire were hardly initiated from the periphery with social forces bursting in upon the political center. Nor were they generated by conflicts between the center and the periphery. Instead, the impulse to change stemmed from within the state, and was transmitted by intra-elite conflict. The focus of change was the state itself, either in the form of restoration or reform. The aim was never the integration of center and periphery, or the structural transformation of society. Modernization movements in the Ottoman Empire were always selective and segregative in scope rather than comprehensive and coalescent, always exclusive and directed toward state-building rather than inclusive and aimed at social integration.

The pattern of relations that prevailed between state and society governed intra-elite relations as well.[9] Elite status in the empire, in contrast to Western Europe, was determined by association with state power. Indeed, there were no other bases of political status independent of such power. Therefore it is apt to characterize elite structure in Turkey as monistic rather than pluralistic. In Western Europe, the center tended to be composed of a multiplicity of elites, most important, the territorial ruler (the king), the feudal lords (or the aristocracy), the burghers, and the church. These elites composed a complex status system which rested on autonomous sources of power and legitimating symbolism. The relationship of a lord to an overlord was marked by *Gefolgschaft* (comradely followership), by contract, and by the principle of dualism in which the ruler and lord associated as two distinct centers of power. In the Ottoman Empire, *Gefolgschaft* reappears in the *kul* ("slave") system, contract disappears into command, and the religious ulema walk the halls of power as part of the imperial-patrimonial bureaucracy.

In the process of centralization under absolutism in the West, against the background of feudalism and *Ständestaat* (state composed of publicly recognized occupational groups), "secondary elites" (the aristocracy and later the burghers) were incorporated into the center in a series of confrontations which were softened by accommodations and compromises and marked by the recognition of the autonomous status of contending elites. The whole process contained within it the embryonic forms of constitutionalism, parliamentary rule, pluralist political order, and institutionalized civil society.[10] Later, in the movement toward the modern state, the process encompassed social groups (e.g., labor), using the same accommodative approach.

In contrast to Western Europe, elite relations in the Ottoman Empire were marked by confrontations that were noncompromising in nature. This same pattern of elite behavior and interaction, informed by the same methodology, remained the distinguishing mark of the Turkish elite throughout the modern state-building process. A similar model of governance informed the outlook of the Young Turks and the Republican elite. Solidarism, and later populism, were conceived as panaceas for conflict, and the philosophy of control was capped by positivism once religion was privatized. The center remained active, segregated, and closed, whereas the periphery continued to be primordial, segmental, and heterodox. The model worked until the elite split and reappeared manning the strategic posts of the multiparty system in 1946.

The period 1946–59 was an important break in Turkish history. Elite competition spilled over into society, and for the first time mobilized hitherto apolitical groups. The theater of conflict among the elite became the society itself, rather than the palace, the bureaus of the civil servants, or the back rooms of the single party. But it was not the expansion in the scope of power competition that was decisive. More important, the rules of the game had to change. Now competition had to take place within democratic rules. It is here—in the incongruence between the lingering effects of the past built into the structure and political culture of the Republic and the mechanisms and rules of democracy—that one of the crucial insights into Turkey's recurrent problems with democratization lies.

### The Precedent Regime: State-Dominant Monoparty Authoritarianism

The founding of a secular Turkish Republic in 1923 was a radical break with the Ottoman past, and yet, in terms of the system of power and its occupants and in its relations between center and periphery, the Republic showed remarkable continuity with the past. It has been rightly suggested that the Turkish Revolution was primarily a revolution of values, a cultural revolution that radically changed the legitimating system of symbols supportive of political authority.[11] A secular, nationalist republic clearly required an act of rupture from an imperial-patrimonial monarchy that rested on religious legitimation. This aspect is important and radical. Moreover, a set of institutions was inserted into the system of power that not only replaced the monarchy but also displaced the religious men of learning, the ulema, from their positions of power. The entire complex of political institutions and the legitimating system of symbols and norms were novel, if not in reference to the immediate past of the Young Turk era (1908–19), then certainly in terms of the classical network of Ottoman institutions. A secular state circumscribed by law, a constitutional parliamentary system, a conception of sovereignty resting ultimately on the will of the people, a party that was reformist, nationalist, and militantly anticlerical and, finally, a new secular system of education, a new style of dress, and even a new alphabet and calendar—all of these, no doubt, were fundamental changes adding up to a revolution. But simply to emphasize the novelties may lead one to overlook the continuities in the system of power, its structure and occupants, and the whole system of relations between state and society. The Turkish Revolution was, as we say, a "revolution from above," intent not on social-structural transformation but on political and cultural change, itself largely confined to the center.[12]

The early republican regime was characterized as a state-dominant monoparty authoritarianism. Such a characterization points up the system and structure of power behind the institutional facade of the regime. In other words, what were the constitutive groups and the core structure of the regime? Was it the party, the state bureaucracy, the military, the Parliament, or some dominant social class? Given the legacy of the Ottoman system, the core group could hardly have been a dominant social class: an aristocracy simply did not exist, the urban commercial class and the landed notables had neither the political organization nor the power to challenge the state elite (military officers and the bureaucracy) who had led the War of Independence (1919–22) and the subsequent revolution from above. To be sure, among the social groups, only the group of landed notables had enough influence to be included in the political (party) alliance of the regime—not, however, as a core group but as subordinate partners of the civil and military elite. The ruling elite was in fact composed of a triarchy: the Republican People's party (RPP), the military, and civil bureaucrats.[13] It was led by the charismatic founding father, Mustafa Kemal Atatürk, and supported enthusiastically by the secularized, progressivist urban intelligentsia made up of university and literary circles, teachers, lawyers, petty officials, and so on.

The military and the bureaucracy were the old, traditional guardians of the state; the party was the only newcomer.[14] In the Ottoman setting, the military, the bureaucracy, and the religious leadership had fused into a guardian (askeri) class to make up the pillars of sultanic power. After the Republic, when the ulema was disbanded, the triarchic structure of the elite remained the same, the ulema being replaced by the party. The legitimation of the new regime fell on the mediating function of the party; its leadership, however, was drawn from among the ranks of the military and the bureaucracy. Core political decisions were articulated by the party, but they were always taken in concert with the nonparty members of the triarchy. In fact, the military and bureaucracy were more cohesive, better institutionalized, consensually more integrated, institutionally more autonomous, socially more homogeneous, and ideologically better socialized than party members. Though the dominant wing of the party was bureaucratic, its influential members included, after all, local notables and even more heterogeneous urban, mercantile groups. Despite this limited pluralism, the power elite, particularly at the "inner circle" level, was highly integrated, cohesive, and closed.

In terms of its formal institutionalization, the regime was in essence a *régime d'assemblée*.[15] It was based on the idea of concentration of functions and the centralization of power. In practice, of course, the Assembly was disciplined into obedience by party leadership, and dominated by the executive. In the perception of the core elite, such concentration and centralization of power were justified in terms of its vanguard role in the realization of the progressivist *telos*, and immanent historical development, on which rested the elite's sense of legitimacy.

The progressivism of the central elite was juxtaposed to the traditionalism of the periphery.[16] The politics of the early Republic was marked by a multiplicity of cleavages, none of which, however, was as penetrating as the cultural bifurcation that crystallized around the progressivism of the center and the traditionalism of local communities. Neither socioeconomic nor ethnic and religious cleavages were as persistent and profound as the clash of values in which the social-cultural heterogeneity of the periphery, now subsumed under the overarching belief in Islam, came into sharp conflict with the new orthodoxy of progressivism, anchored in a secular, positivist ideology. The tension between the Ottoman center and periphery had been partly reduced by the linkage function served by Islam; now, when this major connection to the periphery was disrupted by the secularism of the center, the tension was exacerbated and the distance between the central elite and the ascriptive groups of the periphery greatly increased. The state elite now faced, without much intermediation, a religiously anchored, primordially embedded, segmental society which it was supposed to reshape and reform.

The old Ottoman suspicion of intermediate groups and institutions was an integral characteristic of the reformist republican elite as well; this characteristic explains the absence of dispersion and differentiation of power at the top and the lack of organizationally autonomous intermediary groups which left the regime open to a plebiscitary, populist type of authoritarianism. The regime, however, never evolved in this direction; the center remained highly segregated and closed, with the periphery always diffuse, weak, and unmobilized. There was no attempt to pulverize ascriptive attachments and primordial institutions in order to penetrate and incorporate the periphery. As we shall see, only after the transition to democratic politics did the institutional arrangements of the monoparty regime become convenient for moving toward a populist democracy with restricted liberties.

The authoritarian regime of the early Republic was marked not by its populist incorporation but by its exclusion of the masses. The stability of the monoparty period is only partially explained by the ideological and institutional coherence and integration of the Kemalist elite. In larger part, the explanation lies with the nature of Turkish society and its relations to the political center and the state. In this context, the character of the monoparty regime is best defined as "authoritarian politics in an unincorporated society," for the regime relied for its stability not on the organized incorporation of social groups, but on the unorganized tradition-bound passivity of the masses. It would be seriously misleading to think of the early republican regime as a system of state corporatism.[17] Neither the "exclusionary" nor the "inclusionary" variants of corporatism were relevant to the Turkish case.[18] In the absence of an autonomous, mobilized, and organized society, there was no need to dismantle it, or to use high levels of exclusionary repression. In the absence of attempts to mobilize the population, there was no need to construct an inclusionary corporatist system. The regime made virtually no attempt to disrupt ascriptive attachments of peripheral groups. Rather, the limited access of the periphery to the center, and its segmentalism, traditionalism, and passivism were skillfully combined with the cooptation of local elites to soft-pedal social reforms and to push state reforms at the top in order to consolidate the ideological and organizational cohesion of the central elites. During the monoparty period, the regime was selective in its penetration of society, entering mainly into the economy, specifically into the industrial sector, and then chiefly through state enterprises—a type of penetration that has been properly called economic statism rather than corporatism.[19] Otherwise, the legal, administrative, and ideological penetration of the periphery was limited: republican institutions and values trailed off into the solidary relations of ascriptive groups by the time they reached the periphery. Consequently a large area of social life was independent of the "authoritative allocation of values" by the state, and governed by the primordial ground rules of traditional patterns.

In conclusion, the overall system remained similar in its structure to the Ottoman past. It was organized, cohesive, and closed at the top, with selective penetration and restricted institutional permeation of society. It was primordial, segmented, and disconnected at the bottom. These characteristics had strong effects upon the nature of the later democratic process. The state-dominant, bureaucratically constituted political system, its formal institutionalization in a *régime d'assemblée*, the weakly organized, diffuse, and inert periphery, and the low level of ideological and institutional permeation of the periphery—all of these factors had a shaping effect on the mode of transition to democracy and the democratic process itself.

## Democratization from Above and Its Consequences

The factors that facilitated the transition from monoparty authoritarianism to multiparty politics have been the focus of a number of detailed studies.[20] The Westernizing thrust of Kemalist ideology and reforms, the limited but surviving social and political pluralism of the Republican People's party (RPP), the low levels of repression, the social differentiation generated by economic development, and the international milieu after World War II—no doubt, all had important roles to play in the transition to democracy. What has been overlooked so far is the form of the transition itself, and its consequences for the ensuing process of democratic politics. As Dankwart Rustow put it, when Turkey "received its first democratic regime as a free gift from the hands of a dictator," it was to pay a heavy price for it later.[21] The outcome of an elite-instigated democratization from above was a crippled democratic regime with a short lifespan.

The traditional and weakly penetrated nature of society and the integrated and centralized structure of political power made it unlikely that the transition would involve either a radical rupture with the old regime or require a politics of accommodation negotiated among contending parties. In other words, the centralist alliance was sufficiently organized and cohesive, and the peripheral social groups sufficiently diffuse and inchoate, to permit a mode of transition other than democratization from above. There was, to be sure, an increasing level of conflict among the political elites, and an increasing level of differentiation within society. Nonetheless, the military and civil bureaucratic wings of the alliance were confident that a change in regime would involve neither a challenge to their prominence in the system nor a threat to the Kemalist reforms of which they took themselves to be the ultimate guardians.[22] Hence, after an untroubled period of liberalization initiated and controlled from above, governmental power was peacefully transferred to the challenging Democratic party (DP) in 1950.

This peaceful transition to democracy, allowed by fiat and with limited pressure from below, left intact the institutions and actors of the previous regime. The bureaucratic elites kept their prominent place in a system that was itself bureaucratically constructed, state-dominant, and hence resistant to party politics. Moreover, opposition groups in Turkey had always been libertarian out of power and autocratic once in power.[23] When this tradition combined with the resilient institutions of the monoparty regime and with the prominence and intransigence of bureaucratic elites, the result was a rather short-lived democratic experience (1950–60) in which, true to tradition, the newly incumbent Democratic party leadership turned authoritarian in power, and the RPP, in alliance with the bureaucratic elites, fought back in the name of liberty.

The short-lived Turkish experiment with democracy between 1950 and 1960 validated the general point made by Dankwart Rustow that democracies that are not the outcome of compromise forged in conflict often prove ephemeral.[24] Turkish democracy, it could be said, was won too easily, without a struggle. It emerged out of a background in which there had been no dispersion of power among a plurality of elites with different bases of power, and in which no provision for the institutionalization of conflict and compromise had been made. Hence, when the centralized, Jacobin institutions of the monoparty regime were taken over intact by the Democratic party, they were not changed to accommodate to a democratic form of politics. On the contrary, they were put to use for purposes similar to those of the past: that is, to squelch electoral opposition and to restrict the range of debate over policy. The bureaucratic intelligentsia were just as arrogant in their stance. They were not willing to compromise their prominent place in the system, nor were they in sympathy with electoral politics that challenged their power. Neither the new nor the old elite had struggled for democracy or negotiated for compromise, nor had they forged attitudes and institutions appropriate to them.

The Democratic party was, in fact, established by a faction of the central elite who had been prominent members of the Republican People's party. In contrast to the RPP, however, the DP leadership forged a wide-ranging coalition among a motley of discontented peripheral groups including the more modern (market-oriented) landed interests found in the western parts of Turkey, the urban mercantile class, most of the small peasantry, and religious protest groups. A wide clientelist network, fed by distributive policies, a diffuse populist appeal, a conciliatory attitude toward religious demands, and a relative liberalization of the economy bound this variety of peripheral groups loosely to the DP. The DP, however, was never able to overcome the low institutional penetration of society which it had inherited from the past. The network of patron-client relations, the appeal to religious sentiment, and populism were, in fact, attempts by the DP to overcome its institutional shortcomings by rewarding regional cliques, kinship ties, religious demands, and personal influence networks.[25]

Throughout the 1950s, the RPP remained in opposition. Its leadership continued to be composed of old guard bureaucratic politicians led by the wartime hero and elder statesman Ismet Inönü. Support for the party came largely from the traditional notables of eastern Turkey (the least-developed region of Turkey), the bureaucracy, and the intelligentsia. In the face of the DP attempt to build itself as a mass party, the RPP never tried to break out of bureaucratic, elitist politics, and looked with disdain and suspicion upon the peripheral coalition that united behind the DP. Thus, the opposition of the RPP was deprived of mass support, and confined to the tactics of provoking the administrative and judicial bureaucracy and the intelligentsia to intransigence against the DP. Moreover, the RPP always made it known that in the last resort it relied on the military as the ultimate guardian of Kemalist reforms against what was defined by the RPP leadership as the major threat of the DP: its activation of traditionalism ("reaction") against the progressivism of the Kemalist world outlook. When, therefore, the military intervened in 1960—supported by the RPP, the bureaucracy, and the intelligentsia—it was clear that the leadership of the DP had overestimated its electoral success and underestimated the survival power of the old elite alliance.[26]

Neither the institutions of the antecedent regime nor the mode of transition to democracy foreclosed the outcome for democratic politics. We should be careful not to read determining effects into constraints.[27] Both the DP and the RPP leadership committed grievous errors. The RPP had been created not to compete in mass politics but to hold on to central power in order to transform culture and society. The military and the bureaucracy had been its natural allies; hence, the closeness of the RPP to the bureaucracy made it powerful enough to challenge any majority-based electoral power in Turkey. The DP, barely accepted as a legitimate political force, grew arrogant with its electoral success, and failed to establish a sense of trust in the old bureaucratic elites. Instead of engaging in a politics of compromise with the RPP, it chose confrontation, even when the social coalition behind it had begun to crumble. When the DP leadership attempted to undermine the power of the bureaucracy, made clientelist inroads into the state, conceded religious demands, and frontally attacked the intelligentsia, what it overlooked was a significant variable in Turkish politics: namely, that democracy could survive only on the basis of a compromise with the secular, progressivist bureaucratic intelligentsia. The RPP, on the other hand, provoked the Democrats into a politics of confrontation, encouraged bureaucratic intransigence, and even approved the street politics of university students and politicization of the military. What the RPP did not realize has since become a constant of Turkish politics; namely, that democracy will survive in Turkey only on the basis of compromise with the nonbureaucratic forces of society. What both parties overlooked, however, is a constant of democratic politics: democracy survives not on substantive compromise alone but more fundamentally on the contingent institutionalization of compromise.

## The Imposed Institutional Compromise of 1961 and Its Aftermath

Turkey's second attempt at democratic rule began with another institutionalization imposed from above, this time with the institutions that were established during the military interregnum between 1960 and 1961. What ensued, however, was radically different from the institutions forged during the monoparty regime. The 1961 Constitution had behind it a decade of democratic experience and learning. It reflected the new balance of power and an institutional compromise supportive of such a balance.[28] In the face of the popular support mobilized by the counter-elite—the leadership of the Democratic party—the bureaucratic-intelligentsia and the authors of the constitution were on the defensive against centralization of power and concentration of function. As a consequence, power was dispersed, institutions carefully differentiated, and bureaucratic checks and controls were established against the power of the parties. The organization of parties at the village level was forbidden. A Constitutional Court was established to review legislation. A second chamber, the Senate, was established to counterbalance the power of the Assembly. The prerogatives and functions of the Conseil d'Etat were reinforced and protected. A state planning organization was founded in order to guide and coordinate economic development. A body called the National Security Council, composed of top-ranking commanders and some cabinet ministers, was formed to serve as an advisory organ to the government on security matters. Such public bodies as the universities and the Turkish Radio and Television Corporation were declared autonomous and self-governing. And finally, individual rights, civil liberties, and associative freedoms were enlarged and put under constitutional guarantees. By most criteria, the democratic politics envisioned in the constitution was not plebiscitary, but liberal. The new institutions were, in short, supportive of a politics of reconciliation and incrementalism, and hence, unfavorable to sudden radical change and concentration of power. And yet, within two decades, Turkish democracy failed twice, once in 1971, when the military intervened indirectly, and a second time in 1980, when it took over power directly. What happened? To what extent was it impossible to exercise choice for democratic politics, and to what extent were these failures because of errors of the political actors involved? These are the questions we shall explore below.

Despite the checks and controls placed on the power of the parties after 1961, the permeation of the political system and society by parties steadily increased.[29] What had been devised in 1961 was a liberal constitution, not a liberal society. Especially after the mid-1960s, the weakening and disruption of ascriptive ties, the fast increasing urbanization and growth of shanty towns, the rapid socioeconomic change, and the high level of social mobilization—all these developments greatly magnified the impact of parties.[30] In fact, in the 1960s and 1970s, parties exercised much greater control over the fate of Turkish politics than they ever had before. Hence, the mode of articulation, the form of mass participation, the emerging party system, and the pattern of interaction among party elites were crucial factors in the failure of democracy in 1971 and again in 1980.

After the Democratic party was dissolved by the military in 1960, its heir, the Justice party (JP), kept the tradition of clientelist alliance that had been originally forged by the DP to hold together a divergent set of interests.[31] Thus the JP was electorally successful in the 1960s by relying for its support on the business community, agrarian interests, the small peasantry, and urban marginals. In terms not only of its clientelist incorporation of diverse groups, but also of its economic liberalism, its conciliatory and concessionary attitude toward religion, and populist sentimentality, the JP essentially followed in the footsteps of the DP. The DP had previously failed in its politics toward the old elite alliance composed of the military, the bureaucracy, and the intelligentsia. The new leadership of the JP, under Süleyman Demirel, changed its politics. His strategy was to strike a balance between the requirements of electoral success and the exigencies of elite politics. Hence, while Demirel continued the electoral tactics and alliances of the DP on the one hand, on the other he tried to appease and neutralize the military, to penetrate the upper ranks and to purge the lower ranks of the bureaucracy, to bypass or downgrade the intelligentsia, and ultimately to dissociate the RPP from its old centralist partners.

Throughout the 1960s, the JP tried to carry out a precarious balancing act, the purpose of which was to gain the trust of the military and to convince it of the infeasibility of the dispersion of political power envisioned in the 1961 Constitution, to maintain electoral success, and finally to isolate the RPP and subordinate the bureaucracy. This balancing act was dictated by the successes and failures of the DP on the one hand, and the emergence for the first time in Turkey of a new politics spread out on a Right-Left continuum on the other. Thus, when the JP was caught among the multiple pressures of old centralist elite proclivities, the new Right-Left electoral politics, and the emerging violence and terrorism of a new generation of youthful militants, the politics of juggling easily slipped into a politics of uncertainty, indetermination, and weak governments. The result was inability to cope with violence, tacit acquiescence to the countermobilization of right-wing militants against the Left, loss of governmental efficiency, and the creation of a power vacuum into which the military stepped in 1971.

During the 1960s, the Republicans, on the other hand, were caught between the elitist politics of their past and the electoral defeats they suffered in 1965 and 1969.[32] When the party tried in 1965 to move timidly toward a redefinition of itself as "left-of-center," not only did the major axis of Turkish politics undergo a transformation from the cultural politics of "progressivism versus tradition" to the functional cleavages of "Right and Left," but also the party leadership had to recompose itself. The disagreements between the old-guard bureaucratic politicians and the new crop of populist radicals resulted in 1967 in an open split among the leadership. When some of the old leaders left the party to form another one that represented the centralist-Kemalist outlook, the radical-populist wing increasingly gained domination over the party ranks.

In the aftermath of the 1971 military memorandum, the movement that had initially begun as a timid move toward left-of-center became more radical in terms of ideology, mass politics, and relations with the military. Under the youthful leadership of Bülent Ecevit, the party opted out of the centralist alliance and its official outlook and increasingly defined itself as a mass-oriented populist-Social Democratic party.[33]

Partly as a consequence of the JP's relatively successful courtship of the army, but largely as a result of the growing radicalization of the RPP, the relation between the RPP and the military gradually turned into one of mutual distrust and suspicion. The civil bureaucracy, on the other hand, actually split when the RPP turned radical and drew away from the centralist outlook. Some, especially in the lower echelons, supported the radical-populist RPP, whereas others, particularly in the upper echelons, came to sympathize with the JP or stood firm in their commitment to the Kemalist center. The same split occurred within the ranks of the intelligentsia.

The realignment of the major parties, along with their growing autonomy from the bureaucracy, their penetration of the administrative apparatus, the erosion of the Kemalist center, the largely informal linkages that they formed with professional and interest associations, and the unprecedentedly high levels of political and social mobilization were the prominent characteristics of this new era of politics on the eve of the 1970s. In these developments were both promise and danger. The promise was that a democratic center, composed of the JP and the RPP, could by alliance and compromise forge a new democratically constituted political system that could overcome the bureaucratic dominance of the past. The danger was that, once the old bureaucratic center underwent erosion and fragmentation, and if the two parties failed to construct a new political center, then elite polarization would be transmitted to the mass electoral level, activate traditional cleavages, and overwhelm the democratic process by undermining the reconciliatory incrementalist processes that had emerged since 1961. The danger was realized, despite the serious warning posted by the indirect military intervention in 1971. The promise of democratization was postponed to the indefinite future when the party system plunged into a deep crisis.

### Parties and the Party System in the 1970s

The party system in the 1973–80 period contained the two major parties, the JP and RPP, and several minor ones.[34] In terms of the spread of these parties on the Right-Left continuum—the increasingly predominant line of political cleavage in the 1970s—the JP stood to the right of center, identified with business and landed interests, but as an interclass, mass party, its appeal extended to the popular sector as well, largely through its skillful use of party patronage and manipulation of clientelist ties. Its pragmatic outlook was interspersed with strident anti-Communism, an appeal to religious and nationalist sentiments, and a diffuse sentimental populism. Two minor, splinter parties complemented the JP on the Center-Right: the Democratic party (DemP) which was formed in 1970 following a factional split from the JP; and the Republican Reliance party (RRP) which was founded in 1967 by a dissident group of RPP politicians opposed to the left-of-center movement within the RPP. Neither party, however, survived very long. The DemP, after a strong showing in the 1973 elections, and the RPP, from the start, proved to be failures. They nearly disappeared in the 1977 elections.

The party system had two powerful minor parties on the extreme Right. Each capitalized on a different line of cleavage and displayed a different type of right-wing extremism. The Nationalist Action party (NAP) bore a close resemblance to contemporary neo-Fascist movements in Western Europe and South America. Although the party had limited electoral support, its grip on Turkish politics stemmed largely from its militant, highly disciplined and trained youth organization, which was mobilized against the Left. The other party on the Right, the National Salvation party (NSP), was extremist in a different sense. Its political outlook was based on the fundamentalist Islamic world view, a view based on the *Sharia*.[35] The NSP emerged with forty-eight seats in Parliament in the 1973 elections; in 1977, however, it lost half of its representation, although it continued to play an important role in parliamentary arithmetics.

In the 1970s, there were five parties on the Left which represented the variants of Marxism. The Unity party and the RPP, on the other hand, were the populist-Social Democratic alternatives on the Left. After the suppression of the Marxist Left in 1971 and their exclusion from the 1973 general elections, they were able to draw minuscule electoral support in 1977, and achieved no representation in the Parliament.[36] Despite their lip service to unity, the Marxist Left parties were never able to overcome the fractionalization among their ranks—their influence on Turkish politics stemmed largely from the radical political culture which they disseminated particularly among the youth.

The major party of the Left was the RPP; led by Bülent Ecevit, it adopted the mantle of populist "social democracy" in the 1970s, and sought to project a radical image that was centered around several dominant themes: basic changes in Turkey's socioeconomic order; an increasingly radical rhetoric heavily oriented toward mass appeal to workers, small peasants, and urban marginals; defense of the 1961 Constitution and the individual, associational, and other civil liberties guaranteed within it; and, finally, vehement denunciation of right-wing movements and parties, particularly the NAP.

Two trends characterized the party politics of the 1970s, namely, increasing party fragmentation and a sharpening of ideological confrontation and polarization. Tendencies toward fragmentation became prominent only after 1961. Until then, Turkey had a two-party system at the electoral level, and (largely as a result of electoral laws) a predominant party system at the parliamentary level. In the 1960s, however, the number of parties in the Parliament grew steadily from four in 1961 to six in 1965, to eight in 1969. There was a slight decline in the 1970s from seven in 1973 to six in 1977. The increase in party fragmentation posed important difficulties for government formation in the readjustment period (1961–5) after the military intervention. By 1965, the JP controlled a comfortable majority in Parliament. Therefore, the effect of party fragmentation was not felt until the 1973 elections, when Turkish voters administered a shock to the party system. The losses suffered by the JP and the gains made by the RPP and several minor parties led to the emergence of a competitive and fragmented party system, and a nonmajoritarian and fractionalized Parliament—one in which governments could only be formed by coalitions among parties.

Several factors facilitated the rise of fragmentation in the party system. First, the pluralist thrust of the 1961 Constitution encouraged the emergence of small minor parties, most of which sought to win the loyalties of the former DP supporters. Another factor was the adoption of proportional representation after 1961, which also improved the chances of representation of minor parties. Until then elections had been held under the simple-plurality system which was based on large, multiple-member constituencies with the strongest party winning all the seats. Such an electoral arrangement clearly limited the chances of minor parties entering Parliament. With the switch to proportional representation, these limitations were removed. In addition, the change in the electoral law was also instrumental in encouraging fissiparous tendencies in the party organizations.[37] Both major parties, as well as some of the smaller ones, experienced splits in the 1960s. Finally, shifts in electoral behavior had a special effect on the parliamentary strength of the JP and RPP, and served as a major catalyst in the transformation of the Turkish party system into a highly fragmented one.[38]

It would be wrong to suggest that electoral instability and the rise of party fragmentation were the prime "causes" of the crisis experienced by the Turkish political system. As several Western European democracies show, fragmentation by itself does not necessarily lead to instability and immobilism in parliamentary politics. It only leads to coalitionary governments, and, in some instances, to minority party governments, which may not be durable, but certainly are not inevitably destructive of the democratic process. However, as the experience of some other Western European democracies (e.g., the Weimar Republic and the French Fourth Republic) suggests, when fragmentation is accompanied by the simultaneous rise of polarization among the parties, the result can be destructive; the functioning of democratic regimes is seriously undermined when the party system is both fragmented and polarized.[39]

In the 1970s, along with fragmentation, the intensity of ideological conflicts in Turkey increased substantially in comparison to that of the two previous decades. However, this trend toward greater ideological polarization was more pronounced among the party elites and activists than among the mass public. Since the appeal of extremist parties was limited, the centrifugal pull toward the extremes, characteristic of polarized pluralist systems, remained relatively weak.[40] Electoral outcomes in 1973 and 1977 demonstrate clearly that a substantial majority of the voters supported the centrist political parties of the Left and the Right. In a national survey held in 1977, close to 80 percent of the respondents placed themselves near the center of the party spectrum.[41] The only evidence of growing polarization among the voters was to be found in the support given to the extreme right-wing NAP, which increased its votes from 3.4 percent in 1973 to 6.4 percent in 1977. In short, measured by the preferences of the electorate, the system experienced only a limited degree of ideological polarization skewed toward the Right.

The behavior of the party elites, on the other hand, contrasted with that of the voters. The tradition of intense intra-elite conflicts in Turkish politics became even more accentuated as a result of the increasing ideological division among the parties. Fueled by the extreme antagonism among minor parties, the major party elites as well turned against each other with a vengeance. The Center-Left RPP and the Center-Right JP were drawn into the rhetoric of extremism. While the JP leadership sought to portray the RPP as a party infiltrated with "militant leftists," the RPP, in turn, denounced its principal competitor for collaborating with "Fascist political forces." The result of these acrimonious exchanges was a mutual process of delegitimization. Each branded the other as an antisystem party, while terrorism and violence increased steadily. Acts of terrorism committed by extreme groups, instead of encouraging closer cooperation between the two parties, provided a dangerous excuse for accusing each other of supporting violence. Ideological polarization at the elite level soon seeped down to the mass level, where longstanding religious, sectarian, and ethnic differences were tapped for use in ideological warfare, again largely by the small extremist parties and groups. The major party elites, even in the face of such dangerous cleavages in society, refused to collaborate in the establishment of a grand coalition. How can we explain such a refusal?

Several factors acted as constraints on the forging of an accommodation between the two major parties. The first of these was related to the increase in partisan fragmentation. The overcrowding of the party spectrum exacerbated the problem of projecting ideologically differentiated party images to the electorate—a familiar problem which parties face in most cases of extreme multipartism. Some of the minor parties such as the NAP, the NSP, or the TLP (Turkish Labor Party) tried to resolve this dilemma by steadily expanding toward the extremes. For the system's two major parties near the Center, the need to maintain ideological distinctiveness was compounded by the fact that, as broadly interclass parties, both were basically competing for the same social base. Under these circumstances, the RPP and the JP found it electorally expedient to project sharply contrasting images, striving to increase the ideological distance between themselves. But they did so less through specific policy commitments than through exaggerated rhetoric, manipulation of ideological symbolisms, mutual recriminations in and out of Parliament, and most important, by an adamant refusal to compromise or cooperate with each other. A grand coalition or a similar compromise solution obviously would have created serious tensions with their intended electoral images. Rather than face these tensions, and their unpredictable outcomes, the RPP and the JP preferred to strengthen the images that they subscribed to, with all their polarizing and destabilizing consequences. At the same time, actual or possible tendencies toward fragmentation led each major party to cooperate with the more extremist political forces, and such cooperation, in turn, inhibited compromise between them. They did so either to achieve the realignment of a fragmented electoral base (JP) or to prevent possible splits by the more radical factions (RPP).

A second factor that undermined the chances of an accommodation between the two major Turkish parties concerned the increased degree of competitiveness between them during the 1970s following more than two decades of one-party predominance in electoral and parliamentary politics. It was only with the 1973 and 1977 elections that the distribution of parliamentary seats displayed some rough balance in the strengths of the RPP and the JP—at least in the sense that neither was able to gain a majority. Why did the increased degree of competitiveness and the shift from predominance to dualism prove to be detrimental to a grand coalition? We think that a partial explanation may be found in Robert Dahl's observation that, in party systems in which there is a dual balance without a majority, "the temptation to shift from coalition to competition is bound to be very great, particularly for the party that believes it could win a majority of the votes."[42] The workings of the Turkish party system conformed to Dahl's observation. Both major parties believed that they were in a position to win a parliamentary majority; what was needed was the pursuit of short-term tactics and strategies that would produce this result. This mode of thinking was especially pervasive in the leadership ranks of Ecevit's RPP, which came very close to obtaining a majority. Believing that power was within its grasp if given another chance at the polls, the RPP incessantly campaigned for "early elections" throughout the 1973–80 period. The party was so obsessed with this goal that it gave little serious consideration to other governing formulas, including a grand coalition with the JP. On the other hand, the JP similarly believed that it could recapture its predominant position in the party system if only the fragmented Center-Right vote could realign itself behind the party's banner. Demirel's strategy for realignment rested on winning back those voters who had defected to a splinter party (the newly formed DemP). This process, in turn, was to be completed by projecting the image of the JP as the only alternative to the growing strength of the leftist electoral forces. This strategy was successfully implemented and by 1977 most of the Center-Right votes were realigned behind the JP. However, since the JP's success depended on a strategy of polarization vis-à-vis the RPP, it further undermined the possibilities of accommodation between the two major parties.

Third, there was the role of minor parties, particularly the NAP and the NSP, which figured in several of the coalitions, and which sought to perpetuate the polarization between the RPP and the JP, knowing very well that depolarization would undermine their chances of participating in government. Of course, when the major parties refused to cooperate with each other, they found themselves dependent on the minor parties to form coalitions. But when coalition governments were formed with the minor parties—after lengthy negotiations in the midst of recurrent governmental crises—these coalitions were soon incapacitated because of quarrels and disunity among the partners. While the parties making up the coalition frequently exercised mutual vetoes against each other on key policies, cabinet members publicly accused their ministerial colleagues from other parties of mismanagement and wrongdoing. Hence polarization and lack of compromise were not simply confined to major parties, but permeated elite relations in general.

Finally, organizational concerns and problems within the two major parties proved to have adverse consequences for greater cooperation between them. The shifting and precarious parliamentary arithmetic of the 1970s, with many parliamentarians defecting from their parties to join others, made the task of maintaining party discipline and unity a difficult one. One way of dealing with this problem was the resort to a method that had often been used by party leaders in the past, namely, to keep interparty relations as conflictual and antagonistic as possible. As the relations between the RPP and the JP displayed polarizing tendencies, their leaders could plead for unity within the party ranks with greater ease and justification than would have been possible under more consensual political conditions. In this way, the sense of external threat was conveniently used to legitimize party unity and discipline. It should also be noted that this tactic strengthened the authority of party leaders over rank-and-file members—not an insignificant consideration, since both Ecevit and Demirel faced challenges to their leadership by dissident party members at various points during the period between 1973 and 1980.

Whatever other conjunctural reasons might be adduced, the fact remains that the refusal and inability to cooperate or compromise were in perfect accord with the historical-structural pattern of elite interaction in Turkey.[43] It was fundamentally not the exigencies created by the party system, the internal problems of parties, or the actions of the minor parties that ultimately brought down democracy in Turkey in its latest version. Certainly, these reasons, particularly the disruptive and violent behavior of extreme groups, strongly affected the outcome. Nonetheless, violence could have been eliminated, terrorism suppressed, and the democratic regime could have survived; the outcome was indeterminate. The recent regime failure, more profoundly than ever before, was the result of the inability of the centrist forces and leadership, of democrats on both sides of the political spectrum, to see the logic of the escalating crisis, and to cooperate and collaborate in the face of it, in order to prevent its consequences. When such cooperation did not take place, the polarization of the party system, the instability of coalition governments, the parceling of the bureaucracy into warring camps, the politicization of ethnic, religious, and sectarian cleavages in society, and the violence and terror finally overwhelmed the system and put an end to it on 12 September 1980.

## Trends and Prospects

Since 1950, Turkish society has undergone important transformations. It is no longer the diffuse, powerless, primordially embedded, and vertically controlled peripheral formation that it once was. It has turned from a gelatinous landscape to a social system of differentiated structures, with crosscutting cleavages in which functional-horizontal axes of conflict matter. More specifically, what was once a segmentally compartmentalized periphery suffused with ascriptive attachments is now in an increasing process of articulation with expanding forms of functionally differentiated interests, growing associational groups, and an increasing scope of generalized market transactions. While the older forms of behavior are diluted, and allegiances to kinship, clan, and religious and ethnic community are loosened, they do not altogether disappear, but exist in combination with the new. Therefore, as the older ascriptive attachments begin to take on an instrumental form, the functional modes of interaction are cast in the idiom of primary relations. And again, it is this mix of old and new, born in the absence of a fully institutionalized spread of functional associations and the breakdown of primordial loyalties, that facilitates the emergence of populist appeals and a wide network of clientelist relations, on the one hand, and a mass of people either caught in the counter-pressures of old and new attitudes or simply adrift, on the other.[44] Ever since the periphery has been politicized and penetrated by the market, functional modes of consciousness have subsisted within obligations of ascriptive groups, disenchantment with intense commitment, and organizational capacity to act with traditional forms of protest. In sum, the social scene in Turkey is more complex, more conflict-ridden, and more potentially explosive than ever before.

Neither is the old center the cohesive and closed seat of power and progressivism that it once was. The bureaucracy has been fragmented and the intelligentsia divided, the Republican People's party has opted out of the center, and the military has been caught in the precarious position of being out of step with old allies and unable to rely on new ones. The cultural politics of the early Republic which centered around the value cleavage of the secular-positivist progressivism of the center and the religious, primordial traditionalism of the periphery has begun to lose its salience, and no longer provides the key to Turkish politics.[45] As the old centralist alliance has broken down, so has the loose coalitional unity of the peripheral forces. There are now alliances, associative and clientelist relations, ideological and elite-mass linkages which cut across the center-periphery division and supersede the old relations between them. The old, mutual insulation of center and periphery has given way to the new, mutual penetration of state and society, mediated and shaped by the existence of political parties, patronage networks, and interest associations. In sum, a new pattern of cleavages, new social and economic problems, and a new form of politics have gained ascendancy, particularly in the 1970s, and have provided the background against which, once again under military aegis, Turkey is preparing to return to a democratic form of government.

As we have pointed out, in the last two decades, when Turkey began to move from a state-dominant political system to a party-centered polity, it was hoped that a democratically constituted political center would emerge to replace the bureaucratic control system on which the early Republican regime was based. This hope, however, did not materialize because the party system became fragmented, polarized, inefficacious, and debilitated. The way was paved for military rule under which Parliament was abolished, political parties dissolved, the bureaucracy purged, the activities of labor confederations (with one exception) banned, professional associations suspended, and the university system completely redesigned and centrally bound to state control.[46]

Once again, it was under military surveillance that constitutional and institutional arrangements were made for the resumption of parliamentary politics.[47] The important questions revolved around the efforts of the ruling National Security Council, composed of the five chiefs of the general staff, to strike a balance between stability and democracy. In contrast to 1960, this time there was much emphasis on the centralization and concentration of power, with "strong oversight powers for the military."[48] A provisional article of the new Constitution submitted to national referendum in November 1982 provided for the automatic election of General Kenan Evren to a seven-year presidency. General Evren remained the head of the chiefs of the General Staff and head of the National Security Council until the new Parliament convened in 1982. He then resigned from his military post along with the four commanders who constituted a Presidential Council to advise Evren and the cabinet. Another means for military voice in the political system was provided through powers of the National Security Council which has a majority of military members, and makes its recommendations to the Council of Ministers on matters of external and internal security.

The new constitution promotes the president to the position of a strong executive. He is given important powers of appointment: the chief of the General Staff, the members of the Constitutional Court and the state Supervisory Council, and university rectors are all appointed by the president. He also has important discretionary powers; he can dissolve Parliament and call for national elections, call the National Security Council and the Council of Ministers into session and preside over them, proclaim a state of emergency or martial law, and veto constitutional changes. Moreover, the acts of the president will not be subject to judicial review, and he need not be a candidate elected from among members of the Parliament.

What is envisioned in the 1982 Constitution is a state divorced from politics and a depoliticized society. A state-controlled Council of Higher Education supervises the universities; political parties cannot form auxiliary branches; labor unions, professional associations, and university faculty members cannot engage in politics; and the government is allowed to confiscate newspapers and periodicals before their publication. The former parties have all been banned, a ten-year proscription placed on the political activity of their leaders, and almost all members of the last Parliament have been barred from politics for five years.[49] The party and election laws were designed to favor two major centrist parties; Communist, Fascist, and theocratic parties were outlawed.

While the military played a dominant role in the restructuring of the rules for political participation and representative electoral institutions, it also exercised direct controls on the transition process. The electoral calendar was designed by the ruling National Security Council; it envisaged the formation of new political parties, subject to the approval of the military, and the holding of national elections under the new electoral law. Between April 1983, when the resumption of political activity was authorized, and the national elections of November 1983, the NSC was directly involved in several key decisions concerning the newly emerging party politics: two parties widely recognized as the heirs of Turkey's two major political parties before the 1980 military coup were barred from entering the electoral contest; the NSC exercised veto powers both for the founding members of new parties and candidates nominated by the parties for the Parliament; and strict controls on political activity, aided by the presence of martial law throughout the country, precluded the type of political mobilization that Turkey had witnessed during the election campaigns prior to the military coup.

The military's efforts to restrict the number of parties and to prevent the old political structures from reemerging in the party system enabled only three of the newly founded parties to compete in the November elections. Of these, the Center-Right Nationalist Democracy party (NDP), led by a retired general, was clearly the one favored by the armed forces. Its leadership ranks included several individuals who had held high-ranking positions under military rule. While the military expected the NDP to become the governing party following the elections, it also anticipated that the role of the "loyal opposition" would be played by the Populist party (PP), which claimed to represent the political Center-Left. The third party, the Motherland party (MP), was the one that did not appear to figure significantly in the NSC's plans for controlled transition from military to civilian rule. Led by Turgut Özal, the chief economic policy-maker in the last civilian government before the 1980 coup, who had retained his post during the first two years of the military rule, the MP espoused a strong commitment to liberal economic policies and conservative cultural values.

Contrary to the military's expectations, the results of the 1983 national elections resulted in a landslide victory for Özal and the MP. The MP obtained a comfortable majority in Parliament, and the PP emerged as the main opposition party. The military's favorite, the Nationalist Democracy party, faced a major debacle in the elections and its assumed central role in the transition process dissipated almost overnight. Having strongly associated itself with the NDP, the military faced a serious dilemma. Despite the apparent opposition from the hard-liners among its ranks, however, the armed forces accepted the voters' verdict and the subsequent transfer of governmental power to the MP. Quite clearly, the November elections contributed significantly to the legitimization of representative electoral processes while giving Prime Minister-elect Özal a key role in Turkey's political transition.

This outcome became even more evident when the local elections, held in March 1984, once again provided the MP with a clear plurality of the popular vote. In addition to reinforcing the MP's position as the governing party and the dominant electoral force, the local elections, by replacing appointed mayors with elected civilian officials, represented another important step in the civilianization of the regime. However, the outcome of the local elections also magnified the distortions created in the party system by the military's earlier efforts to control and manipulate electoral politics. The two parties that were permitted in March to compete in elections for the first time, the Center-Left Social Democracy party (SODEP) and the Center-Right True Path party (TPP), came in second and third respectively, well ahead of both the PP and the NDP. The continued exclusion of two fairly strong parties from the legislative arena and the presence of two other apparently artificial political organizations in Parliament appeared to pose problems for the creation of a workable multi-party system in Turkey.

It is clear then that democracy in Turkey, at least in the immediate future, will be required to go through a period of politics with narrowly drawn limits. The provisions for the new regime strongly limit competitive politics. But whether these provisions will be used by the military to disallow any genuine exercise of power by political parties may well depend on the extent to which the parties and party elites themselves avoid a politics of confrontation and cooperate on a number of areas and issues vital for the survival of democracy.

There are serious difficulties and limitations involved in the development of Turkish democracy, but certainly the situation is far from hopeless. A democracy with narrow limits entails, of course, considerable costs: social and economic reforms may be slow in coming, social welfare and justice postponed, and freedoms restricted. The alternative to a restrained process of democratization, however, does not appear, at least for the immediate future, to be a fully competitive democratic politics, let alone its social and economic variants. If the limits have been too narrowly drawn, they may prove to be expendable through a politics of accommodation born of cooperation and compromise; and, if Turkish democracy cannot weather the storms of a fully competitive politics initially, it may be able to move toward it through a carefully orchestrated, consociational transition period with limits. Otherwise, the alternative to a democracy with limits may entail even greater sacrifices and costs. What is required, therefore, for the future consolidation of democracy in Turkey is not empty rhetoric and boundless promise or blind action, but a sober assessment of its current limits and options, and thoughtful evaluation of its possibilities for the future.

# Notes

## Chapter 1  An Introduction to Southern European Transitions from Authoritarian Rule: Italy, Greece, Portugal, Spain, and Turkey

1. Perhaps it would be more accurate to observe that Southern European societies may not have more viable civil societies as a whole, but they tend to have specific regions: Piedmont, Lombardy, Tuscany, Catalonia, Porto, and so on that are more highly developed. Under certain circumstances these areas come to play a particularly significant political role. Latin America may not lack for analogous regions, for example, São Paulo or Córdoba, but they have usually been submerged or suppressed by social and political forces coming from regions organized along different principles.

## Chapter 2  Political Economy, Legitimation, and the State in Southern Europe

*Author's Note:* I am very grateful to Professors Maurizio Cotta, John Macdonald, Edward Malefakis, and Nicos Mouzelis for commenting on this chapter. My special thanks go to Professor Philippe Schmitter for his helpful and thorough criticisms and suggestions.

1. The sociological distinction between center and periphery originates with Edward Shils, *Center and Periphery* (Chicago: University of Chicago Press, 1974) and has been recast in *Marxisant* guise by Immanuel Wallerstein, *The Capitalist World Economy* (New York: Cambridge University Press, 1979). Another significant development of the notion is to be found in Johan Galtung, "On the Last 2,500 Years in Western History," in *The New Cambridge Modern History*, ed. P. Burke (New York: Cambridge University Press, 1979), vol. 12, pp. 318–61. In this chapter I make use of the distinction put forward by these authors, and especially Wallerstein's notice of the "semiperiphery." At one point the entry of the Southern European countries into the advanced, wealthier, and industrialized center is described as a "shift to core" borrowing, an expression from Wallerstein. In the present European context, Galtung's concept for the "inner periphery" (or "outer center") seems particularly appropriate. Except for this matter I am not committed to their more general, and different, views. For a brief discussion of Wallerstein's notion of the semiperiphery as it may be applied to Southern Europe cf. Anne M. Bailey et al., "The Anthropology of Southern Europe: Towards an Integrated Explanatory Framework," a Working Paper of the Southern European Research Group, in *Critique of Anthropology* 4, no. 16 (Spring 1981): 56–62. For the continued use of the center/periphery distinction as applied to the Mediterranean basin cf. S. Amin, "Introduzione Generale al Dibatito" in IASM, *Strategie Alternative di Sviluppo della Regione Mediterranea* (Naples: Istituto per l'Assistenza allo Sviluppo del Mezzogiorno, 1984), pp. 20–25. Finally, for a center/periphery discussion about the relationship between the state and civil society that largely applies to the area examined in this chapter up to the time of its final integration into the Western economic and political order, cf. K. Vergopoulos, "L'Etat dans le capitalisme periphérique," *Revue du Tiers Monde* 24, no. 93 (January–March, 1983): 34–52.

2. The notion of "backward society" (*société arriérée*), linked as it is to traditional ideas about progress, was driven out, for a number of reasons, by the ideologically more

acceptable concept of "underdevelopment." In Spain and its former colonies it is embodied in the abundant literature on *atraso*, meaning both backwardness and delay. The Italian Risorgimento cannot be understood without it. Cf. Carlo Cattaneo's radical liberalism and the efforts made by him to modernize the mentality of his countrymen. C. Cattaneo, *La società umana* (Milan: Mondadori, 1961), pp. 21-48. All the reform movements initiated in Turkey throughout the nineteenth century were obsessively centered upon the issue of "backwardness," as shown, for instance, by R. Davidson, *Reform in the Ottoman Empire, 1856-1876* (Princeton: Princeton University Press, 1963) and in the *locus classicus*, B. Lewis, *The Emergence of Modern Turkey*, 2d ed. (New York: Oxford University Press, 1968).

3. L. Wallerstein, *The Modern World System* (New York: Academic Press, 1974), p. 101. Ironically, subsequent events led to the restoration of a "medieval" society in Catalonia; by "freezing" feudalism, the Catalans attempted to preserve their liberties and privileges under the Spanish crown. See A. Mackay, *Spain in the Middle Ages* (London: Macmillan, 1977), pp. 159-64 and S. Giner, *The Social Structure of Catalonia*, 2d ed. (Sheffield: Sheffield University Press, 1984), pp. 1-13.

4. There were, of course, exceptions to this general decline, such as Venice's remarkable capacity for survival and even continued prosperity, or the development of a Greek merchant bourgeoisie under new masters. On the retrenchment and decline of the area, see F. Braudel, *La Méditerranée et le monde méditerranéen à l'époque de Philippe II*, 2 vols. (Paris: A. Colin, 1966).

5. L. Cafagna, "Italy, 1830-1914," in *The Emergence of Industrial Societies*, ed. C. M. Cipolla, pt 1; J. Fontana and J. Nadal, "Spain, 1914-1970" in *Contemporary Economies*, ed. C. M. Cipolla, pt. 2 (London: Collins, 1975), p. 461; both volumes published in the Fontana Economic History of Europe series.

6. N. Mouzelis, *Modern Greece: Facets of Underdevelopment* (London: Macmillan, 1978), p. 4.

7. L. Cafagna, "Italy, 1830-1914," and J. Fontana and J. Nadal, "Spain, 1914-1970," pp. 460-73. The economic crises that ensued after the war did not destroy the industrial base thus created.

8. As shown by M. V. Cabral in *Portugal na alvorada do século XX* (Lisbon: A Regra do Jogo, 1979), pp. 7-41; cf. also Ramiro da Costa, *O desenvolvimento do capitalismo em Portugal* (Lisbon: Assivio de Alvim, 1975). The phenomenon of the transition to capitalism without industrial expansion or a quantitative growth of commodities has been explored for one Mediterranean country in the eighteenth century by P. Vilar in his *La Catalogne dans l'Espagne moderne* (Paris: SEVPEN, 1962), which Cabral quotes (pp. ix-x). What happened, then, during the pre–World War I period was that the capitalist economy expanded beyond such areas as Catalonia and Piedmont. Yet its expansion did not always necessarily mean "growth" and "industrialization." Cf. also M. Halpern Pereira, *Livre cambio e desenvolvimento económico* (Lisbon: Cosmos, 1971).

9. J. Nadal, *El fracaso de la revolución industrial en España, 1814-1913* (Barcelona: Ariel, 1975), p. 226.

10. M. Izard, *El segle XIX: burgesos i proletaris* (Barcelona: Dopesa, 1978). Protectionism, of course, does not necessarily have to result in the sclerosis of capitalism. Protectionism in the U.S.A. had different consequences.

11. N. Mouzelis, *Modern Greece*, pp. 16-17.

12. For a description of the evolution of the Ottoman state in relation to this issue cf. I. Sunar, "Anthropologie politique et économique: l'Empire Ottoman et sa transformation," *Annales*, nos. 3-4, May-August 1980, pp. 551-79, in which the author describes the system as a "mode d'organisation économique patrimoniale redistributive" (p. 551).

13. For instance, according to Jordi Nadal and other historians, foreign ownership of Spanish firms robbed the country of an industrial takeoff. Though vastly profitable to foreign investors, their concerns in Spain had a detrimental effect upon Spanish devel-

opment. Charles Harvey has attempted to qualify such charges in his study of the Rio Tinto copper mines, but he has not refuted them altogether. C. E. Harvey, *The Rio Tinto Company: An Economic History of a Leading International Mining Concern, 1873–1954* (London: Alison Hodge, 1982).

14. C. Tsoucalas, *The Greek Tragedy* (Harmondsworth: Penguin, 1969), pp. 15–23.

15. "By the 1960's a circle of twenty families—multimillionaires all—virtually controlled the system of pre-Revolutionary Portugal." T. Gallagher, "Controlled Repression in Salazar's Portugal," *Journal of Contemporary History* 14 (1979): 396.

16. P. Schmitter, "The 'Regime d'exception' That Became the Rule: Forty-eight Years of Authoritarian Domination in Portugal," in *Contemporary Portugal: The Revolution and Its Antecedents*, ed. L. Graham and H. M. Makler (Austin: University of Texas Press, 1979), pp. 3–46.

17. On the political importance of the lack of agrarian reform for the breakdown of parliamentary democracy in the area, see E. Malefakis, *Agrarian Reform and Peasant Revolution in Spain* (New Haven: Yale University Press, 1970) and E. Sevilla, *La evolución del campesinado en España* (Barcelona: Península, 1979).

18. About the precise nature of structural dualism in Southern Europe, see the discussion below.

19. On this question, see S. J. Woolf, ed., *The Nature of Fascism* (London: Weidenfeld & Nicolson, 1968).

20. This issue has its parallel in the important, if often neglected, question of how revolutionary (in the "proper" sense of the word) Fascism really was. Since, by definition, Fascism appears as an essentially counterrevolutionary force, most observers have neglected its transformation potential. It is also a most unpalatable issue. For a rigorous approach to the problem, however, see R. de Felice, *Le interpretazioni del fascismo* (Bari: Laterza, 1970).

21. The following model was elaborated first in an essay that appeared in 1974 ("Cuadernos de Ruedo Ibérico") by Eduardo Sevilla and S. Giner. It was refined with the help of M. Pérez Yruela (*Papers, Revista de sociologia*, Barcelona, no. 8, 1978: pp. 103–41) and appears in a more extended English version in S. Giner and E. Sevilla, "From Despotism to Parliamentarianism: Class Domination and Political Order in the Spanish State," in *The State in Western Europe*, ed. R. Scase (London: Croom Helm, 1980), pp. 197–229.

22. Cf. The concept of a "reactionary coalition" as developed in Barrington Moore, Jr., *Social Origins of Dictatorship and Democracy* (Boston: Beacon, 1966), pp. 436ff.

23. The term "means of emotional production" is borrowed from Collins's discussion of the manipulation of the materials and techniques used to stage rituals producing strong emotional bonds—as well as bonds of obedience, I would add. R. Collins, *Conflict Sociology* (New York: Academic Press, 1975), pp. 58–59.

24. "Service class" is meant in a sense akin to that of K. Renner's concept of *Dienstklasse* in his *Wandlungen der Modernen Gessellschaft* (Vienna: Verlag der Wiener Buchhandlung, 1953), p. 119. Cf. M. S. Archer and S. Giner, eds., *Contemporary Europe: Class, Status, and Power* (London: Weidenfeld & Nicolson, 1977), pp. 1–59.

25. With further industrialization and secularization the Spanish church began to divide and to become ideologically more heterogeneous. G. Hermet, *Les Catholiques dans l'Espagne franquiste*, 2 vols. (Paris: Fondation Nationale des Sciences Politiques, 1981).

26. On the crucial importance of selective repression for the maintenance of Salazarism, see T. Gallagher, "Controlled Repression in Salazar's Portugal," pp, 385–402, in which he adduces evidence for the class nature of that repression. In the light of Gallagher's discussion, the description of Salazar's rule (or indeed Franco's or Metaxas's) as a dictatorship of the bourgeoisie seems in order and cannot be considered as a "leftist" oversimplification. By the same token, the "extermination of the enemy" ethos of these Manichaean regimes cannot be forgotten. For the grim data on the Spanish case cf. A.

Reig Tapia, "Consideraciones metodológicas para el estudio de la represión franquista en la guerra civil," *Sistema* (Madrid), no. 33, November 1979, pp. 99–128. For a development of the concept of despotic coercion cf. S. Jackson, B. Russet, D. Snidal, D. Sylvan, "Conflict and Coercion in Dependent States," *Journal of Conflict Resolution* 22, no. 4 (December 1978). In this article the label "coercive authoritarianism" is applied to regimes mostly in certain Third World states that I would call despotic. The authors relate dependence on rich nations to internal violence and political distortions. Although what seems to apply to a much more developed Southern Europe can hardly be extended without modifications to Latin America or (much less so) to Africa, similarities between certain areas are important enough to invite comparison.

27. "Nonclass" does not mean that correlations betweeen religion and class cannot be found; in a great number of cases, the contrary is the case. Yet the exceptions are too abundant and the effects and sources of religious affiliation too varied for their reduction to class and for class analysis to be meaningful. On the other hand, to affirm that "religion is a more important factor than social class" in accounting for the "moderate and conservative choices of voters" may appear too strong a statement. See J. J. Linz, "Europe's Southern Frontier: Evolving Trends toward What?," *Daedalus* 108 (Winter 1979): 180. The moderate choices of the Southern European Left (linked to Social Democratic and moderate Eurocommunist parties) cannot certainly be attributed to that reasoning. When the church was used to "delegitimize" Socialism and Communism and ban them (often with threats of excommunication) these movements were most radical. But this observation raises other issues.

28. M. Kolinsky, *Continuity and Change in European Society* (London: Croom Helm, 1974), p. 17.

29. Cf. the "regeneration" politics of the conservative premier Maura as analyzed by R. Punset, "Maura y el maurismo: Perspectiva histórica de la revolución desde arriba," *Sistema*, no. 33, November 1979, pp. 129–41.

30. J. J. Linz, "Crisis, Breakdown and Reequilibration," in *The Breakdown of Democratic Regimes*, vol. 1, ed. J. J. Linz and A. Stepan (Baltimore: Johns Hopkins University Press, 1978), pp. 11–13.

31. A. Sardinha, *O valor da Raça* (Lisbon: n.p., 1914); Anon., "Traditionalism and Reaction in Greek Education" in *Greece under Military Rule*, ed. R. Clogg and G. Yannopoulos (London: Secker & Warburg, 1972), p. 143. It is curious, however, how, while in opposition in the 1970s, the modern left-wing, anti-Common Market, patriotic, "Third World"-oriented, Socialist PASOK party in Greece showed subtle connections with these feelings which went deeper than its Panhellenic name might suggest.

32. On the limited Greek orthodox revival (foundation of new monasteries, and convents, etc.) see *The Times*, 11 December 1979, p. 5 of special supplement on Greece, by Archimandrite K. Ware. As for Turkey, cf. I. Sunar and B. Toprak, "Islam in Politics: The Case of Turkey," *Government and Opposition* 18, no. 4 (Autumn 1983): 421–41.

33. On the issue of left-wing legitimation and the open question of the current waning of the opposition, cf. S. Tarrow, "Italy in 1978: Where Everybody Governs, Does Anybody Govern?" in *Legitimation of Regimes*, ed. B. Denitch (Beverly Hills: Sage, 1979); ISA Series no. 17, pp. 229–48.

34. The importance of the traditional sector and its integration into the modern economy, not only in Italy but elsewhere in modern societies, has been emphasized by S. Berger and M. J. Piore in *Dualism and Discontinuity in Industrial Societies* (New York: Cambridge University Press, 1980). Their use of the term "dualism" refers to the existence, side by side, of different forms of economic activity which are nevertheless integrated at another level. They do not claim that there are two economies, separated in every sense (a view rejected in this chapter), but rather that there is segmentation of one single economy.

35. J. Caro Baroja, "The City and the Country," in *Mediterranean Countrymen*, ed. J. Pitt-Rivers (Paris, The Hague: Mouton, 1963), pp. 27–40; and *La Ciudad y el campo* (Barcelona/Madrid: Alfaguara, 1966).

36. Again, Naples seems the paradigmatic city in this respect. About the permanence of its sociocultural features, see L. Barzini, "Una grande calamità," *New York Review of Books* (February 1980), pp. 43–45. Of course, one can take a less "culturalist" and fatalistic view of Neapolitan resilience to "modernization," political corruption, and other phenomena, as shown in P. Allum, "Ecologia politica di Napoli," in *Partiti politici e strutture sociali in Italia*, ed. M. Dogan and O. M. Petracca (Milan: Comunità, 1968), pp. 491–542.

37. For an analysis of the place of the Italian IRI within the economic and political structures of Fascism, cf. M. Maraffi, "State/Economy Relationships: The Case of Italian Public Enterprise," *British Journal of Sociology* 31, no. 4 (December 1980): 507–24. Maraffi emphasizes both the "remedial" character of state intervention and the "enclave nature" of public enterprise within the economic order of Fascism. The same, *mutatis mutandis*, applies to Spain.

38. Cf. H. O. Schmitt, *Economic Stabilization and Growth in Portugal* (Washington, D.C.: International Monetary Fund, April 1981).

39. An example is CAMPSA, the Spanish petroleum state monopoly.

40. A major Eurasian manufacturing aircraft deal took place in 1979 between Spain's CASA and Indonesia's Nurtanio. CASA's successful Aviocar plane is to be developed in a bigger version. Yet both American Northrop and German Messerschmitt partly own CASA. In turn the latter has a 4 percent share in the Airbus international jetliner.

41. Cf. S. Giner and J. Salcedo, "Migrant Workers in the European Social Structures," in *Contemporary Europe*, ed. S. Giner and M. S. Archer (London: Routledge & Kegan Paul, 1978), pp. 94–123.

42. The loss of economic leadership does not mean they are powerless or that their respective confederations of managers and industry owners are unimportant. Yet employers' organizations are increasingly channeling the interests of large corporations into the general economy.

43. G. di Palma, "Italia, Portogallo, Spagna: Ipotesi su tre regimi alla prova," *Prospettive Settanta* 3, no. 1 (January–March 1977): 42–61.

44. On this issue see below, and note 54.

45. I. Sunar and S. Sayari, *Turkish Democracy: Changing and Persistent Problems, and Prospects* (Aarhus, Denmark: University of Aarhus, Institute of Political Science, 1982), pp. 1–3; also, E. Özbudun, "La transición del autoritarismo a la democracia en Turquía," in *Transicion a la democracia en el Sur de Europa y América Latina*, ed. J. Santamaría (Madrid: Centro de Investigaciones Sociológicas, 1982), which covers the issue up to 1979.

46. G. di Palma, "Italia, Portogallo, Spagna," p. 43.

47. P. C. Schmitter, "Liberation by *Golpe:* Retrospective Thoughts on the Demise of Authoritarian Rule in Portugal," *Armed Forces and Society* 2, no. 1 (November 1976): 5–33. Schmitter's analysis of the fall of the regime largely in terms of factors inside it deserves much attention. His emphasis on the relative autonomy of the state as a source of weakness, rather than of strength, is most relevant as a cure for excessive emphasis on the congruence that "ought to exist" between social structure and regime. As Schmitter emphasizes, alternative strategies could have been followed by the government and might have led in a different direction, avoiding the ultimate outcome of the 1974 events. For a relatively similar stress on the "autonomy" of political actors, see Mouzelis, *Modern Greece*, in which limits to class determination of government policy are established.

48. "Consociationalism" as it appears in A. Lijphart, *The Politics of Accommodation: Pluralism and Democracy in the Netherlands* (Berkeley and Los Angeles: University of California Press, 1968), and *Democracy in Plural Societies: A Comparative Exploration* (New Haven: Yale University Press, 1977).

49. In this chapter I have refrained from any detailed consideration of some of the subprocesses that can be distinguished within the general process of transition to

democracy, such as regime liberalization, dictatorial recrudescence ("backlash"), democratization, and so forth. For a critical account of the analytical problems involved in such subprocesses, together with a model of the transition patterns, cf. P. C. Schmitter, "The Transition from Authoritarian Rule to Democracy in Modernizing Societies: Can Germani's Proposition (and Pessimism) Be Reversed?" (Paper presented at the Conference on Transitions from Authoritarianism and Prospects for Democracy in Latin America and Southern Europe, Woodrow Wilson Center, Washington, D.C., 1981, mimeographed.)

50. For a detailed view of the corporate society and a critical account of theory about it, see S. Giner and M. Pérez Yruela, *La sociedad corporativa* (Madrid: CIS, 1979).

51. Some observers, however, seem to believe they were not shams. H. J. Wiarda, *Corporatism and Development: The Portuguese Experience* (Amherst: University of Massachusetts Press, 1977).

52. The 1979 $25-million World Bank loan to Greece for reforestation and agricultural development was the last one to be given because of Greece's advanced stage of development. *Finance and Development* 16, no.3 (September 1979): 4.

53. My approach in this chapter has stressed patterns of social inequality and class analysis, but I have refrained from a detailed account of them in order to gain clarity. Although the sources are abundant, the reader may find the following helpful, insofar as they have been used to underpin my arguments: J. Cutileiro, *A Portuguese Rural Society* (Oxford: Clarendon Press, 1971); Mouzelis, *Modern Greece*; chapters on Greece, Portugal and Italy (by M. Attalides and N. Mouzelis, H. Martins, and L. Gallino respectively) in *Contemporary Europe: Class, Status, and Power*, ed. M. S. Archer and S. Giner; S. Giner "La estructura social de España," in *Poder y clases sociales*, ed. A. López Pina (Madrid: Tecnos, 1978), pp. 75–133; P. Sylos Labini, *Saggio sulle classi sociali* (Bari: Laterza, 1974); S. S. Acquaviva and M. Santuccio, *Social Structure in Italy* (Oxford: Martin Robertson, 1976). Finally, a most useful list of sources is to be found in N. Diamandouros, "Southern Europe: An Introductory Bibliographical Essay" (Athens: Center for Mediterranean and Arab Studies, 1979, mimeographed).

54. For a further development of these ideas of S. Giner, "Southern European Socialism in Transition," *West European Politics* 7, no. 2 (1984); also in *The New Mediterranean Democracies: Greece, Spain, and Portugal*, ed. G. Pridham (London: Frank Cass, 1984).

55. For a more detailed account of corporatism in one Mediterranean country, cf. S. Giner and E. Sevilla, "From Corporatism to Corporatism: The Political Transition in Spain," *Southern Europe Transformed*, ed. A. Williams (New York: Harper & Row, 1984), pp. 113–41.

56. The rise of a "southern question" on a European scale rather than on a national one was pointed out above. It is not incompatible—on the contrary—with these wider trends. Cf. M. Nikolinakos, "Il concetto di 'Sud Europa': Il problema Nord-Sud e il Mediterraneo," *Quaderni Mediterranei*, no. 1, 1975, pp. 53–72.

## Chapter 3  The Demise of the First Fascist Regime and Italy's Transition to Democracy: 1943–1948

1. C. F. Delzell, *Mussolini's Enemies: The Italian Anti-Fascist Resistance* (New York: Howard Fertig, 1974), pp. 231–32.

2. A. Aquarone, *L'organizzazione dello Stato totalitario* (Turin: Einaudi, 1965), p. 290.

3. Juan Linz's well-known definition is most appropriate to Italian Fascism: "Authoritarian regimes are political systems with limited, not responsible, political pluralism; without elaborate and guiding ideology (but with distinctive mentalities); without intensive nor extensive political mobilization (except some points in their development); and in which a leader (or occasionally a small group) exercise power

within formally ill-defined limits but actually quite predictable ones." "An Authoritarian Regime: Spain," in *Cleavages, Ideologies, and Party Systems*, ed. E. Allardt and Y. Littunen (Helsinki: Academic Bookstore, 1964), p. 297.

4. Mussolini as quoted by Ciano in his diary (from Aquarone, *L'organizzazione dello Stato totalitario*, p. 292) said: "It is the monarchy which, by its idiotic gassing, prevents the 'Fascistification' of the Army." Translation by H. Gibson, *The Ciano Diaries, 1939–1943* (Garden City: Doubleday, 1946), p. 93.

5. Aquarone, *L'organizzazione dello Stato totalitario*, pp. 301–2.

6. For the composition and the functioning of the Grand Council, last convened 7 December 1939, see G. Binachi, *25 luglio. Crollo di un regime* (Milan: Mursia, 1963), pp. 519–26.

7. See R. A. Webster, *The Cross and the Fasces: Christian Democracy and Fascism in Italy* (Stanford: Stanford University Press, 1960); P. Scoppola and F. Traniello, eds., *I cattolici tra fascismo e democrazia* (Bologna: Il Mulino, 1975) and P. G. Zunino, *La questione cattolica nella sinistra italiana (1940–1945)* (Bologna: Il Mulino, 1976).

8. Specifically, R. De Felice, *Mussolini il duce. Gli anni del consenso (1929–1936)* (Turin: Einaudi, 1974); *Intervista sul fascismo* (Bari: Laterza, 1975); and G. Amendola, *Intervista sull'antifascismo* (Bari: Laterza, 1976).

9. Aquarone, *L'organizzazione dello Stato totalitario*, p. 310. Quotations from Italian sources throughout this chapter were translated by the author of the chapter.

10. Ibid.

11. The first position is held by L. Salvatorelli, "Situazione interna e internazionale dell'Italia nel primo semestra del 1943," in *Il movimento di liberazione in Italia* (1955), pp. 34–35; the second by R. Battaglia, "Un aspetto inedito della crisi del 1943: l'atteggiamento di alcuni gruppi del capitale finanziario," in *Il movimento di liberazione in Italia* (1955), pp. 34–35. Others spoke of "an immense moral pressure" being exercised against Fascism by many sectors.

12. Aquarone, *L'organizzazione dello Stato totalitario*, p. 311.

13. Bianchi, *25 luglio*, p. 566.

14. Ibid., p. 477.

15. P. C. Schmitter, "Speculation about the Prospective Demise of Authoritarian Regimes and Its Possible Consequences" (Occasional Paper no. 60, Woodrow Wilson International Center for Scholars, Washington, D.C., 1981), p. 13.

16. F. W. Deakin, *The Brutal Friendship: Mussolini, Hitler, and the Fall of Italian Fascism* (London: Weidenfeld & Nicolson, 1962).

17. Count Carlo Sforza quoted by Bianchi, *25 luglio*, p. 742. Bianchi also reports De Gasperi's opinion that though those who had overthrown Mussolini may reap political benefits, those who had to negotiate for an armistice will be in a less favorable position. Therefore, De Gasperi thought that it would be a political mistake to participate in such an operation (p. 658).

18. N. Gallerano, "Fascismo: La caduta," in *Il Mondo contemporaneo: Storia d'Italia—3*, ed. F. Levi, U. Levra, and N. Tranfaglia (Florence: La Nuova Italia, 1978), p. 493.

19. Delzell, *Mussolini's Enemies*, pp. 322–23.

20. Ibid., p. 338.

21. E. Ragionieri, *Storia d'Italia: Dall'unitá ad oggi*, vol. 4 (Turin: Einaudi, 1976, p. 2372.

22. Ibid.

23. R. Battaglia, *Storia della Resistenza italiana: 8 settembre 1943–25 aprile 1945* (Turin: Einaudi, 1964), p. 219.

24. G. Quazza, *Resistenza e storia d'Italia. Problemi e ipotesi di ricerca* (Milan: Feltrinelli, 1976), pp. 146–47.

25. Ragionieri, *Storia d'Italia*, p. 2374.

26. Quoted by Quazza, *Resistenza e storia d'Italia*, p. 158. See also the entire chapter

"Il dibattito sulla svolta di Salerno," in P. Spriano, *Storia del Partito comunista italiano. La Resistemza. Togliatti e il partito nuovo*, vol. 5 (Turin: Einaudi, 1975), pp. 314–37.

27. Delzell, *Mussolini's Enemies*, p. 463.

28. Ragionieri, *Storia d'Italia*, pp. 2406 and 2434. See also p. 2450: "Perhaps in no other sector so much as in that of the Ministry of Foreign Affairs and the diplomacy, has there occurred so massive a continuation [between Fascism and post-Fascism] in all executive offices of the top cadres."

29. A famous partisan commander quoted by E. Cerquetti, *Le forze armate italiane dal 1945 al 1975* (Milan: Feltrinelli, 1975), p. 13. For a synthesized excellent overview see also G. Rochat and G. Massobrio, *Breve storia dell'esercito italiano dall 1861 al 1943* (Turin: Einaudi, 1978), especially the last two chapters.

30. For a comprehensive, well-informed account see E. Piscitelli, *De Parri a De Gasperi: Storia del dopoguerra, 1945 / 1948* (Milan: Feltrinelli, 1975).

31. See the chapter "L'ipoteca dei vincitori e la'prospettiva greca'," in Spriano, *Storia del Partito comunista italiano*, pp. 420–50.

32. For a perceptive essay identifying the scope for discretion open to Italian policy-makers and in sharp polemic with Communist views, see E. Di Nolfo, "Sistema internazionale e sistema politico italiano: interazione e compatibilita," in *La crisi italiana*, ed. L. Graziano and S. Tarrow (Turin: Einaudi, 1979), pp. 43–77.

33. See the essay by M. De Cecco, "Economic Policy in the Reconstruction Period, 1945–51," in *The Rebirth of Italy, 1943–50*, ed. S. J. Woolf (New York: Humanities Press, 1972), pp. 156–80. See also the dissertation by John Harper, presented to the School of Advanced International Studies of the Johns Hopkins University, Washington, D.C., 1980.

34. See L. Valiani's chapter in *Azionisti, cattolici e comunisti nella Resistenza*, ed. L. Valiani, G. Bianchi, and E. Ragionieri (Milan: Angeli, 1971) and the essay by G. De Luna, "Partito d'azione (1942–1947)," in *Il mondo contemporaneo. Storia d'Italia—2*, ed. F. Levi, U. Levra, and N. Tranfaglia (Florence: La Nuova Italia, 1978), pp. 836–45.

35. See the data supplied by C. Pavone, "La continuitá dello Stato. Istituzioni e uomini," in the multiauthored *Italia, 1945–48: Le origini della Repubblica* (Turin: Giappichelli, 1974), pp. 137–289.

36. As quoted by R. D. Putnam, "The Italian Communist Politician," in *Communism in Italy and France*, ed. D.L.M. Blackmer and S. Tarrow (Princeton: Princeton University Press, 1975), p. 203.

37. For an elaboration of this point see G. Pasquino, "Italian Democracy in a Period of Change" (presented to the First Conference of Europeanists, Washington, D.C. 29–31 March 1979), now translated and published as "La demócracia italiana en un periodo de cambio," in *Revista de Estudios Politicos*, January–February 1980, pp. 105–43.

38. Appropriately Ragionieri, *Storia d'Italia*, p. 2468, underlines "the extreme swiftness with which the break in the tripartite transformed itself into a head-on confrontation of the component forces that constitutes a posteriori evidence of the depth of the cracks that had undermined it."

39. "What has been conquered is not lost," Togliatti quoted by Ragionieri, ibid., p. 2392.

40. The two most articulate positions are represented by Quazza, *Resistenza e storia d'Italia*, and by the Catholic-Christian Democrat P. Scoppola, *La proposta politica di De Gasperi* (Bologna: Il Mulino, 1977).

41. The point is made in particular and convincingly by B. Salvati, "The Rebirth of Italian Trade Unionism, 1943–1954," in *The Rebirth of Italy*, ed. S. J. Woolf, pp. 181–211.

42. Quoted by Quazza, *Resistenza e storia d'Italia*, p. 171.

43. See the essays edited by R. Ruffilli, *Cultura politica e partiti nell'etá della Costituente* I: *L'area liberal-democratica. Il mondo cattolico e la Democrazia Cristiana*;

II: *L'area socialista. Il Partito Comunista Italiana* (Bologna: Il Mulino, respectively 1978 and 1979).

44. L. Valiani, *L'avvento di De Gasperi. Tre anni di politica italiana* (Turin: Silva, 1949), pp. 38–39.

## Chapter 4 Political Change in Spain and the Prospects for Democracy

1. Daniel Lerner, *The Passing of Traditional Society* (New York: Free Press, 1958); S. M. Lipset, "Some Social Requisites of Democracy: Economic Development and Political Legitimacy," *American Political Science Review* 53, no. 1 (1959): 69–105; Phillips Cutright, "National Political Development: Measurement and Analysis," *American Sociological Review* 28 (1963): 253–64; D. Jaros and L. V. Grant, *Political Behaviour* (Oxford: Basil Blackwell, 1975); G. Almond and S. Verba, *The Civic Culture* (Princeton: Princeton University Press, 1963); Harry Eckstein, *Division and Cohesion in a Democracy* (Princeton: Princeton University Press, 1966).

2. Dankwart A. Rustow, "Transitions to Democracy," *Comparative Politics* 2, no. 3 (April 1970): 337–63.

3. Robert A. Dahl, *Polyarchy* (New Haven: Yale University Press, 1971).

4. Such an emphasis is adapted from the model proposed by Gabriel A. Almond in "Approaches to Developmental Causation," in *Crisis, Choice, and Change,* ed. G. Almond, Scott C. Flanagan, Robert J. Mundt (Boston: Little, Brown, 1973).

5. Philippe C. Schmitter, "Speculations about the Possible Demise of Authoritarian Regimes and Its Possible Consequences" (Woodrow Wilson Center, Latin America Working Papers no. 60, Washington, D.C., 1980).

6. We use this term in the sense given by Samuel P. Huntington in *Political Order in Changing Societies* (New Haven: Yale University Press, 1968).

7. Nevertheless some authors have described the Spanish transition as a process of self-transformation. See Guy Hermet, "Espagne: Changement de la Société, Moderni-zation Autoritaire de la Démocratie Octroyée," *Revue Française de Science Politique* 27, nos. 4–5 (1977): 582–600. Similarly, Gianfranco Pasquino, "La difficile democrazia in Spagna," *Il Mulino* 27, no. 4 (1981): 595–624. Also, José Casanova, "Modernization and Democratization: Reflections on Spain's Transition to Democracy, *Social Research* 50, no. 4 (1983): 929–73.

8. Manuel-Jesús González, *La Economía Política del Franquismo (1940–1970)* (Madrid: Tecnos, 1979), chap. 3.

9. Juan J. Linz, "Opposition in and under an Authoritarian Regime: The Case of Spain," in *Regimes and Oppositions,* ed. Robert A. Dahl (New Haven: Yale University Press, 1973), pp. 171–260.

10. See Julián Santamaría, "Transición controlada y dificultades de consolidación: el ejemplo español," *Transición a la democracia en el Sur de Europa y América Latina* (Madrid: Centro de Investigaciones Sociológicas [CIS], 1982), pp. 382–85. Raymond Carr and Juan Pablo Fusi, *Spain, Dictatorship to Democracy* (London: George Allen & Unwin, 1979).

11. On the workers' movement under Francoism, see J. M. Maravall, *Dictatorship and Political Dissent* (London: Tavistock, 1978).

12. See Rafael López Pintor and R. Buceta, *Los españoles de los años 70* (Madrid: Tecnos, 1975). Also Rafael López Pintor, *La opinión pública española: del franquismo a la democracia* (Madrid: CIS, 1982).

13. Adolfo Suárez expressed himself in similar terms when the king appointed him president of the government. See "Historia de la transición," *El Semanal de Diario-16,* no. 125 (2 December 1984). A theoretical elaboration of a closely related view appears in Miguel Herrero, *El Principio Monárquico* (Madrid: Cuadernos para el Dialogo, 1972).

14. The project was presented in a television address and was never entirely pub-lished. As it was known, it proposed a bicameral parliament. One of the chambers

would be elected by universal suffrage, while the other would be of the corporatist type. The president of the government would be appointed by the king and selected from a set of three proposed by a council, which was not bound to take into account the electoral results.

15. The uncertainty was so great that only 54 percent of the population thought that the approval of the law would lead to democracy, whereas 53 percent of those who abstained in the referendum thought it would not. See *La reforma política* (Madrid: CIS, 1977), p. 33.

16. On the bibliography on nationalism and regionalism in Spain, see Javier García Fernández, "Repertorio Bibliográfica sobre federalismo, nacionalismo y regionalismo," *Revista del Departamento de Derecho Político* 5 (Winter 1979–80), pp. 271–84. On the historical background to the Basque and Catalan question, see Juan Linz, "Early State-building and Late Peripheral Nationalisms against the State: The Case of Spain," in *Building Nations and States,* ed. S. N. Eisenstadt and S. Rokkan (Beverly Hills: Sage, 1973), pp. 32–112.

17. See articles of the Constitution 8, 28, 29, 62, 117, and 149. As for Carl Schmitt, see his "Der Hüter der Verfassuag," *Beiträge zum öffentichen Recht der Gegenwart* 1 (Tubingen, 1931).

18. Otto Kirchheimer, "Confining Conditions and Revolutionary Breakthroughs," *American Political Science Review* 59 (1965): 964–74.

19. Giuseppe Di Palma, "Founding Coalitions in Southern Europe: Legitimacy and Hegemony" *Government and Opposition* 15, no. 2 (Spring 1980): 162–89.

20. Alfred Tovias, "The International Context of Democratic Transition," *West European Politics* 7, no. 2 (April 1984): 158–171.

21. Data come from different surveys of the Centro de Investigaciones Sociológicas (CIS) published in Rafael López Pintor, *La Opinión pública española,*

22. It was commonly accepted that UCD embraced "the entire political spectrum of some European countries." See Antonio Bar, "The Emerging Spanish Party System: Is There a Model?" *West European Politics* 7, no. 4 (October 1984): 128–55. On the original party system, Jonathan Storey, "Spanish Political Parties before and after the Election," *Government and Opposition* 12, no. 4 (1977):474–93.

23. The 1979 elections are analyzed in J. Maravall, "Political Cleavages in Spain and the 1979 General Election," *Government and Opposition* 14, no. 3 (1979): 299–317. An excellent presentation of electoral results can be found in M. Martínez-Cuadrado, *El sistema polítco español y el comportamiento electoral regional en el Sur de Europa* (Madrid: Instituto de Cooperación Iberóamericano, 1980). And in J. de Esteban and L. López-Guerra, *Las Elecciones Legislativas del 1 de Marzo de 1979* (Madrid: CIS, 1980).

24. The differences between these notions are discussed in G. Sani and G. Sartori, "Polarization, Fragmentation, and Competition in Western Democracies," in *Western European Party Systems,* ed. Hans Daalder and Peter Maier (Beverly Hills: Sage, 1983), pp. 307–40.

25. See, for example, J. Linz, "The New Spanish Party System" in *Electoral Participation: A Comparative Analysis,* ed. R. Rose (Beverly Hills: Sage, 1980), pp. 101–30. The concept of "bilateral opposition" was first coined and elaborated as a trait of polarized pluralism by G. Sartori. See especially his *Parties and Party Systems* (Cambridge: Cambridge University Press, 1976). On the evolution of the Spanish party system, see Richard Gunther, Giacomo Sani, and Goldie Shabad, *Spain after Franco: The Making of a Competitive Party System* (Berkeley and Los Angeles: University of California Press, 1985). Also Michael Buse, *La nueva democracia española* (Madrid: Unión Editorial, 1984).

26. See Eusebio Mujal-León, *Communism and Political Change in Spain* (Bloomington: Indiana University Press, 1983). Also Peter Lange and Maurizio Vannicelli, eds., *The Communist Parties of Italy, France, and Spain: Postwar Change and Continuity* (London: George Allen & Unwin, 1981). See also David G. Bell, "The

Spanish Communist Party in Transition," in *Democratic Politics in Spain*, ed. Bell (London: Frances Pinter, 1983).

27. Jean Blondel, *An Introdution to Comparative Government* (London: Weidenfeld & Nicolson, 1969); Mario Caciagli, "Spain: Parties and the Party System in the Transition," *West European Politics* 7, no. 2 (April 1984): 84-98.

28. For this discussion, see the works cited in notes 22 and 25 and, especially, Mario Caciagli, "Spain: Parties and the Party System in the Transition," *West European Politics* 7, no. 2 (April 1984): 84-98.

29. They have twelve and eight seats in Congress respectively but a much greater blackmail potential because of their key roles at the regional level.

## Chapter 5  Regime Overthrow and the Prospects for Democratic Transition in Portugal

1. On the origins and growth of the MFA, see Douglas Porch, *The Portuguese Armed Forces and the Revolution* (Stanford: Hoover Institution Press, 1977); *Insight on Portugal: The Year of the Captains* (London: André Deutsch, 1975); Denis de Almeida, *Origins e evolução do movimento de Capitaes* (Lisbon: Edições Sociais, 1977); and *Ascensão, Apoge e Queda do M.F.A.*, 2 vols. (Lisbon: Edições Sociais n.d.); Otelo Saraiva de Carvalho, *Alvorada em April* (Lisbon: Bertrand, 1977); Jacinto Baptista, *Caminhos para uma Revolução* (Lisbon: Bertrand, 1975); Avelino Rodrigues, Cesario Borga, and Mário Cardoso, *O Movimento de Capitães e o 25 de Abril* (Lisbon: Moraes, 1974); George Grayson, "Portugal and the Armed Forces," *Orbis* 19 (Summer 1975): 335-78. Also see Thomas Bruneau, "The Portuguese Coup: Cause and Probable Consequences," *The World Today* 30, no. 7 (July 1974): 277-88; António Rangel Bandeira, "The Portuguese Armed Forces Movement: Historical Antecedents, Professional Demands, and Class Conflicts," *Politics and Society* 6, no. 1 (1976); and Marcio Moreira Alves, *Les Soldats Socialistes du Portugal* (Paris: Gallimard, 1975). Also Philippe C. Schmitter, "Liberation by *Golpe:* Retrospective Thought on the Demise of Authoritarian Rule in Portugal," *Armed Forces and Society* 2, no. 1 (November 1975): 5-33.

2. For Caetano, see especially his revealing and bitter memoir written soon after the beginning of his exile in Brazil, *Depoimento* (Rio de Janeiro: Record, 1974). There are several good accounts of Salazar and his system. The best account in English is Hugh Kay, *Salazar and Modern Portugal. A Biography* (New York: Hawthorn, 1970), which is written from a sympathetic perspective, and Antonio de Figueiredo, *Portugal, Fifty Years of Dictatorship* (London: Penguin, 1975), which is written from the perspective of the opposition. Also see Franco Nogueira, *Salazar*, 6 vols. (Coimbra: Atlantida, 1977-85); on corporatism in Portugal, see Philippe C. Schmitter, *Corporatism and Public Policy in Authoritarian Portugal* (Beverly Hills: Sage, 1975). The most comprehensive coverage in English is Howard J. Wiarda, *Corporatism and Development: The Portuguese Experience* (Amherst: University of Massachusetts, 1977). Salazar's own view can be seen in *Doctrine and Action: Internal and Foreign Policy of the New Portugal, 1928-1939* by Dr. Antonió de Oliveira Salazar (London: Ministry & Propaganda, 1939); Oliveira Salazar, *Como se levanta um estado* (Lisbon: Golden Books, 2d ed., 1977). A good overview of the Salazar and Caetano periods is Manuel de Lucena, *A evolução do sistema corporativo português*, 2 vols. (Lisbon: Perspectivas Realidades, 1976); and Tom Gallagher, *Portugal: A Twentieth Century Interpretation* (Manchester: University of Manchester, 1982).

3. For useful background on the PCP, see Arnold Hottinger, "The Rise of Portugal's Communists," *Problems of Communism* 24 (July-August 1975); Eusebio Mujal-Leon, "The PCP and the Portuguese Revolution," *Problems of Communism* 26 (January-February 1977); Eusebio Mujal-Leon, "Communism and Revolution in Portugal," in *Eurocommunism and Detente*, ed. R. Tokes (New York: New York University Press,

1978); and *A Report on Western European Communist Parties, Prepared by the Foreign Affairs and National Defense Division of the Congressional Research Service* (Washington, D.C.: Library of Congress, 1977), submitted by Senator Edward W. Brooke to the Committee on Appropriations, U.S. Senate, June 1977. For the early history of the PCP, see João G.P. Quintela, *Para a historia do movimento comunista em Portugal: I. a Construção do Partido (1919-1929)* (Oporto: Afrontamento, 1976). There are some interesting insights in J. A. Silva Marques, *Relatos da Clandestinidade o PCP visto por dentro* (Lisbon: Edições Jornal Expresso, 1976) and the account by former PIDE inspector Fernando Gouveia, *Memorias de um Inspector da PIDE* (Lisbon: Delraux, 1979); for Intersindical, see *Documentos Sindicais, 1970-1974* (Lisbon: Intersindical, 1974). I have discussed the role of Communists in the Portuguese Revolution in "The Portuguese Communists and the Revolution," *Dissent* 27 (Spring 1980): 194-206; and "Portuguese Communism: Theory and Practice," in *Eurocommunism*, ed. G. Schwab (Westport, Conn.: Greenwood, 1981), pp. 269-303.

4. On the Socialists, see especially Mário Soares, *Portugal, Quelle révolution! Entretiens avec D. Pouchin* (Paris: Calmann-Levy, 1976).

5. For constitutional amendments following the 25 April coup d'état, see Orlando Neves, ed., *Textos históricos da Revolução*, 3 vols. (Lisbon: Diabril, 1974-76).

6. For a good account of Portugal after the coup, see Avelino Rodriguês, Cesario Borga, and Mário Cardoso, *Portugal depois de Abril* (Lisbon: Intervoz, 1976).

7. For a good account of this period, see Porch, *The Portuguese Armed Forces* and *Insight on Portugal*. Also see Mário de Lourdes Lima Santos, Marinus Pires e Lima, and Vitor Matias Ferreira, *O 25 de Abril e as lutas socias nas empresas* (Oporto: Afrontamento, 1976) and José Pires, *Greves e o 25 da Abril* (Lisbon: Base, 1976). On schools, see B. Pimlott and J. Seaton, "How Revolution Came to the Schools of Portugal," *New Society*, 9 December 1976; for Spinola's own account of this period, see António de Spinola, *Pais sem Rumo; Contributo para a história de uma Revolução* (Lisbon: Scire, 1978). For other analyses of the first year of the revolution, see Robin Blackburn, "The Test in Portugal," *New Left Review*, September–December 1974, pp. 87–88; Paul M. Sweezy, "Class Struggles in Portugal," *Monthly Review* 26-27 (September–October 1975); Michael Harsgor, "Portugal in Revolution," *The Washington Papers* (Beverly Hills: Sage, 1976). For COPCON, see Almeida, *Ascensão*, pp. 370-72.

8. I have discussed the background of decolonization in the Portuguese African territories in "The Last Empire: Portugal in Africa," in *The Transfer of Power in Africa*, ed. Prosser Gifford and W. Roger Louis (New Haven: Yale University Press, 1982), pp. 337-85. For the linkages between events in Africa and Portugal see Kenneth Maxwell, "As colonias portugueses e a sua descolonização," in *Revista Critica de Ciências Sociais*, nos. 15, 16, 17, May 1985, pp. 529-47.

9. For the elections, see especially Nuno Vitorino and Jorge Gaspar, *As Eleições de 25 Abril: Geografia e imagem dos partidos* (Lisbon, Horizonte, 1976); B. Pimlott, "Parties and Voters in the Portuguese Revolution," *Parliamentary Affairs*, Winter 1977. Also see the important analysis by John Hammond in *Contemporary Portugal: The Revolution and Its Antecedents*, ed. Lawrence Graham and Harry Makler (Austin: University of Texas, 1979). For good background analyses of this period, see Avelino Rodrigues, Cesario Borga, and Mário Cardosa, *Portugal: Depois de Abril* (Lisbon, Betrand, 1976) and Gianfranco Pasquino, *Le Portugal: De la dictature corporatiste à la démocratie socialiste* (Association française de Science politique, Round Table 6-7 May 1977); T. Bruneau, "Portugal: Problems and Prospects in the Creation of a New Regime," *Naval War College Review* 29 (Summer 1976); Jonathan Story, "Portugal's Revolution of Carnations," *International Affairs* 52, no. 3 (July 1976).

10. Ambassador Carlucci's comment from "Military and Economic Assistance to Portugal." Hearings before the Subcommittee on Foreign Assistance of the Committee on Foreign Relations, U.S. Senate, S.844, 95th Cong., 1st sess. 25 February 1977 (Washington, D.C.: Government Printing Office, 1977); Carlucci became deputy director of the CIA on his return from Lisbon to Washington.

11. Cunhal's comments from Alvaro Cunhal, *A Revolução Portuguêsa, o passado e o futuro* (Lisbon: Avante 1976) p. 152. The translations of this citation and all further ones from Portuguese are the author's.

12. The most perceptive analysis in a comparative perspective of agrarian radicalism in Portugal can be found in Edward Malefakis, "Two Iberian Land Reforms Compared: Spain, 1931-1936, and Portugal, 1974-1978," *Agrarian Reform* (Lisbon: Gulbenkian Foundation, 1981), and the review essay by Ian Rutledge, "Land Reform and the Portuguese Revolution," *Journal of Peasant Studies* 5, no. 1 (October 1977): 79-97. See also Afonso de Barros, *A reforma agraria em Portugal: Das ocupações de terras a formação das novas unidades de produção* (Oeiras: Instituto Gulbenkian de Oeiras, 1979); A. de Vale Estrela, "A reforma agraria portuguesa," *Análise Social* 54 (1978); and Fernando Oliveira Baptista, *Portugal 1975—Os Campos* (Oporto: Afrontamento, 1978). There is useful background information in Manuel Villaverde Cabral, "Agrarian Structures and Recent Rural Movements in Portugal," *Journal of Peasant Studies* 5, no. 4 (July 1978), and Claude Collin, "Enquête sur les cooperatives agricoles au Portugal," *Les Temps Modernes*, November 1976. There are useful data in *Portugal Agricultural Sector Survey* (Washington, D.C.: World Bank, November 1978).

13. For economy, see the volumes of the two international conferences on Portuguese Economy (1977, 1979) held in Lisbon, sponsored by the Gulbenkian Foundation and the German Marshall Fund of the United States. On the popular movement, see Phil Mailer, *Portugal: The Impossible Revolution?* (London: Solidarity, 1977); Maria de Lurdes Lima Santos, Marinus Pires de Lima, and Vitor Matias Ferreira, *O 25 de Abril e as lutas sociais nas empresas* (Oporto: Afrontamento, 1976); José Pires, *Greves e o 25 de Abril* (Lisbon: Base, 1976); F. Avila, C. Ferreira, B. Lory, C. Orsoni, and Ch. Reeve, *Portugal: L'autre combat—classes et conflits dans la société* (Paris: Spartacus, 1975); Orlando Neves, ed., *Mil dias: Diario de uma Revolução* (Lisbon: Mil Dias, 1978); Chip Downs, Fernando Nunes da Silva, Helena Gonçalves, and Isabel Seará, *Os Moradores a conquista da cidade* (Lisbon: Armazem das Letras, 1978); Victor Matias Ferreira, *Movimentos sociais urbanos e intervenção politica* (Oporto: Afrontamento, 1975), and "Movimentos de Moradores: Luta pela Habitação," *Intervenção social* 2 (September 1979); also Luis Leitão, Antonio Dias, Jorge Manuel, and Laurent Dianoux, "Mouvements urbains et commissions de moradores au Portugal: 1974-1976," *Les Temps Modernes*, November 1978.

14. Alvaro Cunhal, *Pela Revolução democrática e nacional* (Lisbon: Editorial Estampa, 23 July 1975), esp. pp. 7 10.

15. Alvaro Cunhal, *Radicalismo pequeno burgês da façada socialista* (Lisbon: Avante, 1974), p. 82; see also Cunhal, *A Revolução Portuguesa* (Lisbon: Avante, 1970), p. 383.

16. *L'Europeo* (Milan), 15 June 1975.

17. For the struggle in the military, see Avelino Rodrigues, Cesario Borgia, and Mário Cardoso, *Abril nos quarteis de Novembro* (Lisbon: Bertrand, 1979). Also, José Gomes Mota, *A Resistência* (Lisbon: Edições Jornal Expresso, 1976).

18. Alvaro Cunhal claimed a party membership of 115,000 in November 1976; see *A Revolução Portuguesa*, p. 402; U.S. intelligence sources put the figure at closer to 50,000: *CIA Factbook*, p. 107, cited in Congressional Research Service, *A Report on West European Communist Parties.*

19. For the speeches of the prime minister, see Vasco Gonçalves, *Discursos, conferências, entrevistas* (Oporto: Edições popular, 1976). See also Vasco Gonçalves, *Livro verde da Revolução* (Amadora, 1975). The PCP's view of the summer is contained in Alvaro Cunhal, *A crisis politico-militar discursos politicos 15* (Documentos Políticos do PCP, May–November 1975; Lisbon: Avante, 1976), which publishes comments made by Cunhal at meetings for the central committee but suppressed in the party's transcriptions put out at the time. The PCP had abandoned Vasco Gonçalves on 10 August 1975. See also Jean Pierre Faye, *Portugal: The Revolution in the Labyrinth* (Nottingham: Solidarity, 1976).

20. For summer disputes in the military, see Ramiro Correia, Pedro Soldado, and Joao Marujo, *MFA e luta de classes; Subsídios para a compreensão do processo histórico português* (Lisbon: Edições Sõciais, n.d.). This collection contains important extracts from speeches in MFA assemblies and the like. For a collection of articles from the MFA *Bulletin*, see *MFA, Motor da Revolução Portuguesa*, ed. Serafim Ferreira (Lisbon, Diabril, 1975).

21. For background on the Soviet view, see Robert Legvold, "The Soviet Union and West European Communism" (Council on Foreign Relations, 11 February 1977), and his "Four Policy Perspectives: The Soviet Union and Western Europe" (Text of state project, Russian Research Center, Harvard University, 30 January 1978). A Communist-dominated Portugal would also have required substantial economic backing from the Soviet Union. There is no evidence that Moscow was prepared to undertake so heavy a burden. President Ford also made it plain to President Brezhnev in the summer of 1975 that there would be no Helsinki accords if the Soviets backed a Communist seizure of power in Lisbon. See Alex MacLeod, "The French and Italian Communist Parties and the Portuguese Revolution," in *In Search of Modern Portugal: The Revolution and Its Consequences*, ed. L. Graham and D. Wheeler (Madison: University of Wisconsin Press, 1983), pp. 297-320; Joan Barth Urban, "Contemporary Soviet Perspectives on Revolution in the West," *Orbis* 19, no. 4 (Winter 1976): 1359-1402; Robert Legvold, "The Soviet Union and West European Communism," *Eurocommunism and Détente*, ed. R. Tokes, pp. 314-84; see esp. pp. 331-76, where Legvold deals with the conflicting Soviet Communist party and Italian Communist party interpretations of the "lessons" of Chile and Portugal. For a Soviet view, see V. V. Zagladin, "Preconditions of Socialism and the Struggle for Socialism," *Voprosy Filosafii* 11 (November 1975).

22. For figures on aid (overt, covert), see Lester A. Sobel, ed., *Portuguese Revolution, 1974-1976* (New York: Facts on File, 1976). On Western reactions, see Tad Szulc, "Lisbon and Washington: Behind Portugal's Revolution," *Foreign Policy*, Winter 1975-76, and Kenneth Maxwell, "The Thorns of the Portuguese Revolution," *Foreign Affairs*, January 1976. Also, Kenneth Maxwell, ed., *The Press and the Rebirth of Iberian Democracy* (Westport, Conn.: Greenwood, 1983).

23. For the 1976 Constitution and politics after 1976, see Bruneau, "Portugal: Problems and Prospects in the Creation of a New Regime," pp. 65-83; "The Left and the Emergence of Portuguese Liberal Democracy," in *Eurocommunism and Eurosocialism: The Left Confronts Modernity*, ed. Bernard E. Brown (New York: Cyro, 1979); Thomas Bruneau and Mário Bacalhau, *Os Portugueses e a política quatro anos depois do 25 de Abril* (Lisbon: Meseta, 1978). For constitutional changes in 1982, see *Constituição da Republica Portuguesa* (Coimbra: Livraia Almedina, 1982). For a succinct overview of problems of the diffusion of power and the role of political parties, see J. M. Barroso, *Le système politique portugais face à l'integration Européenne* (Lisbon: Associação Portuguesa para as relações internacionais, 1983). Also, Tom Gallagher, "Portugal's Bid for Democracy: The Role of the Socialist Party, 1973-1978," *West European Politics* 2, no. 1 (May 1979).

24. For an economic overview, see Paul Krugman and Jorge Braga de Macedo, "The Economic Consequences of the April 25th Revolution," in *Portugal since the Revolution: Economic and Political Perspectives*, ed. Jorge Borges de Macedo and Simon Serfaty (Boulder, Colo: Westview Press, 1981).

## Chapter 6  Regime Change and the Prospects for Democracy in Greece: 1974-1983

*Editors' Note:* An earlier and shorter version of this chapter appeared in Spanish in *Transisión a la democracia en el sur de Europa y América Latina*, ed. Julián Santamaría (Madrid: Centro de Investigaciones Sociológicas, 1982), pp. 199-241.

1. Works, mostly in English, dealing with regime transitions in Spain and Portugal and with Southern Europe as a whole, include Geoffrey Pridham, ed., *The New Mediterranean Democracies: Regime Transition in Spain, Greece, and Portugal* (London: Frank Cass, 1984); Julián Santamaría, ed., *Transición a la democracia en el Sur de Europa y América Latina* (Madrid: Centro de Investigaciones Sociológicas, 1982); Allan Williams, ed., *Southern Europe Transformed: Political and Economic Change in Greece, Italy, Portugal, and Spain* (New York: Harper & Row, 1984); and Beate Kohler, *Political Forces in Spain, Greece, and Portugal* (London: Butterworth, 1982); Juan Linz, "Europe's Southern Frontier: Evolving Trends Toward What?" *Daedalus* 108, no. 1 (Winter 1979): 175–209, and his "Spain and Portugal: Critical Choices," in *Western Europe: The Trials of Partnership*, ed. David S. Landes (Lexington, Mass.: Heath, 1977), pp. 237–96; Giuseppe Di Palma, "Italia, Portogallo, Spagna: Ipotesi su tre regime alla prova," *Prospettive Settanta* 3, no. 1 (January–March 1977): 42–61; Ferdinand A. Hermen and Peter-Hugo Köppinger, "Von Diktatur zur Demokratie: Das Beispiel Spaniens und Portugals," *Verfassung und Verfassungswirklichkeit* 10 (Jahrbuch 1976): 13–190. For a short article on Portugal and Greece, see Gianfranco Pasquino, "L'instaurazione di regimi democratici in Grecia e Portogallo," *Il Mulino* 24 (1975): 217–37.

Among works focusing on one country, see, for Spain, José Maravall, *The Transition to Democracy in Spain* (London: Croom Helm, 1982), and the chapters by Julián Santamaría, in *Transición a la democracia*, ed. Santamaría, pp. 371–417; Kenneth Medhurst and Mario Caciagli, *New Mediterranean Democracies*, ed. Pridham, pp. 30–49 and 84–98 respectively; Giner and Sevilla, in *Southern Europe Transformed*, ed. Williams, pp. 113–41; and Edward E. Malefakis, in *From Dictatorship to Democracy: Coping with the Legacies of Authoritarianism and Totalitarianism*, ed. John H. Herz (Westport, CT: Greenwood, 1982), pp. 215–30. See also the article by José Casanova, "Modernization and Democractization: Reflections on Spain's Transition to Democracy," *Social Research* 50, no. 4 (Winter 1983): 929–73 and the monographic works by Raymond Carr and Juan P. Fusi, *Spain: Dictatorship to Democracy* (London: George Allen & Unwin, 1979); John F. Coverdale, *The Political Transformation of Spain after Franco* (New York: Praeger, 1979); Lothar Maier, *Spaniens Weg zur Demokratie* (Meisenheim am Glan: Anton Hain, 1977); Jose Amodia, *Franco's Political Legacy: From Dictatorship to Facade Democracy* (London: Penguin, 1977). For Portugal, see Thomas C. Bruneau, *Politics and Nationhood: Post-Revolutionary Portugal* (New York: Praeger, 1984); Jorge Braga de Macedo and Simon Serfaty, eds., *Portugal Since the Revolution: Economic and Political Perspectives* (Boulder, Colo.: Westview Press, 1981); Lawrence S. Graham and Douglas L. Wheeler, eds., *In Search of Modern Portugal: The Revolution and its Consequences* (Madison: University of Wisconsin Press, 1983); and Rainer Eisfeld, *Sozialistischer Pluralismus in Europa: Ansätze und Scheitern am Beispiel Portugal* (Cologne: Wissenschaft & Politik, 1984). See also Kenneth Maxwell, "The Emergence of Portuguese Democracy," in *From Dictatorship to Democracy*, ed. Herz, pp. 230–50; Thomas C. Bruneau, "Problems and Prospects in the Creation of a New Regime," *Naval War College Review* 29, no. 1 (Summer 1976): 65–82; Gianfranco Pasquino, "L'evoluzione dei regimi autoritari: Il caso di Portogallo," *Critica Sociale* 66, no. 5 (May 1974), pp. 249–51; and especially Philippe C. Schmitter, "Liberation by *Golpe*: Retrospective Thoughts on the Demise of Authoritarian Rule in Portugal," *Armed Forces and Society* 2, no. 1 (November 1975): 5–33, as well as his paper "Historical Bloc Formation and Regime Consolidation in Post-Authoritarian Portugal" (1976). For an excellent and far-ranging bibliography of works dealing with the Portuguese Revolution, and focusing on the question of regime transition, see William Lomax, *Revolution in Portugal: 1974–1976: A Bibliography* (Durham, N.H.: The International Conference Group on Modern Portugal, 1978).

For a more general inquiry into the dynamics of regime change, see also the special issue of the *International Political Science Review* I, no. 1 (January 1980). Schmitter's article mentioned in the text is "Liberation by *Golpe*," just cited. For an incisive analysis of the significance of confining conditions, see Otto Kirchheimer, "Confining Conditions and Revolutionary Breakthroughs," *American Political Science Review* 49 (1965): 964–74. Finally, Linz's description of an authoritarian regime can be found in his "Authoritarian Regime: Spain," in *Cleavages, Ideologies and Party Systems*, ed. E. Allardt and Y. Littunen (Helsinki: Westermarck Society, 1964), pp. 291–341; see also Linz's more recent, more encyclopedic article "Totalitarian Authoritarian Regimes," in *Handbook of Political Science*, ed. Fred I. Greenstein and Nelson W. Polsby (Reading, Mass.: Addison-Wesley, 1975), vol. 3, pp. 175–411.

2. Despite a lot of discussion in the press, scholarly analyses of the nature of the Greek authoritarian regime and of the 1974 transition to democratic rule in Greece are few. Some of the best works are available only in Greek. On the regime itself, see George Catiforis, *He nomothesia ton varvaron* [The Legislation of the Barbarians] (Athens: Themelio, 1975), parts of which, especially the chapter dealing with attempts by the colonels to institutionalize their regime, have also appeared in French as "L'organization institutionelle d'une 'société défensive' en Grèce," *Les Temps Modernes* 276 bis (1969), pp. 153ff. See also the excellent and wide-ranging doctoral dissertation by Nicolas-Michel Alivizatos, "Les institutions politiques de la Grèce à travers les crises. Constantes et spécificités d'un parcours constitutionel agité (1922–1974)" (Doctorat d'Etat en Droit, University of Paris II, 1977), pp. 254–95, 570–617, published as *Les institutions politiques de la Grèce à travers les crises, 1922–1974* (Paris: Librairie Générale de Droit et de Jurisprudence, 1979). Other works dealing with the Greek authoritarian regime include Richard Clogg and George Yannopoulos, eds., *Greece under Military Rule* (New York: Basic Books, 1972); [Rodes Roufos], *Inside the Colonels' Greece* (London: Chatto & Windus, 1972); and the uneven work by Hariton Korizis, *To aftarchiko kathestos, 1967–1974* [The Authoritarian Regime, 1967–1974] (Athens: Gutenberg, 1975).

3. For the theory that the democratic restoration of 1974 represents nothing more than a "mere change of guard," see Andreas Papandreou's statement broadcast from Deutsche Welle radio station on 26 July 1974, and printed in the Greek newspaper *He Kathimerine* [The Daily], 22–23 July 1979. On the long history of foreign intervention in Greece, see Theodore A. Couloumbis, John A. Petropulos, and Harry J. Psomides, *Foreign Intervention in Greek Politics: A Historical Perspective* (New York: Pella, 1976).

4. The best discussion of the 1974 and 1977 elections in English is to be found in Howard R. Penniman, ed., *Greece at the Polls: The National Elections of 1974 and 1977* (Washington, D.C.: American Enterprise Institute, 1981). For the 1981 elections, see George Th. Mavrogordatos, *Rise of the Greek Sun: The Greek Election of 1981* (London: King's College, Centre for Contemporary Greek Studies, Occasional Paper 1, 1983), and, in Greek, P. N. Diamandouros, P. M. Kitromilides, and G. Th. Mavrogordatos, eds., *Hoi Ekloges tou 1981* [The 1981 Elections] (Athens: Hestia, 1984). On PASOK, more generally, the best work to date is Christos Lyrintzis, "Between Socialism and Populism: The Rise of the Penhellenic Socialist Movement" (Ph.D. diss., London School of Economics, 1983). See also his "Political Parties in Post-Junta Greece: A Case of 'Bureaucratic Clientelism'?" in *New Mediterranean Democracies*, pp. 99–118. See also Heinz-Jürgen Axt, "On the Way to Self-Reliance? PASOK's Government Policy in Greece," *Journal of Modern Greek Studies* 2, no. 2 (October 1984): 189–207. Finally, for a negative assessment of PASOK, see Roy C. Macridis, *Greek Politics at a Crossroads* (Stanford, Calif.: Hoover Institution, 1984).

5. The most recent, and by far the most thorough, attempt to analyze the social bases of the schism is George Th. Mavrogordatos, *Stillborn Republic: Social Coalitions and Party Strategies in Greece, 1922–1936* (Berkeley and Los Angeles: University of California Press, 1983). The best study in Greek is George Ventires, *He Hellas tou 1910–1920* [The Greece of 1910–1920] (Athens: Ikaros, 1970), originally published in 1930.

On social and economic change in Greece during the late nineteenth and early twentieth centuries, see George Dertilis, "Social Change and Military Intervention in Politics: Greece, 1881-1928" (Ph.D. diss., University of Sheffield, 1976); Constantine Tsoucalas, "Dependance et réproduction: Le rôle de l'appareil scolaire dans une formation trans-territoriale" (Ph.D. diss., University of Paris-Sorbonne, 1976); and Nicos P. Mouzelis, *Modern Greece: Facets of Underdevelopment* (London: Macmillan, 1978), pp. 3-29.

6. On the Greek-Turkish War of 1919-22, the most recent published work in English is Michael Llewellyn Smith, *Ionian Vision: Greece in Asia Minor, 1919-1922* (London: Allen Lane, 1973). Victoria Solomonides's unfinished Ph.D. dissertation "The Greek Administration of the Izmir Vilayet, 1919-1922" (King's College, University of London) casts new light onto these important years. See also the old and controversial work by Arnold Toynbee, *The Western Question in Greece and Turkey* (London, 1922) and the worthwhile study by A. A. Pallis, *Greece's Anatolian Venture—and After* (London: Methuen 1937). In Greek, see the Marxist analysis by Nikos Psyroukes, *He Mikrasiatike Katastrophe* [The Asia Minor Catastrophe] (Athens: Epikairoteta, 1974), and the more traditional narrative account by Spyros B. Markezines, *He synchronos Hellas* [Contemporary Greece], vol. I, 1920-1922 (Athens: Papyros, 1973). A good, though brief analysis of the 1919-22 events can be found in L. S. Stavrianos, *The Balkans since 1453* (New York: Holt, Rinehart & Winston, 1958); see also Douglas Dakin, *The Unification of Greece, 1770-1923* (New York: St. Martin's Press, 1972). On the refugee question, and on its impact on Greek society, see Dimitri Pentzopoulos, *The Balkan Exchange of Minorities and Its Impact upon Greece* (The Hague: Mouton, 1962); and Stephen P. Ladas, *The Exchange of Minorities, Bulgaria, Greece, and Turkey* (London: Macmillan, 1932). More generally, see André Andreades, ed., *Les effets économiques et sociaux de la Guerre en Grèce* (New Haven: Yale University Press, 1929), as well as the more recent work by John Campbell and Philip Sherrard, *Modern Greece* (London: Benn, 1968), pp. 127-55.

On the Great Idea, see Campbell and Sherrard, *Modern Greece*, pp. 83-126; John A. Petropulos, *Politics and Statecraft in the Kingdom of Greece, 1833-1843* (Princeton: Princeton University Press, 1968), pp. 345-48; Dakin, cited above, pp. 82-86; and, in Greek, C. Th. Dimaras, "*Tes Megales Taftes Ideas*" ["Of this Great Idea"] (Athens: By the Author, 1970).

On the ideological vacuum, and on the moral crisis produced by the death of the Great Idea, and by defeat in Asia Minor, see the important literary work by George Theotakas, *Argo* (London: Methuen, 1951), and the more recent scholarly study Thomas Doulis, *Disaster and Fiction: Modern Greek Fiction and the Impact of the Asia Minor Disaster of 1922* (Berkeley and Los Angeles: University of California Press, 1977).

Finally, on various aspects of the pressures that rapid social and economic change placed upon the interwar political system, see: Angelos Elefantes, *He epangelia tes adynates epanastases. . .* [The Promise of the Impossible Revolution. The Communist Party of Greece and the Bourgeoisie in the Interwar Period] (Athens: Olkos, 1976); Mouzelis, *Modern Greece,* and Mavrogordatos, *Stillborn Republic.* See also Roussos Koundouros, "Law and the Obstruction of Social Change: A Case Study of Laws for the Security of the Apparently Prevailing Social Order in Greece" (Master of Philosophy thesis, Brunel University, 1974).

7. The historical account of interwar Greece to date is Gregorios Dafnes, *He Hellas metaxy dyo polemon* [Greece between Two Wars] (Athens: Ikaros, 1955). In languages other than Greek, see Mavrogordatos, *Stillborn Republic;* Keith R. Legg, *Politics in Modern Greece* (Stanford: Stanford University Press, 1969; John S. Koliopoulos, *Greece and the British Connection, 1935-1941* (Oxford: Oxford University Press, 1978); and the small classic by Nicolas G. Svoronos, *Histoire de la Grèce moderne,* 3d ed. (Paris: Presses Universitaires de France, 1972).

On the role of the armed forces during the same period, see Thanos Veremis, "The

Greek Army in Politics, 1922-1935" (Ph.D. diss., Oxford University, 1974). See also Mouzelis, *Modern Greece*, pp. 104-14.

On the rise of the anti-Communist state in Greece, see Koundouros, "Law and the Obstruction of Social Change," as well as Catiforis, [The Legislation of the Barbarians], pp. 31-88.

8. On the 1940s, see the valuable John O. Iatrides, ed., *Greece in the 1940s: A Nation in Crisis* (Hanover, N.H.: University Press of New England, 1981) and John O. Iatrides, ed., *Ambassador MacVeagh Reports: Greece, 1933-1947* (Princeton: Princeton University Press, 1980). The most authoritative accounts from the Right are: C. M. Woodhouse, *Apple of Discord: A Survey of Recent Greek Politics in Their International Setting* (London: Hutchinson, 1948), and his more recent *The Struggle for Greece, 1941-1949* (London: Hart-Davis MacGibbon, 1976), which is more sympathetic to the rebel side than the earlier work. William Hardy McNeill, *The Greek Dilemma: War and Aftermath* (Philadelphia: Lippincott, 1947) is more sympathetic to the Left. For a superb, annotated bibliography on the years 1941-44, see Hagen Fleischer, "Greece under Axis Occupation, 1941-1944," *Modern Greek Society: A Social Science Newsletter* 5, no. 1 (December 1977), and 6, no. 1 (December 1978).

On the institutionalization of the anti-Communist state during the Civil War years, see Catiforis, [The Legislation of the Barbarians], pp. 31-88; and Alivizatos, "Les institutions politiques, pp. 117-84, 421-95 which provides an excellent analysis of the legal weapons used to safeguard the anti-Communist state. The quotation in the text is on p. 427.

9. On the autonomy of the Greek armed forces vis-à-vis civilian authorities, see: Nicos C. Alivizatos, "The Greek Army in the Late Forties: Towards an Institutional Autonomy," *Journal of the Hellenic Diaspora* 5, no. 3 (Fall 1978): 37-45.

10. For a good narrative account in English of events since the Civil War, see Richard Clogg, *A Short History of Modern Greece* (Cambridge: Cambridge University Press, 1979), pp. 166-86, as well as Campbell and Sherrard, *Modern Greece*, pp. 247-98. The best work in Greek is probably Spyros Linardatos's multivolume history *Apo ton emfylio ste hounta* [From Civil War to the Junta] (Athens: Papazeses, 1977-), still to be completed. The importance of the United States and of NATO for Greek politics during the same period is discussed in Theodore A. Couloumbis, *Greek Political Reaction to American and NATO Influences* (New Haven: Yale University Press, 1966), and also in Michael Mark Amen, "American Institutional Penetration into Greek Military and Political Policymaking Structures: June 1947-October 1949," *Journal of the Hellenic Diaspora* 5, no. 3 (Fall 1978): 89-113. Finally, a good analysis of politics and society in postwar Greece is contained in Jean Meynaud, *Les forces politiques en Grèce* (Lausanne: Etudes de Science Politique, no. 10, 1965).

11. On the growth of the Greek economy in the postwar period, see Nicolas Vernicos, "L'économie de la Grèce, 1950-1970" (Ph.D. diss., University of Paris, 1974); Howard S. Ellis, *Industrial Capital in Greek Development* (Athens: Center of Planning and Economic Research, 1964); E. Kartakis, *Le développement industriel de la Grèce* (Lausanne: Centre de Recherches Européennes 1970); Wray O. Candilis, *The Economy of Greece 1944-1966. Efforts for Stability and Development* (New York: Praeger, 1968); and Michales Malios, *He synchrone phase anaptyxes. . .* [The Contemporary Phase of Capitalist Development in Greece] (Athens: Synchrone Epoche, 1977).

On the relationship between economic development and politics during the same period, see: Mouzelis, *Modern Greece* pp. 115-33; Melina Serafetinidis, "The Breakdown of Parliamentary Institutions in Greece" (Ph.D. diss., London School of Economics, 1979; Michael J. Bucuvalas, "The Breakdown of a Political System Experiencing Economic Development: Greece, 1950-1967," in *Columbia Essays in International Affairs*, ed. Andrew W. Cordier, vol. 7, *The Dean's Papers, 1971* (New York: Columbia University Press, 1972), pp. 131-48; and Campbell and Sherrard, *Modern Greece*, pp. 299-322.

12. The conditions under which the authoritarian regimes were established and consolidated in Spain and Portugal have not received adequate attention. For Spain, see Juan Linz, "From Falange to Movimiento-Organización: The Spanish Single Party and the Franco Regime, 1936–1968," in *Authoritarian Politics in Modern Society: The Dynamics of Established One-Party Systems*, ed. Samuel P. Huntington and Clement H. Moore (New York: Basic Books, 1970), pp. 128–203, as well as Stanley G. Payne's *Falange: A History of Spanish Fascism* (Stanford: Stanford University Press, 1961). Among the more general works, see Stanley G. Payne, *History of Spain and Portugal*, 2 vols. (Madison: University of Wisconsin Press, 1973), his *Franco's Spain* (New York: Crowell, 1967); and George Hills, *Franco: The Man and His Nation* (New York: Macmillan, 1968).

For Portugal, the best work is undoubtedly Manuel de Lucena, *A evolução do sistema corporativo português*, 2 vols. (Lisbon: Perspectives & Realidades, 1976). In English, see Hermínio Martins, "Portugal," in S. J. Woolf, ed., *European Fascism* (London: Weidenfeld & Nicolson, 1968), pp. 302–36 which, though short, is probably the best on Salazar's New State; see also Tom Gallagher, *Portugal: A Twentieth-Century Interpretation* (Manchester: Manchester University Press, 1983); Antonio de Figueiredo, *Portugal: Fifty Years of Dictatorship* (New York: Holmes & Meier, 1976); Hugh Kay, *Salazar and Modern Portugal* (London: Eyre & Spottiswood, 1970); and A. H. de Oliveira Marques, "Revolution and Counterrevolution in Portugal—Problems in Portuguese History, 1900–1930," in *Studien über die Revolution* (Berlin: Akademie-Verlag, 1969), pp. 403–18, as well as the same author's general work, *History of Portugal*, 2d ed. (New York: Columbia University Press, 1976).

13. Studies on the problems associated with systemic crises, include Leonard Binder et al., *Crises and Sequences in Political Development* (Princeton: Princeton University Press, 1971); Dankwart A. Rustow, *A World of Nations* (Washington, D.C.: The Brookings Institution, 1967), esp. pp. 120–35; Gabriel A. Almond, Scott C. Flanagan, and Robert J. Mundt, eds. *Crisis, Choice, and Change: Historical Studies of Political Development* (Boston: Little Brown, 1973); and more recently Raymond Grew, ed., *Crises of Political Development in Europe and the United States* (Princeton: Princeton University Press, 1978); esp. pp. 3–40.

For a different perspective, see Barrington Moore, *The Social Origins of Dictatorship and Democracy* (Boston: Beacon, 1966); and Schmitter, "Historical Bloc Formation and Regime Consolidation in Post-Authoritarian Portugal," cited in note 1, Juan J. Linz, "The Consolidation of Regimes: A Theoretical Problem Approach" (Paper presented at the VIII World Congress of Sociology, Toronto, 19 August 1974); and Giuseppe Di Palma, "Left, Right, Left, Right—or Center? On the Legitimation of Parties and Coalitions in Southern Europe" (Paper presented at the International Political Science Association Round Table on "The Politics of Mediterranean Europe," Athens, May 28–June 1978).

14. In English, the best narrative of events during the 1967–74 period is Clogg, *A Short History of Modern Greece*, pp. 186–99. In Greek, the most detailed source is Solon N. Gregoriades, *Historia tes Synchronou Hellados, 1941–1974. He Diktatoria* [History of Contemporary Greece, 1941–1974. The Dictatorship], vols. 5–7 (Athens: Kapopoulos, 1975).

15. There were two major exceptions to this rule: one was Panagiotes Pipeneles, a longtime and devoted friend of the Greek court who had served in a number of governments of the Right between 1955 and 1963. Shortly after the coup, Pipineles became foreign minister, a post, in an apparent switch of loyalties, he kept after the failure of the king's countercoup in December 1967. The second, and even more significant exception was Spyros Markezinis who will be discussed in the context of the regime's attempt to achieve legitimation through liberalization, and the establishment of a "guided democracy."

16. The utterances of the colonels on the decrepitude of the "old regime" can be

found in the Greek press during the period of the authoritarian regime, and especially in the earlier years. Another source is the propaganda publications produced by offices of the regime, such as *The Undermining of the Greek Nation by Communism. The Records Reveal the Truth* (Athens: Ministry to the Prime Minister, Press and Information Department, 1968). By far the most authoritative source is the series containing Papagopoulos's speeches and public statements, *To Pistevo mas* [Our Credo], 7 vols. (Athens: Press and Information Office, 1968–72).

For a defense of the Greek parliamentary elite by one of its prominent members, see: Georgios I. Ralles, *He Aletheia gia tous Hellenes Politikous* [The Truth Regarding the Greek Politicians], 2d ed. (Athens: Hermeias, 1971).

17. Viewed from the perspective of the evolution of the Greek political system, on the other hand, the break in the unity of the Greek Right was a decisively significant development to the extent that it helped break down the deep polarization between Left and Right which the Civil War had created, and, in the process, established the preconditions for the modernization of the Greek Right.

18. On the polarization brought about by the collapse of the Republic and the Civil War in Spain a great deal has been written. Among the best studies are: Gerald Brenan, *The Spanish Labyrinth: An Account of the Social and Political Background of the Spanish Civil War* (Cambridge: Cambridge University Press, 1960); Edward E. Malefakis, *Agrarian Reform and Peasant Revolution in Spain: The Origins of the Civil War* (New Haven: Yale University Press, 1970); Stanley G. Payne, *The Spanish Revolution: A Study of the Social and Political Tensions that Culminated in the Civil War in Spain* (New York: Norton, 1970); Richard Robinson, *The Right, the Republic and Revolution: The Origins of Franco's Spain* (Pittsburgh: University of Pittsburgh Press, 1970); Gabriel Jackson, *The Spanish Republic and the Civil War*, rev. ed. (New York: Harper & Row, 1977); Burnett Bolloten, *The Spanish Revolution: The Left and the Struggle for Power during the Civil War* (Chapel Hill: University of North Carolina Press, 1979); and Juan J. Linz, "From Great Hopes to Civil War: The Breakdown of Democracy in Spain," in *The Breakdown of Democratic Regimes: Europe*, ed. Juan J. Linz and Alfred Stepan (Baltimore: Johns Hopkins University Press, 1978).

The conditions in Portugal that led to the collapse of the Republic receive a detailed examination in Douglas L. Wheeler, *Republican Portugal: A Political History, 1910–1926* (Madison: University of Wisconsin Press, 1978), and in the important article by Marques, "Revolution and Counterrevolution in Portugal," cited in note 12.

19. For Franco's attitudes toward the Republic which his regime replaced, see the biographies by Payne and by Hills already cited in note 12, as well as the work by J.W.D. Trythall, *Franco: A Biography* (London: Hart-Davis, 1970). For Salazar, see Antonio Ferro, *Salazar: Portugal and Her Leader* (London: Faber & Faber, 1939) which has the advantage of having been written by one of Salazar's followers; P. Fryer and P. M. Pinheiro, *Oldest Ally: A Portrait of Salazar's Portugal* (London: D. Dobson, 1961); Christian Rudel, *Salazar* (Paris: Mercure de France, 1969), as well as Kay, *Salazar and Modern Portugal*, and Figueiredo, *Portugal*.

20. The political mobilization of the early sixties, starting with George Papandreou's "unrelenting struggle" (to bring down the Karamanlis government of the time), and culminating in the series of constitutional and political confrontations involving the crown, the opposition forces, and successive palace governments arguably damaged the fragile fabric of democratic rule in Greece. Nevertheless, I believe that it is equally true that popular commitment to democratic values remained strong despite these actions which, at any rate, were aimed at opening up the political system, and in rendering it more democratic, not in abolishing it.

21. Mouzelis, *Modern Greece*, pp. 114–33. More generally, on the relation of economic development, economic growth, and politics, see note 11. For the purposes of this discussion, "economic growth" refers to a process of economic change that involves measurable magnitudes, and does not necessarily encompass the entire econ-

omy, but can, instead, be confined to certain selected sectors. Economic development, by contrast, implies a much broader process involving structural change in an economy, and resulting in a wider participation in the goods and services, as well as in the decision-making process affecting that economy.

22. On Spanish economic development, see above all Jaime Vicens Vives, *An Economic History of Spain* (Princeton: Princeton University Press, 1969) which, though uneven in quality, is clearly the best general account in English. See also *The Economic Development of Spain: Report of a Mission of the International Bank for Reconstruction and Development* (Baltimore: Johns Hopkins University Press, 1963), and Charles W. Anderson, *The Political Economy of Modern Spain* (Madison: University of Wisconsin Press, 1970). For Portugal, see V. Xavier Pintado, *Structure and Growth of the Portuguese Economy* (Geneva: European Free Trade Association, 1964), and the general account by Marques, cited in note 12.

23. For an extensive and excellent analysis of the 1968 Constitution, see Alivizatos, "Les institutions politiques de la Grèce à travers les crises," pp. 254-64, 570-617 passim. See also Phaedon Vegleris, "La constitution de la terreur," *Les Temps Modernes* 269 bis (1969): 103 ff., and Catiforis, "L'organisation institutionelle . . . en Grèce," in the same issue of *Les Temps Modernes*, pp. 153 ff.

24. For details on the institutional arrangements designed to ensure the permanent ascendancy of the military within the state, see Alivizatos, "Les institutions politiques," pp. 270-79, and Catiforis [The Legislation of the Barbarians], pp. 109-39.

25. Alivizatos, "Les institutions politiques," pp. 278-79.

26. For a discussion of the 1973 Constitution and of its more overtly authoritarian features, see Alivizatos, "Les institutions politiques," pp. 264-70, and esp. pp. 279-87.

27. For a narrative of events leading up to the Polytechnic confrontation, see Gregoriades, [History of Contemporary Greece, 1941-1974], vol. 7, pp. 9-170, and, in English, Clogg, *A Short History of Modern Greece*, pp. 194-99. Especially revealing and valuable for this period is Markezinis's own account, *Anamneseis 1972-1974* [Reminiscences, 1972-1974] (Athens: By the Author, 1979), pp. 213-507.

28. For the period between the Polytechnic uprising and the collapse of the regime in July 1974, see Gregoriades, vol. 7, pp. 171-361; Markezinis, pp. 507-626, and Clogg, cited in note 27.

29. For the quotation from Schmitter, see page 20 of his "Liberation by *Golpe*," cited in note 1, which also contains works dealing with the regime transitions in Spain and Portugal. For Greece, the best work so far is Stavros P. Psychares, *Ta paraskenia tes allages* [The Change Viewed from behind the Scenes], 3d rev. ed. (Athens: By the Author, 1975). In English, see Clogg, *A Short History of Modern Greece*, pp. 200-25.

30. For a fuller discussion of these issues, see P. Nikiforos Diamandouros, "Transition to, and Consolidation of, Democratic Politics in Greece, 1974-1983: A Tentative Assessment," in *New Mediterranean Democracies*, ed. Pridham, pp. 50-71.

31. For a discussion of the concept of the "popular emergence," see Guillermo O'Donnell and Philippe C. Schmitter, "Political Life after Authoritarian Rule: Tentative Conclusions about Uncertain Transitions," Volume 4 in this series.

32. Schmitter points out that a "transfer of power" involves handing power over to a segment of the authoritarian regime's moderate supporters; by contrast, in a "surrender of power" the outgoing regime's moderate opponents are the beneficiaries of change. See Philippe C. Schmitter, "Speculations about the Prospective Demise of Authoritarian Regimes and Its Possible Consequences" (Paper presented at the workshop on "Prospects for Democracy: Transitions from Authoritarian Rule," at the Woodrow Wilson Center, September 1980, pp. 9-15, subsequently revised and reprinted as Working Paper of the European University Institute, Florence, Italy, 1984) and Figure 1.

33. For a discussion of these events in English, see Diamandouros, "Transition and Consolidation," pp. 53-54, as well as Harry J. Psomiades, "Greece: From the Colonels' Rule to Democracy," in *From Dictatorship to Democracy*, ed. John H. Herz, pp. 250-55.

In Greek, see Psychares, [The Change], 5–130, and Markezinis, [Reminiscences], pp. 507–40.

34. See Psychares, [The Change], for the role of the participants: Kanellopoulos, pp. 131–40; Mavros, pp. 143–47; Averoff-Tossizza, pp. 149–56; Air Vice-Marshal Alexander Papanikolaou, chief of the air force, pp. 179–89; and Vice-Admiral Petros Arapakes, chief of the navy, pp. 198–210. For Markezinis's own account, see [Reminiscences], pp. 541–80.

35. On the decision to substitute Karamanlis for Kanellopoulos and Mavros, see Psychares, [The Change], pp. 140–43, 147–49, 156–60, 189–91, and 210–12.

36. Karamanlis's handling of the transition and his subsequent behavior, initially as leader of the Right which he tried to modernize, and eventually as head of state, have won him quasi-universal approbation, but his earlier role as the standard bearer of the anti-Communist forces in the 1950s and early 1960s remains much more controversial. To this day, there exists no satisfactory treatment of the life of this complex man, and of the slow evolution of his style of leadership, if not his thought, toward increasingly more liberal and democratic positions. Despite their hagiographical qualities, the best works to date are C. M. Woodhouse, *Karamanlis: Restorer of Greek Democracy* (Oxford: Clarendon Press, 1982), and Maurice Genevoix, *La Grèce de Caramanlis ou la démocratie difficile* (Paris: Plon, 1972).

37. The best source on the 1974 elections is Howard R. Penniman, ed., *Greece at the Polls*.

38. A detailed treatment and listing of the acts and decrees that provided the legal foundation for the instauration of the new regime are contained in Petros I. Pararas, "To chronikon epanodou eis ten Demokratian" [The Chronicle of the Return to Democracy], *To Syntagma* [The Constitution], 1, no. 1 (January–February 1975): 55–62.

39. On the threat of a military reaction and on Karamanlis's handling of the situation, see the interesting comments by Psomiades, "Greece: From the Colonels' Rule to Democracy," in *From Dictatorship to Democracy*, ed. Herz, pp. 255–58.

40. On the failed coup of February 1975, see Clogg, *A Short History of Modern Greece*, pp. 207–9.

41. See *Facts on File*, 30 August 1975, p. 637 for the quotation. The decision not to proceed with the execution of the three leaders of the 1967 coup was motivated as much by a desire to prevent a possible military reaction as by the determination to avoid the type of profound and traumatic polarization brought about by the execution of six conservative political leaders in the wake of the Greek defeat in Asia Minor in 1922. The so-called execution of the Six remained a haunting and lasting reference point in the interwar and postwar liberal-conservative cleavage in Greek politics.

42. On the legacy problem, see John H. Herz, "Introduction: Method and Boundaries," and "Conclusion," in *From Dictatorship to Democracy*, ed. Herz, pp. 3–11 and 275–91 respectively.

43. See Pararas, [Return to Democracy], pp. 58–59 for the various measures designed to put an end to restrictive legislation and to provide for an open political system.

44. On the role of the monarchy in Greek politics, see Jean Meynaud, *Les forces politiques*, and his *Rapport sur l'abolition de la démocratie en Grèce. 15 juillet–21 avril 1967* (Montreal: Etudes de Science Politique, 1967). See also Clogg, *A Short History of Modern Greece*, pp. 166–99, and Nicos Mouzelis, "Capitalism and Dictatorship in Post-War Greece," in *Modern Greece*, pp. 115–33. On the Greek military, in general, see the interpretative essays by Mouzelis, "Class Structure and the Role of the Military in Greece: An Interpretation," in *Modern Greece*, pp. 105–14, and Thanos Veremis, "Security Considerations and Civil-Military Relations in Post-War Greece," in *Greece in the 1980s*, ed. Richard Clogg (New York: Macmillan, 1983), pp. 173–83, as well as the fine study by Nikolaos A. Stavrou, *Allied Politics and Military Interventions: The Political Role of the Greek Military* (Athens: Papazisis, 1977).

## Chapter 7  Democracy in Turkey: Problems and Prospects

1.  The seminal essay on the breakdown of democracy and the establishment of authoritarian rule in Latin America was Guillermo O'Donnell's *Modernization and Bureaucratic Authoritarianism* (Berkeley: University of California, Institute of International Relations, 1973); evaluation of O'Donnell's thesis by various authors is found in David Collier, ed., *The New Authoritarianism in Latin America* (Princeton: Princeton University Press, 1979); see also Juan Linz and Alfred Stepan, eds., *Breakdown of Democratic Regimes* (Baltimore: Johns Hopkins University Press, 1978); and the chapters in this volume.

2.  The extent to which old regime legacies exercise constraints on revolutionary outcomes is discussed in Otto Kircheimer's seminal essay, "Confining Conditions and Revolutionary Breakthroughs," *American Political Science Review* 59, no. 4 (December 1965): 964–74.

3.  In recent years, there has been a growing emphasis on the important role that the state plays in society and history. For an earlier and insightful attempt to relate democratic outcomes to state and elite structures, see Hans Daalder, "Parties, Elites, and Political Developments in Western Europe," in *Political Parties and Political Developments*, ed. Joseph LaPalombara and Myron Weiner (Princeton: Princeton University Press, 1966), chap. 2.

4.  For information on the classical network of ruling institutions in the Ottoman Empire, see Halil Inalcik, *The Ottoman Empire: The Classical Age, 1300–1600* (London: Weidenfeld & Nicolson, 1973); and H.A.R. Gibb and Harold Bowen, *Islam and the West*, 2 vols. (Oxford: Oxford University Press, 1950 and 1957).

5.  Halil Inalcik, "Capital Formation in the Ottoman Empire," *Journal of Economic History* (March 1969): 97–140; also Ilkay Sunar, "L'Antropologie politique et économique: L'Empire Ottoman et sa transformation," *Annales, E.S.C.*, May–August 1980: 551–79.

6.  For a good discussion of stratification in the Ottoman Empire, see Serif Mardin, "Historical Determinants of Stratification: Social Class and Class Consciousness in the Ottoman Empire," *Siyasal Bilgiler Fakülesi Dergisi* 22, no. 4 (1967).

7.  On local elites and notables, see especially the following: Yücel Ozankaya, *Osmanli Imparatorlugunda Ayanlik* (Ankara: Ankara University Press, 1977); Albert Hourani, "Ottoman Reform and the Politics of Notables," in *The Beginning of Modernization in the Middle East*, ed. William R. Polk and Richard Chambers (Chicago: University of Chicago Press, 1968); Halil Inalcik, "Centralization and Decentralization in Ottoman Administration," *Studies in Eighteenth-century Islamic History*, ed. Thomas Naff and Roger Owen (Carbondale: Southern Illinois University Press, 1977).

8.  An excellent essay which discusses the relation between the political Center and local communities in terms of the lack of "civil society" in the Ottoman Empire is Serif Mardin, "Power, Civil Society, and Culture in the Ottoman Empire," *Comparative Studies in Society and History* 11, no. 3 (June 1969): 258–81; also his "Center-Periphery Relations: A Key to Turkish Politics," *Daedalus* 102 (Winter 1973).

9.  See Halil Inalcik, "The Nature of Traditional Society," in *Political Modernization in Japan and Turkey*, ed. Robert Ward and Dankwart Rustow (Princeton: Princeton University Press, 1964); also, Serif Mardin, "Opposition and Control in Turkey," *Government and Opposition* 1 (April 1966): 375–87.

10.  See Reinhard Bendix, "Social Stratification and Political Community," in *Philosophy, Politics, and Society*, ed. Peter Lasslett and W. G. Runciman (New York: Barnes & Noble, 1962); also, Gianfranco Poggi, *The Development of the Modern State* (London: Hutchinson, 1978).

11.  See, for instance, Serif Mardin, "Ideology and Religion in the Turkish Revolution," *International Journal of Middle East Studies* 2, no. 3 (July 1971): 197–211.

12.  A study that puts special emphasis on this aspect of the Turkish Revolution is

Elley Kay Trimberger, *Revolution from Above: Military Bureaucrats in Japan, Turkey, Egypt, and Peru* (New Brunswick, NJ.: Transaction Books, 1978).

13. The best study on Turkish political elites is Frederic Frey, *The Turkish Political Elite* (Cambridge, Mass.: MIT Press, 1965).

14. On the organization, ideology, and nucleus of social support of the RPP, see Ergun Ozbudun, "The Nature of the Kemalist Political Regime," in *Atatürk: Founder of a Modern State*, ed. Ergun Ozbudun and Ali Kazancigil (London: Duckworth, 1981).

15. A brief disscussion of the formal institutions of the early Republic can be found in Bernard Lewis, *The Emergence of Modern Turkey* (Oxford: Oxford University Press, 1968).

16. Parts of the following analysis draw on Ilkay Sunar's article, written in cooperation with Binnaz Toprak, on "Islam in Politics: The Case of Turkey," *Government and Opposition* 18, no. 4 (1983): 423-41.

17. The quoted phrase is the title of Clement H. Moore's article on Nasser's Egypt. It aptly describes the character of the early republican regime as well: "Authoritarian Politics in an Unincorporated Society," *Comparative Politics* 6, no. 2 (January 1974): 193-218.

18. On such variants of corporatism see Alfred Stepan, *The State and Society: Peru in Comparative Perspective* (Princeton: Princeton University Press, 1978), chap. 2; and Ruth Berrins Collier and David Collier, "Inducements versus Constraints: Disaggregating Corporatism," *American Political Science Review* 73, no. 4 (December 1979): 967-86.

19. On the statism in the early Republic, see especially Korkut Boratav, "Kemalist Economic Policies and Etatisme," in *Atatürk*, ed. Ozbudun and Kazancigil; also his *Türkiye'de Devletcilik* (Istanbul: Gerçek Yayinevi, 1974). For the Young Turk period, see the excellent study by Zafer Toprak, *Türkiye'de Milli Iktisat* (Ankara: Yurt Yayinevi, 1982).

20. See, for instance, Kemal Karpat, *Turkey's Politics: The Transition to a Multi-Party System* (Princeton: Princeton University Press, 1959); Metin Toker, *Tek Partiden Çok Partive* (Istanbul: Milliyet Yayinlari, 1970); Mahmut Gologlu, *Demokrasive Geçis: 1946-1950* (Istanbul: Kaynak Yayinlari, 1982).

21. Dankwart Rustow, "Transitions to Democracy," *Comparative Politics* 2, no. 3 (April 1970): 362.

22. On the attitude of the military toward the transition, see George Harris, "The Role of the Military in Turkish Politics," *Middle East Journal* 19, no. 1, pt. 1 (Winter 1964): 54-66, and no. 2, pt. 2 (Spring 1965): 169-76.

23. See Arif Payaslioglu, "Political Leadership and Political Parties," in *Political Modernization in Japan and Turkey*, ed. Ward and Rustow, chap. 9 B; also Dankwart Rustow, "The Development of Parties in Turkey," in *Political Parties*, LaPalombara and Weiner, chap. 4.

24. Rustow, "Transitions to Democracy," pp. 337-63.

25. The politics of the Democratic party is yet to be seriously studied; for information, see Cem Erogul, *Demokrat Parti* (Ankara: S.B.F. Yayinlari, 1970); and Karpat, *Turkey's Politics*.

26. For analyses of the 1960 military intervention, see Ergun Ozbudun, *The Role of the Military in Recent Turkish Politics* (Cambridge: Harvard University, Center for International Affairs, Occasional Papers, 1966); and Kemal Karpat, "The Military and Politics in Turkey: 1960-64," *American Historical Review* 65, no. 6 (October 1970): 1654-83.

27. A possibilist approach to political analysis is exemplified in Juan Linz, *Crisis, Breakdown, and Reequilibration* (Baltimore: Johns Hopkins University Press, 1978).

28. For a good discussion of the 1961 Constitution, see C. H. Dodd, *Politics and Government in Turkey* (Berkeley: University of California Press, 1969), chap. 8.

29. For detailed information on the politics of the 1960s and early 1970s, see Feroz

Ahmad, *The Turkish Experiment in Democracy, 1950–1975* (London: Duckworth, 1977); for party permeation of society, see Arnold Leder, "Kemalist Rule and Party Competition in Rural Turkey" (Ph.D. diss., Indiana University, microfilm, 1974).

30. For the social and economic changes that Turkey underwent in the 1960s and 1970s, see Kemal Karpat, ed., *Social Change and Politics in Turkey* (Leiden: E. J. Brill, 1973); William Hale, *Aspects of Modern Turkey* (London: Bowker, 1976); and Walter Weiker, *The Modernization of Turkey* (New York: Holmes & Meier, 1981).

31. A good study of the Justice party is yet to be published; for information, see W. H. Sherwood, "The Rise of the Justice Party," *World Politics* 20, no. 1 (October 1967): 54–65; and Ahmad, *The Turkish Experiment.*

32. For information on the changing politics of the RPP during this period, see Michael Hyland, "Crisis at the Polls: Turkey's 1969 Elections," *Middle East Journal* 24, no. 1 (Winter 1970): 1–16.

33. See Ecevit's own writings, especially: *Bu Düzen Degismeldir* (Ankara: Ulusal Basimevi, 1968); *Atatürk ve Devrimcilik* (Ankara: Tekin Yayinevi, 1970); and the 1973 party program, *Ak Günlere* (Ankara: Ajans Türk, 1973).

34. Parts of the following analysis draw from Sabri Sayari, "The Turkish Party Sytem in Transition," *Government and Opposition* 13, no. 1 (Winter 1978); see also his "Some Notes on the Beginnings of Mass Political Participation," in *Political Participation in Turkey,* ed. Engin Akarli and Gabriel Ben-Dor (Istanbul: Bogazici University Press, 1975).

35. On the politics of the NSP, see Binnaz Toprak, *Islam and Political Development in Turkey* (Leiden: E. J. Brill, 1981); also Sunar and Toprak, "Islam in Politics."

36. For information on Marxist parties in the 1970s, see George S. Harris, "The Left in Turkey," *Problems of Communism* 29 (July 1980).

37. For the impact of electoral laws on party politics, see William Hale, "The Role of the Electoral System in Turkish Politics," *International Journal of Middle East Studies* 11 (1980): 401–17.

38. See Ergun Ozbudun and Frank Tachau, "Social Change and Electoral Behavior in Turkey: Toward a Critical Realignment?," *International Journal of Middle East Studies* 6 (1979).

39. See Giacomo Sani and Giovanni Sartori, "Polarization, Fragmentation, and Competition in Western Democracies," in *Western European Party Systems: Continuity and Change,* ed. H. Daalder and P. Mair (Beverly Hills: Sage, 1983).

40. For an analysis of polarized pluralism, see Giovanni Sartori, *Parties and Party Systems* (Cambridge: Cambridge University Press, 1976), esp. pp. 131–73.

41. See Ustün Ergüder, "Changing Patterns of Electoral Behavior in Turkey" (Paper delivered at the IPSA World Congress, Moscow, August 1979).

42. Robert Dahl ed., *Political Opposition in Western Democracies* (New Haven: Yale University Press, 1966), p. 337.

43. An impressionistic but insightful study of elite behavior in Turkey is Frederick Frey, "Patterns of Elite Politics in Turkey," in *Political Elites in the Middle East,* ed. George Lenczowski (Washington D.C.: American Enterprise Institute, 1975).

44. For an interesting discussion of youth violence in Turkey, see Serif Mardin, "Youth and Violence in Turkey," *Archives Europeennes de Sociologie* 19 (1978).

45. For a discussion of the changing axes of political cleavage, see Ergun Ozbudun, *Social Change and Political Participation in Turkey* (Princeton: Princeton University Press, 1979); on clientelism and patronage, see Sabri Sayari, "Political Patronage in Turkey," in *Patrons and Clients,* ed. Ernest Gellner and John Waterbury (London: Duckworth, 1977).

46. For the recent relations between the civil bureaucracy and the military, see the interesting article by Metin Keper, "Bureaucrats, Politicians, and Officers in Turkey" (Paper delivered at the Colloquium on Continuity and Change in Turkey, Philadelphia, April 1982).

47. See Nicholas S. Ludington and James W. Spain, "Dateline Turkey: The Case for Patience," *Foreign Policy* 50 (Spring 1983): 150–68.

48. Ibid., p. 150.

49. The total number of former politicians barred from politics is 723 (242 for ten years, 481 for five years).

# Index

Action party (Italy); dissolution of, 61–62; and purge programs, 55–57; and transition to democracy, 67

Africa: and failure of PCP, 125; and Portuguese coup, 109–10, 115, 134

Agrarian reform: in Portugal, 124, 126; and societal dualism, 22

Agricultural sector, Spanish, 74–75

Alexander, Harold H.R.G., 55

Alianza Popular (Spain), 85; and democratic consolidation, 90; electoral support of, 94, 95, 98; after 1982 election, 103, 104, 105, 107

Allies, 48–51

Alphonse XIII (king of Spain), 76

Amendola, Giorgio, 54

Andalusia, 92, 107

Angola, 109, 110, 121, 134

Anticlericalism, 30–34

Anti-Communism, Greek, 142–43

Antunes, Melo, 111, 117, 127, 128

Argentina, 56

Armed Forces Movement. See MFA

Army. See Military

ASP. See Portuguese Socialist Association

Associated Press, 130

Athanassiades-Novas, George, 157

Authoritarianism, Turkish state-dominant monoparty, 168–71

Authoritarian regimes: breakdown of, 45–50; fall into disrepute, 146; institutionalization of, 154–55

Authoritarian regimes, transition to democracy in: causes of, 72; in Greece, 138–64; in Italy, 45–70; in Portugal, 109–37; in Spain, 39–40, 71–108; in Turkey, 165–186

Averoff-Tossizza, Evangelos, 157

Backwardness, 15, 187n. 2

Badoglio, Pietro, 29, 49, 50

Badoglio government, 51

Banks, Spanish, 75

Basic Law of the Press, 77

Basque region, and democratic consolidation, 91–92; after 1982 elections, 107–8; and regional devolution, 86–87

Berlinguer, Enrico, 34

Bianchi, G., 193n. 17

"Black Week" (Spain), 84

Blanco, Carrero, 74, 78, 79

Blondel, Jean, 100

Bonanos, Gregorios, 157

Bonomi, Ivanoe, 48, 52, 55

Bourgeois consolidation, 13–14

Brandt, Willy, 117

Brazil, 130

Brezhnev, Leonid, 200n. 21

Bunker (Spain), 90

Caciagli, Mario, 100

*Caciquismo*, 20

Caetano, Marcello das Neves, 112–15, 197n. 2

Calamandrei, Piero, 64, 68

CAMPSA, 191n. 39

Capitalism: Greek, 144; in late-developing societies, 15–17; in Southern Europe, 14–15

Capitalist corporations, in Southern Europe, 14–15

Carlucci, Frank, 123, 131

Carmona, Oscar, 148

Carneiro, Francisco Sá, 38, 119

Carrillo, Santiago, 34, 116

CASA, 191n. 40

Castro, Fidel, 116

Catalonia: and democratic consolidation, 91–92; after 1982 elections, 107–8; and regional devolution, 86–87

Catholic church, 63, 64, 68, 121–22; in Italy, 47, 50; in Spain, 76, 78

Cattaneo, Carlo, 188n. 2

Cavour, Ernesto, 22

CD. See Coordinacion Democrática

CDE. See Democratic election commissions

CDS. See Social and Democratic Center (Spain)

CDS. See Social Democratic Center (Portugal)

Censorship, 113

Center and periphery, 11, 187n. 1; in Turkey, 166–68, 171

Center Union party, 144, 157, 158, 162

Chile, 5

Christian Democrats (DC) (Italy): and cold war, 60–61; drafting of Constitution by, 64; and free elections, 63–65; hegemony of, 58–59; and purge process, 57; and transition to democracy, 45

213

Political cooptation, 28, 29
Political parties. *See* Party system; *party names*
Pombal, Marquês de, 16
Popular Coalition (CP) (Spain), 103, 107
Popular Democratic party (PPD) (Portugal), 118-19; and democratic consolidation, 132-34; electoral support of, 122-23; and failure of Communists, 127
Popular Democratic party (PDP) (Spain), 95
Popular Front, 45-46, 61, 65, 66
Popular Socialist party (PSP) (Spain), 79
Population, 74
Populist party (PP) (Turkey), 185
Portugal: Constitution, 132-33, 135; coups in, 109-15; democratic consolidation in, 133-34; democratic transition in, 39-40, 109-37; economy of, 114-15, 134-36; Fascism in, 25; foreign aid to, 130; foreign intelligence in, 130-31; industrialization of, 16-18; labor force in, 114-16, 118; military in (*see under* Military); nationalism in, 137; party system in, 116-18, 122-25; political polarization in, 99; secret police in, 113
*Portugal and the Future*, 118
Portuguese Democratic Movement (MDP/CDE), 117
Portuguese Revolution, 109, 115, 135-36
Portuguese Socialist Association (ASP), 116-17
PP. *See* Populist party
PPD. *See* Popular Democratic party (Portugal)
PRD. *See* Partido Reformista Democrático
Primo de Rivera y Orbaneja, Miguel, 24
Protectionism, 18, 19
Prussia, 20
PS. *See* Socialist party (Portugal)
PSD. *See* Social Democratic party (Portugal)
PSDI. *See* Social Democratic party (Italy)
PSI. *See* Socialist party (Italy)
PSOE. *See* Socialist party (Spain)
PSP. *See* Popular Socialist party
Purge process, in Italy, 55-57

Radicalism, 22
Ragionieri, E., 194n. 38
Reactionary coalitions, 25-28
Regime Transitions, research on, 165-66. *See also* Authoritarian regimes; Democracy
Regional devolution (Spain), 86-87; and democratic consolidation, 91-92; and party system, 97, 107-8
Rego, Raul, 117
Religion, 30-34. *See also* Catholic church
Renaissance, 15
Repression, 5-6, 78, 80
Republican People's party (RPP) (Turkey), 169, 172-82

Republican Reliance party (RRP) (Turkey), 177
Resistance movement, 51-59
Restoration (1875-1923), 86
Revolution, and Italian transition, 67
Rio Tinto copper mines, 189n. 13
RPP. *See* Republican People's party
RRP. *See* Republican Reliance party
Rustow, Dankwart, 72, 172

Salazar, Oliveira, 24, 33, 112, 113, 145-46, 148
Saraiva de Carvalho, Otelo, 111, 120, 129
Sartori, G., 196n. 25
Schmitter, Philippe, 138, 154, 156, 163, 191n. 47, 207n. 32
*Seará Nova*, 117
Second Republic, (1931-36), 86
Semipresidentialism, 9
Sergio, Antonio, 117
Service class, 26-28
Sforza, Carlo, 55
Sindicatos Verticales, 84
Soares, Mário, 38, 113, 117, 118, 122, 128, 134
Social and Democratic Center (CDS) (Spain), 95, 107
Social Democracy party (SODEP) (Turkey), 176, 186
Social Democratic Center (CDS) (Portugal), 117, 118, 122-23, 132-34
Social Democratic party (PSDI) (Italy), 64
Social Democratic party (PSD) (Portugal), 134
Socialism, 42-43
Socialist Andalusian party (Spain), 92, 96
Socialist party (PSI) (Italy), 45, 55-57 64-65, 67-68
Socialist party (PS) (Portugal), 116-17, 122-23, 127, 128, 130, 133-37
Socialist party (PSOE) (Spain), 79; electoral support of, 85, 95-99; in 1982 election, 100, 102-8
Societal dualism, 22
SODEP. *See* Social Democracy party
Sotelo, Calvo, 38
Southern Europe: civil societies in, 6-7; compared to Latin America, 3-10; history of, 12-15; scholarly view of, 3
Soviet Union, 52-54, 61, 130
Spain: agricultural sector in, 74-75; attempted coup in, 93, 101, 102; banks in, 75; Catholic church in, 76, 78; civil societies in, 5, 8; coalition building in, 97-98; Constitution in, 87-89; 91-92; coups in, 93, 101-2; democratic consolidation in, 73, 89-93, 101-2, 104, 106; democratic transition in, 39-40, 71-108; economy of, 74-76, 92-93; elections in, 85-89, 100-108; Fascism in,